AF505806

CHSP
HUNGARIAN STUDIES SERIES
NO. 13

EDITORS
Peter Pastor
Ivan Sanders

REMEMBER HUNGARY 1956

Essays on the Hungarian Revolution and War of Independence in American Memory

Tibor Glant

With an Introduction by
ISTVÁN DEÁK

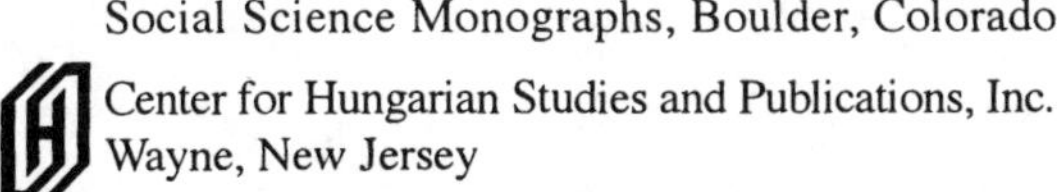

Social Science Monographs, Boulder, Colorado

Center for Hungarian Studies and Publications, Inc.
Wayne, New Jersey

Distributed by Columbia University Press, New York

2007

EAST EUROPEAN MONOGRAPHS
NO. 718

This publication was suported by a grant from the
REMEMBER HUNGARY 1956 COMMITTEE,
California Hungarians.

Library of Congress Control Number 2007933040
ISBN 978–0–88033–616–1

Printed in the United States of America

CONTENTS

*To Antal Bejczy and the California Hungarians,
and to all Hungarian refugees of 1956
in the United States*

PREFACE

The 1956 Hungarian Revolution and War of Independence is the single best-known Hungarian historical event in the United States. The Revolution, and the Soviet crackdown on Hungary, was the first major television experience for a whole generation; it is just about the only event that is regularly mentioned in American history textbooks in connection with Hungary. Hungarians living in the States have worked strenuously to preserve its memory. Nineteen fifty-six feeds into, and confirms, one of the two key images of Hungarians in America: that of a freedom-loving and freedom-fighting nation. This positive image was first created by the extremely successful public relations tour of Lajos Kossuth in 1851–52, and was duly revived in 1956 and 1989. And although Hungary's contribution to tearing down the Iron Curtain in 1989 will certainly go down in history as the more important of the two events, it is still 1956 that has been immortalized in the West.

This volume is the product of a research project initiated by the Remember Hungary 1956 Committee of the California Hungarians and the University of Debrecen in 2005. The initial project went through many changes, and at one point Montclair State University (MSU) joined the program. My original task was to survey various American history textbooks for information on the 1956 Revolution, but when I asked for a free hand and more options everyone agreed. I wrote five essays on the various aspects of the memory of the Revolution in the United States. Professor István Deák of Columbia University agreed to provide an introductory essay on what he saw as the major features of the various Hungarian revolutions and wars for independence. Csaba Békés of the 1956 Institute of Budapest commented on the final draft. In it the reader will find selected documents and reports on the fiftieth anniversary commemorations in the United States. Professor Peter Pastor of MSU, my long-time friend, mentor, and publisher, has agreed to publish the results. This is the book you are holding in your hand.

At the time of the inception of the project I was fully aware of the various efforts by Hungarians living in America to tell their own stories about the Revolution and of its many memories in the New World. Through books, websites, oral history projects, documentary and feature films, concerts, conferences and joint celebrations with their American friends, they have indeed told their own stories. I chose to focus on what seems to be a neglected aspect of the Revolution: the American (non-Hungarian) memories of the events. Memory and strategies of remembering manifested themselves in very different ways in the five essays that deal with what I consider the five most important aspects American memory: media, political memory, academic memory, literature, and art. Bearing in mind that there is no such thing as a monolithic American mind, and therefore no traceable American memory exists, I have focused on the willingness to remember and remind others about the 1956 Hungarian Revolution and War of Independence.

The five essays are admittedly limited in scope and represent my personal preferences and interest. They are intended to provoke discussion as well as further research. They also reflect the limitations of access to information up to August 2006, when I concluded my field work. What follows next is an introductory guide to the five essays.

Media

The first essay looks at how the *New York Times*, arguably the most internationally-minded American daily, has remembered and reminded others of Hungary and 1956. This became the linchpin of the whole project, and it is a mini-dissertation. I also would have liked to work with the electronic media (news coverage of the anniversaries, American documentaries, etc.), but the various television companies and news agencies were not prepared for such cooperation. Another possible topic for research in the field of the media would have been, and still is, the internet subculture of the Revolution; it is the easiest to trace and record, and can be done later.

POLITICAL MEMORY

Of the various dimensions of political memory ranging from diplomatic notes through presidential proclamations and Congressional resolutions to remake (borrowed images)[1] I chose the political memoirs of four American ambassadors to Hungary. Relations between the United States and Hungary hit rock bottom as a result of 1956, and diplomatic relations were restored fully only in 1966, when the two countries agreed to raise them to the ambassadorial level. Between 1967 and 1989 eight American ambassadors served in Hungary, and four published memoirs. I looked at how they represented the Revolution, Kádár, and Hungary.

ACADEMIC MEMORY

Books on the 1956 Hungarian Revolution fill bookshelves in the major academic libraries in the world. The 1956 Institute in Budapest (www.rev.hu) was created to research the Revolution, and it coordinates and monitors both Hungarian and international research in the field. So I chose to go with the original project of the Remember Hungary 1956 Committee and looked at some thirty American history textbooks and their representation of 1956. I was somewhat disappointed to find that unconditional support for the Revolution rarely goes hand in hand with balanced historical accounts.

LITERATURE

One of the most exciting yet underrated aspects of the American memories of 1956 are the literary representations—memoirs and fictions—of the Revolution. From the total of about forty personal and journalistic recollections and works of fiction only about half a dozen have been translated into Hungarian. For the purposes of this essay the real challenge was not digesting the material but piecing it together. There are no lists available, no fixed search terms, and I oftentimes found it quite difficult to establish whether a particular book fits my criteria or not. The books covered here range from the recollections of American journalists in Budapest through personal histories of freedom fighters and Jewish family histories covering their tragic experiences from World War II to 1956 to various works of fiction (novels, crime stories, popular fictions, and juvenile literature). I also included books published in Canada, and some works from Britain and even New Zealand when I could establish that these works are relevant and available in the United States.

FINE ART

In 2001 Professor Michael Steiner of CalState Fullerton took me to the Richard Nixon Presidential Library and Museum in Yorba Linda, California, and I was more than surprised to find a huge painting by a Hungarian artist (Ferenc Daday) depicting Richard Nixon (then Eisenhower's vice president) at Andau, on the Austro-Hungarian border in December 1956. Neither the full story of Nixon's trip nor the history of the painting has been written yet, so I did that for the fifth and final essay in my book. Daday's painting at the Nixon library is a prime example of the interaction between imagined history, memory, and strategies of reminding others of 1956.

Debrecen, March 2007   *TIBOR GLANT*

NOTE

1. The toppling of Saddam Hussein's giant statue in Baghdad in 2003 was a remake of the toppling of the Stalin statue in Budapest in 1956, and the Bush administration tried to justify its actions in Iraq by linking it to 1956.

ACKNOWLEDGMENTS

The Remember Hungary 1956 Committee (RHC) of Los Angeles approached the University of Debrecen in 2005 and proposed that they work together to commemorate the fiftieth anniversary of the 1956 Hungarian Revolution and War of Independence. The driving force behind the RHC proposal was Éva Szörényi, the beloved Hungarian actress. My personal contact with the RHC was Antal Bejczy, a senior professor of robotics and a 1956 refugee. Besides keeping in touch with me, he invited me to California to meet the California Hungarians at their *Széchenyi Tea* in May 2006, raised the necessary funds for publishing this volume, and went out of his way to meet all my requests. Without his (and through him RHC's) unconditional support, I would never have been able to complete this manuscript. Their warm hospitality on my two trips to Los Angeles was an added bonus.

Professor Peter Pastor has been a long-time friend and mentor, and he readily involved his school, Montclair State University (MSU), in the project. Besides sharing his time, office, books and ideas with me, he also agreed to publish this volume. The Global Education Center at MSU was instrumental in providing the academic background for my work. Its director, Dr. Marina Cunningham, embraced the project with enthusiasm and lent me her full support. At times I made her staff (especially Wendy, Karen, and Jackie) work very hard, but they readily cooperated. Credit should also go to the university library at MSU for helping me identify the books for the essay on the literary memory of 1956 and for helping me get some of the volumes I could not obtain otherwise. Last but not least, I would like to thank the faculty and staff of the Department of History at MSU for their support and good company.

At Debrecen, my gratitude goes to Professor Zoltán Abádi-Nagy, who first awakened my interest in the project, Professor Péter Szaffkó, the director of the Institute of English and American Studies, who on very short notice gave me a leave, my colleagues at the North American Department, who held the fort in my absence, and to Professor János Mazsu of History, who represented the university in its negotiations with the RHC.

In the New York-New Jersey area the Hungarian intellectual circle that centers around Professor Deák has been extremely helpful with comments, ideas and guidance. Ivan Sanders, Susan Glanz and Gábor Vermes come to mind first, as well as Professor Károly Nagy from Piscataway, NJ. In California, my fond memories and gratitude go to Antal Bejczy again and again, as well as to Professor Michael Steiner and his lovely wife, Lucy. On my two trips to Los Angeles Bejczy and the Steiners took me wherever and whenever I wished to go, and helped me meet all the people I wanted to meet. The Daday painting at the Nixon library became an obsession for me (from 2001 on, when I first saw it), and they helped me meet the painter himself. Ferenc Daday, ninety-three years of age, granted me a lengthy interview at the library, and I was able to discuss the painting with him while standing in front of it. For the same project (the Tracy S. Voorhees papers) I also received invaluable support from Jim Niessen, a senior university librarian at Rutgers.

As usual, my family proved to be extremely supportive. My father and his wife Kati gave me all the support I needed to travel in the United States, and they put up with most of my grumbling when things were not going smoothly. Yet the real *sine qua non* of this project and book is my wife, Kata, who not only let me be away from home for almost half a year but tried to make separation as easy as possible for both of us. It is only now that I understand why writers dedicate their books to spouses and families.

As regards the publication of this volume, thanks are due to Ivan Sanders of Columbia for proofreading and language editing, Edit Völgyesi for the graphics, typesetting, and preparing the index, István Deák for his contribution and Csaba Békés for his suggestions, and, of course, Antal Bejczy and Peter Pastor for actually making the entire work possible.

INTRODUCTION

REVOLUTIONARY TRADITIONS IN HUNGARY

It is one of the peculiarities of Hungarian history that its revolutions have regularly been sparked by the real or perceived grievances of the social elite. Even though the grievances were directed primarily at the foreign power that held sway over the country, every one of these movements also contained a demand for substantial domestic reform. In each case, however, the movement for reform was hijacked, we might say, by people outside the social elite who turned it into a violent upheaval. This, then, caused an ever-growing section of the elite to demand the restoration of law and order by the very same foreign power against which the social elite had rebelled in the first place.

And now for an attempt at an explanation: Like Poland, its historic soul brother, Hungary was a respected and dynamic middle-sized kingdom in medieval times. Later, however, both kingdoms fell on hard times. In the mid-sixteenth century, Hungary was divided into three parts, regaining its unity and political sovereignty only in 1867; Poland, which was literally abolished late in the eighteenth century, did not regain its unity and independence until 1918. Yet throughout the centuries of division and foreign rule, the existence of these nations was never in doubt simply because in both countries the historic landowning nobility remained firmly in control. This nobility arrogated to itself the very concept of the nation: they were the *populus*, the *gens*, the *natio*, the citizens, the tribe, the nation; the others were the *misera plebs contribuens*, the poor tax-paying population. The traditional concept of Hungary and Poland as two noble, warrior nations remained alive over the centuries and, once foreign rule had come to an end, both countries

became militantly nationalistic. Thus we must consider that the reform movements in Hungary and Poland invariably aimed not only at freeing the country from foreign domination but also at tackling the problem of noble rule. Some in the
reform movements wished to overthrow the ruling elite; others hoped to make the country free and more prosperous in cooperation with the old elite; again others fought for liberty and reform in order to perpetuate the predominant position of the old elite.

What complicated matters enormously was the practical absence of a native urban middle class, which meant that the reformers themselves generally stemmed from the noble estate. Thus, with every radical action the reformers threatened the welfare of their own families and friends. As a consequence, most of the noble revolutionaries were eager to achieve national independence as well as to improve conditions in their country without thereby fatally endangering the pre-eminent position of their own class. The effort wasn't always successful because, inevitably, the continued pre-eminence of the old social elite was endangered by new elements of society who had come to the fore as a result of the upheavals.

Prince Ferenc II Rákóczi's rebellion or uprising in 1703 against Habsburg rule marked the culmination of growing public discontent with the way the Habsburg dynasty treated Hungary, or rather its ruling elite. In the sixteenth and seventeenth centuries, Hungary was divided between an Ottoman dominated center, an autonomous Principality of Transylvania, and a rather small sliver in the west called Royal Hungary. Until the 1680s, only the latter part recognized a Habsburg king as its ruler but then, in an extraordinary effort, Europeans combined their forces to rid Central Europe of the Ottomans. By 1699, almost all of Hungary, including Transylvania, had fallen into the hands of European history's last crusaders.

The campaign represented a great victory for Western Christianity, to which Hungary belonged, but the crusaders exacted a heavy price from the Hungarians for their liberation. As a result, Hungarians in 1699 were no more grateful to their Christian liberators than their descendants were to the Red Army in 1945. Among other things, the Hungarian Diet had to recognize the Habsburgs' hereditary right to the Hungarian crown; the nobility had to give up its right to resist an unlawfully acting ruler; much of the devastated countryside was ceded to foreign money lenders and purveyors; and Catholicism, the religion of the Habsburgs, was force-fed to the mostly Protestant Hungarian nobility. On the opposite side, the Habsburg administration saw little reason for treating the Hungarians any better: the country was infested with bandits and was economically almost worthless; moreover, the Hungarian nobles had proven themselves most fickle in their loyalties. During the previous two centuries, the greatest dignitaries in the realm switched sides again and again from Turks to Habsburgs to Transylvanian princes, often immensely benefiting from the change of loyalties. How could one forget the Turkish and Tatar marauders of the great Hungarian magnate Count Imre Thököly who had repeatedly invaded and devastated the country? Or the Hungarian hussars, who had participated in the Christian reconquest of Buda Castle in 1686 from the Turks and had fought on the kuruc—that is on the Turkish side—just a few weeks earlier. Similarly, in February 1945, some Hungarian troops participated bravely in the Soviet siege of Buda Castle, but the Soviets would not easily forget that the same Hungarians had been serving on the German side only a few days earlier.

Hungarians at the turn of eighteenth century regarded every Habsburg move as a humiliation and a mark of oppression. At last, a countrywide rebellion broke out under Prince Rákóczi, a Catholic magnate, who led an army made up of mostly Protestant nobles and of peasants of all nationalities and denominations. The peasants or better, serfs, had been suffering much less from Habsburg rule than from their heavy feudal obligations and the near-total devastation of the land. True, Prince Rákóczi now proclaimed the unity of all the estates and promised freedom to the serfs who had served him well; still, when the other kuruc leaders spoke of the grievances of the "noble Hungarian nation," they meant precisely that: the injustices that had been visited on the nobility, which alone constituted the nation.

It would be good to know how many people in the country sympathized with the imperial Austrian side and how many with the revolutionary Hungarian side. Thousands of Hungarian subjects of the Habsburg emperor-king served in both armies, but we must keep in mind that more than half of the king's Hungarian subjects were not Magyar-speakers. In any case, in those times, nationality counted for next-to-nothing and membership in one or another estate for nearly everything. Young men had become soldiers so as not to be killed by the marauding military, or in order not to starve to death, or simply, because they had been pressed into service. The pattern would be repeated in every revolution. Still, it is also certain that a good number of young men joined the Hungarian ranks voluntarily in order to fight "Pro Libertate," for freedom. It must be pointed out, however, that for noble recruits, freedom meant national independence and the preservation of noble privilege whereas for the serfs in the revolutionary ranks, it meant freedom from feudal dues and services as well as, hopefully, a piece of land to be held in hereditary tenure. The two different goals could not really be reconciled.

Habsburg military victories, as well as the devastation of the land and terrible human losses because of the plague, caused Rákóczi's followers gradually to abandon his flag. The rebellion ended in 1711 in a great compromise, not the last in Hungarian revolutionary history. According to the terms of Hungarian surrender, no rebel soldier was punished; the kuruc troops were to swear fealty to the emperor-king, and the nobility was to be confirmed in its privileges and rights. Yet one of the country's main problems remained unresolved, namely the complex relationship between the center of power in Vienna and the periphery, that is the fifty-odd Hungarian counties dominated by the landowning nobility. The question throughout the century was who would reform the country: the central bureaucracy or enlightened elements among the nobility. Cooperation between the two was not inconceivable, but it occurred rarely. More often, the grievances of the county nobility and the arbitrariness of the Court in Vienna paralyzed each other.

Things changed fundamentally with the rise of European nationalisms and the growing conviction within the Hungarian elite that the nation would perish unless Hungarian was established as the language of official communications, and when all the inhabitants of the realm accepted the notion that they were Hungarian patriots, irrespective of the language they were speaking. Moreover, all the inhabitants of the kingdom were to be given the rights and privileges of the nobility so that together they might constitute a great nation.

Reforms came gradually until events sped up immeasurably with the outbreak of the European revolutions in 1848, which temporarily paralyzed Vienna and allowed the more radical elements in the Hungarian noble establishment to introduce drastic reforms. Even though the Hungarian reformers exploited the temporary weakness of the central power in Vienna, the liberal constitution of March–April 1848 marked the triumph of legality; theirs was a bloodless revolution, or as I like to say, a lawful revolution. Bloodshed came several months later because Vienna wished to undo some of the concessions it had made to the Hungarians, concessions that, it is true, had made the efficient governing of the Monarchy very difficult. In addition, during the summer of 1848, Lajos Kossuth and his colleagues considerably sharpened Hungarian governmental policy toward the Court, the Austrian government, Croatia, and the national minorities. On the other side, the national minorities, who together constituted an absolute majority of the kingdom's inhabitants, wished to achieve some of the same liberties and privileges that the Hungarians had wrested from the king. In other words, the ethnic minorities opposed the centralizing policy of the Hungarian leaders in the same way that the Hungarians opposed the centralizing tendencies of Vienna. The result was war between Hungary and the rest of the Monarchy as well as a civil war within Hungary.

By the time the followers of Kossuth were definitely defeated, in August 1849, most Hungarians had abandoned his cause. But the revolution had not been fought in vain; the Hungarians had lost the war but they would win the peace for the simple reason that the Habsburg Monarchy of that time was no longer a great power. Rather, it was a combination of many territorial entities which could function only if these entities were willing to co-operate. Because without Hungary the Habsburg Monarchy was inoperable, a compromise agreement became inevitable, and it was concluded, in 1867, making Hungary an equal partner with the rest of the Monarchy.

The ensuing liberal era allowed for unprecedented prosperity and progress but the liberal government's tough nationalist policy exasperated the increasingly dynamic ethnic minorities. Moreover, the Monarchy's shortsighted foreign policy as well as the aggressive hostility of some of Austria-Hungary's neighbors led to World War I; here, the Dual Monarchy could not but lose.

The democratic "Chrysanthemum Revolution," at the end of October 1918, represented a dramatic departure from Hungary's entire political and social tradition. Hungary became a democratic republic that hoped to align itself not with Germany, its traditional protector, but with the Western democracies. The revolution also brought into the government, besides the usual nobles and bureaucrats of gentry origin, a good number of Social Democrats and radically-inclined Jewish intellectuals.

The republic of the Red Count, Mihály Károlyi, ended within a few months for such reasons as the incompetence of Károlyi; the utopian ideas of some of his underlings; the rapaciousness of Hungary's neighbors; and the narrow-minded hostility of the Western democracies. A take-over by the Communists and left-wing Social Democrats, in March 1919, was as inevitable as their ultimate collapse a mere four months later. The causes of that debacle were, again, the incompetence and utopian ideas of the Bolshevik leadership, the rapaciousness of Hungary's neighbors, and the hostility of the Western democracies. But there was one more important force to cause the collapse, namely the implacable hostility of the Hungarian social, business, and political elite toward the Soviet Republic. Counts István Bethlen and Pál Teleki, not to speak of Admiral Miklós Horthy, would rather have Romanian and French colonial troops occupy the country than to tolerate Reds in power.

The conservatives' dream of violently restoring the status-quo-ante proved to be just a dream. During the counterrevolution, new, dubious elements came to the fore whom the old elite both needed and treated with contempt. These newcomers on the political scene wished to discard the Hungarian liberal-conservative constitutional tradition and to replace it with some kind of an anti-Semitic dictatorship. Although this extreme right was never able completely to overcome the resistance of the conservative establishment, it succeeded in bringing about a fundamental social change by gradually expropriating the wealth of Hungary's Jewish population. In this way, between 1938 and 1944, approximately one fourth of the national wealth changed hands. Add to this the utter destruction wrought by the war and it then becomes clear that the post-1945 democratic regime confronted a tabula rasa situation. Consequently, when the Communists seized power in 1947–1948, they had a relatively easy time in expropriating whatever had not already been plundered.

What took place between 1938 and approximately 1952 was a genuine social revolution. True, rather than having been brought about by mass upheaval, it was the work of relatively small domestic forces operating under the tutelage of two successive great powers. The German occupation of Hungary in March 1944, and the Soviet liberation in the spring of 1945 allowed for more change—political, cultural, social, and economic—than all the previous and later revolutions combined. In all this, the Hungarian people played mostly a passive role, either as beneficiaries of plunder or as the victims of plunder.

In 1953, measures were taken to remedy some of the economic and moral damage caused to national life by the Nazi and Soviet takeovers and the cruel as well as often mindless social revolution. The summer and early fall of 1956 represented the culmination of the attempt to undo the damage and to institute a more humane form of Communist government.

In many ways the revolution of 1956 represented a repetition of the old pattern: progressive members of the old elite, in this case dissident Communist intellectuals, had created a radical reformist movement which, in turn, brought forward such elements from other strata of society who had new and very different goals, and who threatened the security and welfare of the Communist cadres. These new elements, mostly workers and students, brought the conflict into the streets thereby precipitating armed intervention from abroad. Foreign intervention then put an end to both domestic reform and the nation's striving for political independence. As in the early 1700s, in 1848–1849, and in 1919, armed intervention from abroad dissipated the dreams of the elite reformers while simultaneously securing the future of the elite to which the reformers belonged.

The word "revolution" has been endlessly debased and abused, witness such terms as "revolution in the making of false eyelashes," yet the only valid definition of the term is that of a violent attempt, by a large number of people, to institute drastic change through the overthrow of the political system and of the prevailing social order. Measured by this definition, not all of the great historical events I have mentioned qualify as revolutions. Certainly, October 1918 and October 1956 were true revolutions because of their mass character and their overarching aims, but the proper characterization of the other great events is debatable. Consider that the professed aim of the Rákóczi and the Kossuth rebellions was not to overthrow the existing social and political order but to put an end to the abuses perpetrated by the king's evil advisers and to restore the ancient rights of the nation. While it is true, as far as the events of March 1919 are concerned, that Béla Kun and his companions advocated the annihilation of the existing social order (for which they were able to mobilize a considerable number of people), the Communists had come to power through peaceful negotiations. Still, it is best and simplest to regard the Rákóczi Rebellion of 1703–1711; the War of Independence in 1848–1849; the democratic and Communist takeovers in 1918–1919, and the events of 1956 as revolutions.

Back in the summer of 1849, much of the Hungarian elite quietly welcomed the law and order brought back by the invading Austrian and Russian armies. In 1919, the Romanian occupation of Budapest enabled the counterrevolutionary Whites to punish the unruly elements among the rural population and to make scapegoats out of the Jews. Finally on November 4, 1956, many sighed in relief that law and order was being reestablished. Let us remember that the hundreds of thousands who marched carrying red flags on May 1, 1957, had not all been coerced to do so by the Communist authorities.

Yet, let us also remember that it was ultimately always a foreign power that put an end to the revolutions: at the Battle of Trencsén [Trenčin], on August 3, 1708, where Habsburg troops irrevocably defeated Prince Ferenc II Rákóczi's forces; at Temesvár [Timişoara], on August 9, 1849, where General Julius Haynau triumphed over Kossuth's honvéd army; on August 1, 1919, when Romanian troops crossed the Tisza River and wiped out the Hungarian Red Army, and on November 4, 1956, when Soviet tanks rolled into the Hungarian capital. Nor were the Hungarian revolutions completely unsuccessful because, with or without a compromise agreement, many of the revolutionary ideas were gradually translated into reality. This is true whether under Maria Theresa and Leopold II in the second half of the eighteenth century, or in 1867, or in 1945 or, finally, in 1989.

ISTVÁN DEÁK
Columbia University

THE *NEW YORK TIMES* AND THE MEMORY OF THE 1956 REVOLUTION

INTRODUCTION

The New York Times is one of the "big five," the best-known American dailies in Europe, including, of course, Hungary.[1] Carefully monitored by the Hungarian Ministry of Foreign Affairs during the Cold War, it is now freely available in the EU, and is a recognized trend setter, especially among liberal intellectuals and media actors. The *Times* now has a searchable database covering all published articles since 1851. This makes it possible to conduct a complete survey of the paper and see what it has had to say about the Hungarian Revolution of 1956, since the beginning of 1957. The *Times* was selected for review for two main reasons. Firstly, it published more articles about the Revolution than the other four of the "big five" (of the American dailies) combined, and, secondly, the paper has been the target of some well-founded but also some unfounded criticism from the politically active '56ers in the United States. The fiftieth anniversary of the Revolution calls for historical analysis and offers the possibility to reconsider some of the criticism directed at the paper.

Historians rarely get to play the numbers game, but when they do they enjoy it. The historical *New York Times* database returns 1,944 hits for an advanced keyword search combining Hungary and 1956, covering the period between January 1, 1957, and March 31, 2006. Excluding accidental hits, Olympic scores and irrelevant articles, the total score is well over five hundred articles of interest. The same keyword search with a shorter time frame, January 1, 1957, to December

31, 1989, yields 1,638 hits. This means that the *Times* devoted over 1,500 articles to the Revolution (and related issues) for the first thirty-two years, and only three hundred during the next sixteen years, since 1990. This goes a long way toward showing that we are dealing not simply with memory but with strategies of remembering. In other words, before 1989, during the communist period in Hungary, the *New York Times* wanted to remember and remind its readers of the Revolution on a regular basis. Since 1989, when Hungary officially recognized the October–November 1956 events as a "Revolution," the paper felt it no longer had such a mission, and confined its coverage to factual reporting on anniversaries and new historical revelations. In the broader time frame mentioned above, the Hungarian Communist leader, János Kádár, gets 1,039 mentions, with 307 linking him to 1956, and 207 to both 1956 and the Soviets. When combined with 1956, the leader of the revolutionary government, Imre Nagy, gets 207 hits, while Cardinal József Mindszenty gets 125. This clearly indicates that the *Times* repeatedly connected all three of them to the Revolution of 1956. Before offering more statistics about choice of words at the end of this essay, we must look at the general tone and attitude of the paper and the types of articles it printed in connection with the Revolution.

Overview: The Changing Tone and Attitude of the *Times*

Initially, the *New York Times* was taken aback by the brutal repression of the Revolution by superior Soviet force. Its tone remained hostile toward Kádár, the Soviet occupation, and Hungary. Regular reports, sometimes exaggerated, of the execution of young freedom fighters helped maintain this attitude. The next shock came in June 1958, when Imre Nagy and three others were executed, despite the safe conduct Kádár had granted them initially. The official statement released by the Hungarian authorities was taken apart by Soviet expert Harry Schwartz. Hostile reporting was combined with extensive reviews of books dealing with the Revolution, with regular references to Cardinal Mindszenty's asylum at the American Legation (later Embassy) in Budapest, and even with such reports as the Greek government releasing a commemorative Imre Nagy stamp in 1961.

The partial amnesty granted by Kádár for those who did not take part in the armed conflict brought about the first editorial calling for possible normalization of relations with Hungary. Yet the real turning point was President Lyndon B. Johnson's "bridge building" speech in 1964. It encouraged the new tone reflecting surprise that Kádár could consolidate his power so fast. The *Times* began to display a less bellicose, more tolerant stand in the matter of communist Hungary, a sort of wait-and-see attitude. Heated exchanges between Washington and Budapest were reported word for word, but so was the American offer to raise the level of diplomatic relations from temporary chargé d'affaires to ambassador.

Chargé d'Affaires ad Interim János Radványi's defection from the Hungarian Embassy in Washington in 1967, set back relations for three years, yet it was rarely mentioned in connection with the Revolution. Anniversary coverage continued, and the general tone remained resentful. The joint Warsaw Pact intervention against the Prague Spring during the presidential election campaign in 1968 was perceived in the paper as the revival of the spirit and the ghosts of 1956.

Richard Nixon's election to the White House, and his new policy toward Eastern Europe, marked the beginning of a new phase in US-Hungarian relations. Four major talking points were agreed upon in the summer of 1969, and by 1973 all but two outstanding issues had been settled. Cardinal Mindszenty left Hungary, the two countries signed a consular agreement, and wartime claims (some dating back to World War I) were settled. William P. Rogers became the first American secretary of state to visit Hungary while in office, a Hungarian travel agency (IBUSZ) office was opened in New York City, and Hungarians could legally manufacture blue jeans (Trapper farmer). The two countries cooperated in the preparations for the Helsinki Conference on European Security, and Hungary was invited to supervise the armistice in Vietnam. President Nixon's resignation over the Watergate scandal set back his policy of détente as well as US-Hungarian relations. The Carter administration agreed to return the Holy Crown and the coronation regalia to the Hungarian people in January 1978, and a bilateral Most Favored Nation (MFN) trade agreement was signed two months later.

The *New York Times* had the beat of these developments, and reported on them favorably. Hungary became a "favorite son" for the paper, and Hungary profiles became more regular and more positive. So much so, that in 1977 a one-page tourist guide was printed for the country, and by the early 1980s Hungarians had come to "fight the Russians" with the "one weapon available," anti-regime street jokes. The tone of these articles was appreciative, especially of Kádár's achievement of some level of legitimacy through improvements in the standard of living, while anniversary reporting remained resentful. And this duality in tone was maintained until Hungary broke free from Soviet rule in 1989–1990.

A general review of the ever-changing attitude of the *Times* towards the Kádár regime and Hungary indicates that editorial preferences revolved around two major issues: maintaining Cold War pressure on Budapest on the one hand, and trying to encourage Hungary to loosen its ties with the Soviet Union via preferential treatment and complimentary remarks on the other. It is hardly surprising that letters to the editor from émigré Hungarians carried repeated, and often justifiable, criticism of this policy of the paper. After all, the *New York Times* did use a double standard in reporting that other dailies such as the *Wall Street Journal* or the *Chicago Tribune* did not. While the *Times* spoke of an "affluent" Hungary in 1972, the *Wall Street Journal* in 1986 declared that "Hungary Doesn't Deserve Model Communist Image."[2]

There was, there simply had to be, a third editorial concern about choice of words about the Revolution, but before reviewing it, we shall take a closer look at the different types of articles dealing with the Revolution and its many memories. In an admittedly arbitrary system of categorization with multiple overlaps, ten different types of articles will be identified and analyzed with a view to gaining further insights into the editorial preferences and strategies of remembering on the part of the *New York Times*. The ten categories are: memory, country profiles of Hungary, political coverage, editorial comments, letters to the editor, Mindszenty articles, human interest stories, obituaries, book reviews, plays, movies, TV programs, and political advertisements.

Memory

The most relevant type of article published in the *New York Times* dealt with the memory, anniversaries and anniversary celebrations of the 1956 Hungarian Revolution; therefore, these get extended review and special attention in this paper. Nineteen sixty-one and 1971 passed almost unnoticed, 1971 brought the first open call for reconciliation (by Professor Charles Gati), while 1976 and 1986 got most of the attention. Two thousand and one was the first major anniversary without a single commemorative article or editorial in October–November. These commemorative articles covered a wide range of issues from Hungarians and Americans in the US celebrating the anniversary through personal recollections of "the 13 days that shook the Kremlin" to Kádár and official Hungary trying to forget, or misrepresent, the events of 1956. Next is a chronological survey of the most interesting articles and tendencies in these articles on memory.

Although the year of 1958 was dominated by the execution of Imre Nagy and some of his fellow revolutionaries, it also saw the publication of three different articles dealing with the memory of the Revolution. Lisa Larsen authored a photographic essay on "Hungary, Twenty Months After," in which she recalled her experiences of a visit to Budapest.[3] She reports on the physical destruction still apparent, and maintains that

> Hungarians do not believe their revolution was in vain. They become strangely alive when they talk about it, as if it had been the most wonderful event in their lives. They are proud of the way they acted. They did the best they could, and now that they realize they never could have won they try to make the best of life as it is.

She goes on to say that Hungarians resent high food prices, and that most Hungarians dream of owning a car. She then tells an anecdote: one Hungarian told her that he would not get a car even if he could, because his neighbors would think he had become a communist, referring to the fact that only high-ranking Party officials could afford an automobile.

Two other articles from 1958 deserve attention. The *New York Times* reported on a rally held at Carnegie Hall, attended by more than 2,000 people. On October 20, Republican and Democratic keynote speakers convened to make this tribute bipartisan. A commemorative plaque was awarded posthumously to *Times* reporter John MacCormack, and presented to his widow by a prominent freedon fighter, Gergely Pongrátz. Governor Averell Harriman addressed the rally by letter and announced his decision to make October 23 "Hungarian Freedom Fighters' Day."[4] On December 4, M. S. Handler reported from Vienna on the official Hungarian "recollection" of the "counterrevolution." Citing information acquired during a short visit to Hungary, Handler correctly identified the official Party rhetoric revolving around two major themes. Mistakes had indeed been made before 1956 by the erstwhile dictator, Mátyás Rákosi, and his Stalinist associates, but the revolt soon turned into a counterrevolution (when demands were made to return private property to its prewar owners) and students and workers abandoned it. From then on, events were driven by criminal elements.[5] In fact, this remained the official Party rhetoric in the press, textbooks and pseudo-academic publications until 1989.[6]

1958 thus confirmed and further developed some key myths about the Revolution. The Larsen piece inadvertently strengthened the communist-generated myth that freedom fighters were really just people who fled Hungary in hope of a better life and a car; the rally at Carnegie Hall earned additional rhetorical support for the myth of the freedom fighters,[7] while the Handler article introduced the official Hungarian Party line (and self-explanatory mythology) on the Revolution to the American public. This trend continued throughout the first half of the 1960s with some interesting extensions on the basic themes. In 1959, on the anniversary of the outbreak of the Revolution, the State Department issued an official statement praising the Revolution and saying that it failed "in the face of ruthless Soviet military intervention."[8] A similar statement was issued and reported in 1960.[9] Also in 1959, Nikita S. Khrushchev paid an official visit to Hungary, and remarked in one of his speeches that there had been some disagreement in the Kremlin over Hungary in 1956. The paper also quotes him saying, "The saliva of the imperialists was running in their mouths at the prospect of Hungary's leaving the Socialist camp."[10] The beginning of the UN debate of the Hungarian question was welcomed by the *Times* in the form of a half-page, day-by-day chronology of the revolutionary events in Hungary.[11] In 1960 and 1961, the Vienna correspondent (Handler) reported on Hungarian expatriates and Austrian students remembering the Revolution,[12] and in 1962 the paper featured an Imre Nagy commemorative stamp issued by the Greek government.[13] Reports on Hungarian economic recovery (by Handler) also commented on the communist version of the events, and reference was made to a picketing of the Soviet UN mission building on the fifth anniversary of the Revolution.[14] By 1965 Hungary had become synonymous with unjustifiable military intervention: the American Socialist Party compared the American intervention in the Dominican Republic to the Soviet invasion of Hungary.[15] Former Vice President and future President Richard Nixon got into a heated verbal exchange with Soviet students at Moscow University over the American use of force, and he replied, "If you want to talk about force, then we should talk about Soviet action against the Freedom Fighters in Hungary."[16]

By 1966, the tenth anniversary of the Revolution, the image of freedom-fighting Hungary, originally created by Louis Kossuth during his tour of the United States in 1850–51, had been fully revived and was deeply embedded in the American political mind and in American memory. Over time, this memory would fade, but in 1966 it provided sound basis for the first big anniversary. Accordingly, another commemorative rally was held at Carnegie Hall, this time a musical event with some political speeches mixed in.[17] The first official Hungarian commemoration of the crushing of the "counterrevolution" was also reported (from Vienna). The article cites a *Népszabadság* editorial admitting some of the mistakes of Rákosi and his associates, and describes Kádár as the Party chief "who came to power after Russian tanks crushed the uprising."[18] This article represents two major trends already identified in the *Times*. On the one hand, it recites the official Hungarian myth of mistakes and criminal elements in the Revolution, and automatically dismisses it as a lie. On the other hand, the stern tone of the piece, especially the comment on Kádár, did not match the tone of earlier articles reporting the improvement of American-Hungarian relations, most notably the raising of diplomatic relations to ambassadorial level. As has been pointed out above, such a dichotomy of tone seemed acceptable to the paper on the whole.

The most important output in 1966 was Timothy Foote's seven-page feature article on Hungary in the Sunday magazine section on November 20, titled "The Road Back to Budapest." Foote was a foreign correspondent in Hungary during the Revolution and revisited Budapest ten years after in the capacity of book editor of *Time-Life*. Much of the article is Foote's own recollection of the events and his impressions of October–November 1956, all of them frank, shocking and bloody, as he himself was slightly wounded. The final third of the piece takes an extended look at Hungary in 1966. He claims that the Cold War changed into some sort of peaceful coexistence, and both major blocs have learnt their lessons. He touches upon, and then dismisses, another myth about the Revolution:

> As far as Hungarians are concerned, the dislocation brought about by the rebellion merely delayed reforms and rewards which would have come sooner by themselves. Since it is probable that, if the uprising could have been peaceably stopped at midcourse, reforms would have been made with less bloodshed, this argument bears the shadow image of one kind of truth. Such talk, however, is both seductive and destructive of the will.

He draws a parallel with the American Revolution, claiming that a similar argument could possibly be made: the colonies should have waited another few years and asserted themselves economically, thus breaking away from Britain without bloodshed. Then he goes on to ask, "But would we have stood for anything in history? Would we, in fact, have been the same country and people we have become?" He then points to the fact that the Kádár regime "has done its best to erase not only many of the grievances which gave birth to the rebellion but the fact of its existence at all." He reminds the reader that there is still an electric fence surrounding the country, that there are 60,000 Soviet troops stationed in Hungary, and that the mine fields around the borders were removed in a face-saving operation, after several Austrian schoolchildren had been blown up. He takes on the new myth of economic prosperity in Kádár's Hungary, but calls it a disappointment by Western standards. He notices a subdued rather than cheerful attitude, and attributes it to the rather low standard of living. He then records the disappointment of Hungarians with America and maintains that Hungarians in the US and in the mother country confirm that the apparent lack of interest on the part of Hungarians in Hungary in talking about or thinking about their rebellion is genuine.

> They are not interested in having far-off relations from a distant country stir them to discontent with what they have. That is a road they have already trod, only to see their hopes crushed. They believe that what they have is what they must live with. They expect no help from the Russian Government, and they no longer look to America for leadership. In this sense they are profoundly neutralist, and sadly realistic. Hungary is still a one-party country, and they know that what the Government permits today it can repress tomorrow.

The passages above speak for themselves. Such sympathetic yet accurate analysis from an American journalist would not be printed in the paper for quite some time. Foote's article is a textbook example of topical overlap: it is an article on memory and a profile of Hungary at the same time.

The next ten years brought political turmoil and East-West détente, and the *New York Times* focused on these issues. This left little room for remembering. Two lengthy articles reviewed the political achievements of President Dwight D. Eisenhower in 1969 and 1971 respectively.[19] The latter was a feature article in the Sunday magazine section on February 7, and it marks the beginning of "Eisenhower revisionism," of seeing the former war hero-turned-president as a political genius in the White House. The Revolution in Hungary gets but a passing mention here. Two articles on Radio Free Europe (hereafter RFE) raised questions about American responsibility for 1956. Unsurprisingly, in "Embattled Radio Free Europe Defends Role," David Binder devotes a whole subsection to 1956, and describes it as a watershed. He reports on the large-scale changes in personnel after the Revolution, and quotes one employee saying that before 1956 RFE was an "agitation station," but since then is has become a "detached, constructive critic."[20] Next year, in 1972, RFE got six-page Sunday magazine section coverage from Henry Kamm, under the title, "The Station That Fulbright Wants to Shut Down." The timing was by no means accidental: the CIA had just admitted that it had been secretly financing RFE and Radio Liberty, and the two stations were under fire in Congress. Kamm deals with 1956 extensively. In a fair summary he recalls that after the Revolution RFE was accused of inciting rebellion and promising the "rebels foreign assistance." He quotes RFE research department head James F. Brown saying that "there was an absence of control during the critical four days." This, in turn, brought about the realization that "RFE had a potential for provoking violence," the decision that it should not use this potential and the realization that it would be accused of doing it nonetheless.[21] He too lists personnel changes and changes in the strategy of the station, and offers an insightful interview with István Bede, the head of the Hungarian service. Bede recalls a classic joke: the Hungarian economic reforms in 1968 were supported only by Kádár and RFE. He also claims the days of "rollback" rhetoric are gone, and he has to accept "goulash Communism," if the people in Hungary believe that socialism is here to stay. He says RFE would "not broadcast the views of Hungarian émigré politicians because they live in the past."[22] Détente had clearly arrived at the English Garden in Munich by 1972, and RFE and Voice of America journalists would officially be allowed into Hungary six years later to cover the return of the Holy Crown and coronation regalia.

The Prague Spring and the joint Warsaw Pact invasion of Czechoslovakia earned extensive coverage in 1968. Comparisons between 1956 and 1968 were offered on a regular basis. A July 19 article in the *Times* went beyond the general trend by reviving the memory the Revolution: "Czech Crisis Recalls Crushing of Hungarian Rebellion in 1956." The unsigned article claims that besides the obvious similarities the one key difference between 1956 and 1968 is that while in 1968 the two superpowers were trying to improve relations, in 1956 the "United States was…actively calling in radio broadcasts for the revolt of Eastern European nations." It then tells the story of the first Soviet withdrawal from Budapest and, for the first time in the *Times*, recalls the Soviet trapping and arrest of Pál Maléter. On November 5 the *New York Times* ran a short article noting that Kádár and other Hungarian officials commemorated the "martyrs" of the "counterrevolution."[23]

Kádár's attempts to win acceptance and reconciliation hit home with prominent 1956ers by 1971, the fifteenth anniversary of the Revolution. Columbia University Soviet expert Charles Gati penned a longer piece with the tell-tale title, "In Hungary, It's Now a Question of Making the Best of It."[24] He correctly identifies the sweeping changes in Hungary since 1956, but cannot help being amazed by the very same changes: "What is most difficult to understand is that this is not the country we left behind." He reports that the general feeling in Hungary is that Kádár is "the best man Hungary can have under the circumstances." He points to a marked shift in the frame of reference: Hungarians look to the West to see what they want (computers) and to the East "to learn what you should be careful not to want (tanks)." He sees the political subculture of antiregime jokes, and sees them as some kind of a political safety valve. He concludes his piece by saying that Kádár's (by Soviet standards extended) liberalism "goes a long way to explain why most Hungarians have come to accept, if only grudgingly, their present situation. After all, with the high hopes of '56 gone, perhaps forever, they have the best of what can be had under the circumstances."

1976 was a special year for Americans and Hungarians alike. The United States celebrated her bicentennial, while Hungarians abroad remembered their suppressed Revolution of twenty years before.[25] It was also election year in the US, and one of the Ford-Carter TV debates had a peculiar effect on both memory and voter behavior. As usual, the *New York Times* covered the events with great interest. Articles on memory are discussed here, while the nature and political implications of the TV debate will be addressed in the subsequent chapter on political reporting.

The first commemorative piece, in fact an article on memory combined with a country profile of Hungary, came from the pen of the former freedom fighter Charles Fenyvesi.[26] He recalls his return to Hungary as "bittersweet." He records the achievements of the Kádár regime in pacifying the country and bringing about, to a certain degree, an acceptable life in Hungary. He then reminisces about the Revolution and the subsequent repression, and identifies by full name all three people who were executed together with Imre Nagy in June 1958. He then goes on to argue that "in some ways, the 1956 revolution has won." Fenyvesi supports his argument by citing some of the key demands of the Revolution and explaining how these have been met. Stalinist terror is gone, and so are the old Stalinists, and with them the all-pervading fear of the 1950s; which is basically correct. He tries to demonstrate, however, with less success, that three other demands of the Revolution have also been met. We now know from historical analysis that the Soviet stranglehold on the Hungarian economy was never relaxed, the "nationalism" of the Kádár regime did not prevent the Romanian dictator, Nicolae Ceausescu, from destroying ethnic Hungarian villages in Transylvania even as late as the 1980s, and discrimination against non-Communists and the interwar elite of Hungary never really ceased. He also looks at the philosophical followers of György Lukács, recalls the deportation of the aristocratic families in the early 1950s, and concludes the article on a somewhat melancholic note. Commenting on the Hungarians' "fatalistic acceptance of Moscow's suzerainty for generations to come," he wonders what inspired armed resistance twenty years before:

> There was no plan for a revolution, only a momentum that was unstoppable. There was no rational calculation, only total desperation….It was a historic dream of glorious defiance that united fiery Social Democrats and bitter ex-Stalinists, silver-tongued writers and workers who felt they had nothing to lose but their chains, students possessed of the all the righteousness of youth, and all the nameless people of Budapest who took to the streets.

Fenyvesi here revives some of the key myths of the Revolution and challenges the official Hungarian view, which he too cites earlier. The Revolution in Budapest was indeed spontaneous, and not preplanned as Kádár's official history claimed, but national unity behind the Revolution did not last long.[27] Fenyvesi, like Gati five years before, accepts the new reality of the 1970s: "For my generation, now middle-aged with dreams discounted or abandoned and horizons narrowing, October of 1956 is a sacred corner in time when we were beautiful and powerful and pure—a youth that can never come again."

A week later a one-page article (with a half-page photo) was published by the exiled General Béla K. Király, the commander of the National Guard (i. e. the freedom fighter forces) in 1956.[28] The picture shows two (presumably) Soviet tanks in the background, and a dead freedom fighter stretched out in the front. Király tells a story form the Revolution, when the former head of the secret police, General Béla

Berecz, came to him to surrender. Without concluding the story, he switches to memory, and tells the story of a successful revolution, and then identifies three reasons why the Soviets invaded Hungary: (1) the USSR needed Hungary for missile bases, (2) Moscow had its own domino theory for the possible collapse of its empire if Hungary "fell," and (3) the Chinese Communists pressured Moscow into intervention. Just as in his academic publications, Király calls the Soviet intervention in Hungary "the first war between socialist states." By way of conclusion, he recalls his final encounter and conversation with Prime Minister Imre Nagy, a story he would tell over and over again, after returning to Hungary.

Two articles round out the 1976 coverage on the memory of the Revolution. On October 29 Malcolm W. Browne reported from Budapest that the anniversary had passed "nearly unnoticed" in Hungary.[29] He states that 60,000 of the 200,000 refugees have returned since the Revolution, and that limited criticism of the government has become acceptable. He reports peaceful student demonstrations but "no violent clashes since 1956." And with a final quote from an unidentified Hungarian he shares the conclusions of Gati and Fenyvesi before him: "It's better to be practical and have whipped cream for your coffee than to spend the rest of your life nursing old sores." Equally important was a special article by David Binder on November 30, in which he linked recent CIA revelations to the Revolution.[30] Citing two contradictory sources, Binder contends that the Eisenhower administration tried to combine the publication of Nikita Khrushchev's secret speech of February 25, 1956, given at the Twentieth Congress of the Communist Party of the Soviet Union, with armed uprisings started by specially trained CIA operatives behind the Iron Curtain. He quotes one of his sources, saying that the "premature release of the speech, which The [New York] *Times* published on June 4, 1956, provoked nationalist risings in Poland, Hungary and Romania too soon for the covert operational groups to respond." These special CIA units were disbanded in 1958. Both his sources, Binders says, are critical of the détente policies of the Nixon and Ford administrations.

The next ten years brought about the most symbolic and most contested American gesture toward Hungary during the Cold War: the return of the King St. Stephen's coronation regalia to Budapest.[31] Such demonstrations of goodwill were soon gone, following the Soviet invasion of Afghanistan and the Iran hostage crisis in 1979. A new Soviet-American confrontation loomed large on the horizon, the two superpowers mutually boycotted the Olympic Games on the territory of the other, and Solidarity surfaced in Poland and questioned the very ideological basis of the regime. "The second Cold War" was in full flow. By the thirtieth anniversary of the Revolution the "old guard" in Moscow was dead and gone, and Mikhail Gorbachev was teaching Russian words like "glasnost" and "perestroika" to the American public and press. Memory again was linked to political developments, with one notable exception. In 1978 Stephen G. Esrati wrote a lengthy piece on shortwave radio and radio memories. He listed five formative radio memories, among them Henry Cabot Lodge's UN speech during the Soviet invasion of Budapest on November 4, 1956, and "Radio Free Budapest signing off with 'help us' and an unidentified march; and then returning to the air some time later as Radio Budapest with a Soviet view of events."[32]

Nineteen eighty-six, which turned out to be the last decennial anniversary of the Revolution before communism collapsed in Hungary, followed the trends set by 1966 and 1976: the *New York Times* reported anniversary celebrations in the United States and commented on the attempts on the part of the Kádár regime to suppress, or reinvent, the memory in Hungary. Skeletons were out of the closet as early as June 23, when Michael T. Kaufman reported from Budapest on the obscure cemetery parcel, "Section 301, Where Hungary's Past Is Buried." This was the first time the paper told the story of the relatives trying to locate the remains of their beloved and trying to get a proper reburial for Kádár's victims. In October and November Kaufman reported from Budapest, Szolnok, and Warsaw. The first article begins with a summary of and some statistics about the Revolution, and continues (along the familiar line) with a look at Kádár's status in the country: "[He] is still very much in power, but these days no one calls him the 'butcher of Budapest' as once they did." He quotes the dissident intellectual Miklós Haraszti about Poland and Hungary: "for the Poles the most important thing is remembering, while for many Hungarians the most important thing is forgetting." This, in turn, is followed by the official version of the Hungarian government, but with an amazing twist. Kaufman tells of a three-part series on TV about the "counterrevolution," and supplements it with sections of an interview with the director of the series. This director, whom he identifies as a Dezső Rodzianyi, claimed that after carefully studying still photographs of the demonstrators he concluded that the students had been gradually replaced by gypsies, thus equating the "criminal elements" of the Kádár mythology with an ethnic minority.[33] In his article penned in Szolnok, Kaufman tells about the celebrations Kádár and Party official János Berecz (whom he identifies as an historian) staged to commemorate the birth of their regime on November 4, 1956. Kaufman quotes Berecz extensively, but points out the inconsistencies in his statements. When asked about "the gaps in the historical account" and Kádár's sudden turnaround, Berecz responded, "We still do not have a minute-by-minute account of what happened between the first and fourth of November."[34]

Kaufman contributed a third piece printed on November 10, this time from a Warsaw suburb, where he attended a Catholic mass and rally that unveiled a marble plaque to the memory of "the Hungarians killed in the 1956 uprising." He quotes Father Leon Kantorski saying that Poles do not want any socialism anymore. He concludes with an insightful remark about Hungarian dissidents: "The model they admittedly dream about is that of Poland, where an underground culture actively competes with the official one" about interpretations of the past.[35] Articles like this explain why there was no street access to the *New York Times* in Hungary during the 1980s, and why the Hungarian Ministry of Foreign Affairs paid special attention to the paper.

In an article from New Brunswick that sounds more like a flashback to the sixties than a product of the Reagan era, Priscilla Van Tassel adds a hitherto undiscussed dimension to the study of strategies of remembering: ethnic revival mixed with academic memory.[36] She contends that "bittersweet" celebrations of the thirtieth anniversary of the Revolution have triggered wholesale demands from students in the area to be offered courses in Hungarian history and culture. Rutgers University hastily revived its Hungarian program dropped twenty years earlier, and Mercer County College joined the project. Van Tassel attributes this new interest to the coming of age of the second and third generations of the refugees and quotes five students of Hungarian origin supporting these programs and telling about rediscovering their roots. References are made to the contributions of the American Hungarian Foundation, and its president, August (Ágoston) Molnár, is interviewed. Molnár expresses his doubts about the sustainability of such high level of interest in things Hungarian. Of course in 1986 no one could imagine what 1989 would bring.

Nineteen eighty-nine is remembered in Hungary as "the year of miracles." It witnessed the total collapse of the Soviet empire in a mostly peaceful way, but at amazing speed. In Hungary, 1989 was as much about 1956 as it was about the future. "Counterrevolution" became "popular uprising" in late January, Imre Nagy turned out to be a national hero and not a criminal and a traitor, and both Kádár and his victims were buried in a proper way during the summer. By October Hungary became a republic (and not a people's republic), and 1956 officially became a Revolution and War of Independence, as well as a national holiday. The *New York Times* published more than 150 articles about Hungary in 1989, in which memory and political reporting mixed inseparably. The reburial of Imre Nagy and his fellow victims received more coverage from the paper than any other event since the Revolution. Like the Revolution in 1956, the diplomatic accord between the Vatican and Hungary, Mindszenty's departure from Budapest, and the return of the Holy Crown, the reburial also became front-page news and a topic for several editorials. Still, the general trend the paper followed was to let Hungarians speak their mind.

The *Times* dutifully reported Minister of State Imre Pozsgay's famous speech about the "popular uprising," raised the issue of the reburial as early as February 8, and on February 11 quoted a liberal Soviet view supporting Hungarian neutrality in 1956. It lauded the rebroadcasting of Imre Nagy's famous November 4 speech on May 7, and welcomed revelations by historian Mária Ormos that Kádár had a hand in kidnapping and executing Nagy.[37] Coverage of the reburial was followed by a report that the Hungarian Supreme Court fully rehabilitated Imre Nagy on July 6.[38] Kádár was presented as a respected elder statesman following his death, and Henry Kamm filed a special article on his funeral.[39] The anniversary was reported from Budapest under the title, "New Hungary Marks '56 Uprising: 'Gorby!' and 'Russians Out!' Mix. A New Hungary Celebrating the 1956 Rebellion."[40] By the end of 1989, 1956 had taken its due place in Hungarian memory. Hungarians legitimately could and have ever since remembered their Revolution.

Unsurprisingly, since 1990 the *New York Times* has pursued a more factual, and less spectacular, policy of remembering. In 1991 two major issues dominated *Times* reporting: what East European historians could (and perhaps should) do about the Communist past, and how far should retaliation for Communist crimes and abuses go. The former issue was briefly revisited in 1996 and 1997,[41] while the latter was repeatedly revived, most notably in 1994 and 1999.[42] The big scoop in 1992 was the so-called Yeltsin-dossier, a compilation of Soviet Politburo documents on Kremlin decision making in 1956.[43] The dubious role of RFE was on the table again in 1995 and 1996, when radio archives were opened.[44] The 1996 Atlanta Olympic Games revived memories of the bloody battle during the Melbourne Olympics in the pool between the Hungarian and Soviet water polo teams, just when the Soviet invasion was taking place in Budapest.[45] In 2006, a documentary (*Freedom's Fury*) and a feature film dealt with this topic. (For the record, Hungarians went a perfect 2–0 in these two games.)

SPECIALS FROM HUNGARY: COUNTRY PROFILES

The second major group of articles of interest for the purposes of memory preservation is a series of special articles on Hungary; for want of a better term, country profiles. These articles range from half-page single-topic pieces to multi-page coverage in the Sunday magazine section. With a few early but notable exceptions, they share a positive, approving attitude towards Kádár's Hungary. They usually present Kádár as a tragic hero-turned-master-politician, and maintain that Hungary had a "tragic" uprising in 1956, but since the restoration of communist power the country came a long way to become the happiest barrack behind the Iron Curtain. In this regard, country profiles have, in some way, balanced the critical tone of the anniversary articles. What follows is a sampling of the most interesting pieces, with a focus on memory preservation and/or strategies of forgetting.

"Defiance in Hungary" by Handler from 1961 is the first interesting piece.[46] It reports on the post-1956 state of the arts and literature in

Hungary, and identifies "internal emigration" as the underling trend. Soccer games are more of a concern for Hungarians than nuclear tests or Soviet Party congresses, and the only cheerful thing the author sees is "bright-eyed, handsome children, well dressed and pampered by parents who are hard pressed to make both ends meet." Quiet resistance to the regime, total state control of culture (even composing at the Liszt Academy of Music), and poverty taken with pride are the key themes for Handler. Nineteen sixty-two marks a change in tone, and the turnaround is completed by 1964. By December, Hungary and Kádár would become the "favorite sons" of the paper and would remain that until 1989.

Nineteen sixty-two saw the publication of two interesting pieces in the *Times*. Drama critic Howard Taubman touring the Iron Curtain countries, reported from Budapest that the Kádár regime had developed a new, rather liberal attitude toward the arts.[47] In an article that is mostly concerned with a shift in theme from cooperative farms to human interest stories on stage since 1956, Taubman comments on the Revolution and its official Hungarian interpretation. He cites the Party line that liberalization was well on its way and the "counterrevolution" had set it back considerably, because enemies of the regime forced "renewed surveillance after 1956," although the will to liberalize on the part of the government overcame all such obstacles within a year. Taubman did not have to dig too deep to find that this view was not widely shared, as not many of the people he contacted considered the events leading up the Revolution as "liberalization." Paul Underwood went a step further and began his piece printed on September 27 with the following remark: "Liberalization in Communist-ruled Hungary has gone so far as to raise the question in some minds of who did win the 1956 revolt, after all." He reports that non-Communist Western newspapers are freely available in Budapest (even for Hungarians), that "Kádár has curbed the powers of the secret police," and that the "new atmosphere of 'humanism' has induced many of the 'silent' writers, who had retired from active work in protest against the crushing of the 1956 revolt, to resume their creative effort."[48]

Max Frankel's special from Budapest on the state of US-Hungarian relations,[49] like the Taubman piece cited above, represents a transition between the extremes of Handler on the one hand and Underwood on the other. Frankel correctly identifies sources of tension between the two countries, then points to signals of goodwill on both sides: Kádár's partial amnesty granted to those who did not fight in the Revolution and the US decision to remove the Hungarian Question from the UN agenda. He sees Cardinal Mindszenty's stay at the American Legation in Budapest as the key issue to be settled before relations could be "normalized." The Revolution gets two mentions in the article: first, it is identified as the point in time when bilateral relations cooled off, and it is mentioned again in connection with Mindszenty. He does call the events a "revolution."

"Bridge-building" brought about a supportive public relations campaign in the paper on behalf of Kádár—not because he suddenly came to live up to American ideals of democracy but because his Hungary could be perhaps an example for other Iron Curtain countries. Genuine enthusiasm about major positive developments in Hungary and in international relations mingle with mixed acceptance of the status quo and the unconscious desire to praise the regime to death. As will be shown later, such reporting earned critical remarks in the letters to the editor section of the paper. The all-around change in the tone of reporting in the paper was largely due to the efforts of Max Frankel and David Binder. Frankel describes Hungary as "A land of Euphemism" and is the first to observe the effects and role of political humor in stabilizing the Kádár regime.[50] In a highly controversial, six-page Sunday magazine article Binder claims that "10,000,000 Hungarians Can't Be Wrong."[51] Turning evil into virtue, he describes Kádár's ascension to power as a rags-to-riches story, elegantly dodging disturbing details by saying that the "complete story of Kádár's activities during that fateful year of 1956 has yet to be disclosed." He describes Kádár as a victim and survivor of Stalinist purges, who knows all too well what to do and what not to do. He calls the challenges facing the ruler of Hungary "large and familiar:" Kádár must be able to toe the line, adjusting to changes in Moscow, must reform the economic system of Hungary, must "contend with Magyar nationalism," and must find a solution to "the corruption, apathy and cynicism that are endemic to East European societies." He concludes with words of praise for Kádár's character. This article, like Binder's "Pleasantly Pampered Hungary" from a year later,[52] stands out as the classic country profile piece identified in the introduction of the present chapter.

Two possible ways to further develop the positive image of Hungary were to narrow and/or widen the focus of reporting. Accordingly, single-topic pieces were printed on the one hand, while the broader context was provided with the new slogan, "A Thaw in East Europe's 'Ice Age.'" In two articles published two days apart and echoing earlier catch-phrases, C. L. Sulzberger analyzed Hungarian foreign policy. In "Foreign Affairs: Not Titoist or Polycentrist"[53] he describes Kádár as a supporter of better East-West relations and bilateral contacts, and calls him a liberal and a nationalist: "The interesting thing about Kádár, who has followed a rocky road from prison to opposition to revolution and counterrevolution and then to power, is that he is neither a Communist intellectual nor a pragmatic technician, but in between." Sulzberger continues by saying that "although he was primarily responsible for inviting in Soviet troops in 1956, there is no doubt he is a nationalist," and supports peaceful competition between "the Communist and capitalist blocs." In "Foreign Affairs: Hungary between Two Symbols,"[54] Sulzberger raises the already familiar concept of the Revolution winning through the back door, and compares Kádár to Nagy. He is presented as a tragic hero-turned-master of Realpolitik, bringing a "human aspect" and "liberalism" to his country. Sulzberger explains the "two symbols" in his title the following ways: "Human and responsible, he seems bigamously wedded to Hungary's national pride and to Communism, a man caught between the symbols of the ideological tyrant Rákosi and the ideological renegade Nagy."

Widening the focus meant coverage of the various Soviet satellites in a single article. In this, Frankel was the trend-setter, reporting from Vienna on January 18, 1965, with the headline, "Changes in Eastern Europe: A Country-by-Country Profile," and the subheading, "Speed of Thaw Varies in Region." He cites Western analysts marking changes in the Eastern bloc by degrees of "de-Stalinization" and "de-satellization," and claims that East Europeans "use much the same standards" in evaluating their own lives. He discusses seven countries in the region and contends that they are all different cases—the first open challenge to the image of the monolithic Soviet bloc in the paper. Hungary stands out not just as an example to follow in the text, but Kádár's photo is also placed in the center of the article. Frankel proposes an interesting thesis, which became the underlying theme of reporting on Hungary: "Hungary, which eight years ago made the most dramatic bid for escape from the Soviet bloc is today the best example of how far de-Stalinization can proceed without much significant de-satellization."[55] Kádár's achievements are listed but are contrasted with his loyalty to Moscow: "National pride was encouraged, but there was never a suggestion that the national interest deviated in the slightest from that of the Soviet Union." Quoting unidentified Hungarian sources, he lists three possible explanations: (1) he is loyal to Khrushchev, who put him into power after 1956; (2) domestic opposition forces him closer to Moscow; and/or (3) he wants to control reforms so that they would not get out of hand like before. The "thaw" theme was further developed by Edmund Stillman in a nine-page Sunday magazine special on August 21, 1966.[56] Stillman, a former diplomat, looks at the region with a diplomat's eye and sees clear signs of decay in the bloc: "snubbing Russians" is "common sport," he says, the Russian military has become invisible, and resistance to Moscow and "challenge to the Soviet hegemony" is spearheaded by Ceausescu's Romania. Hungary gets two mentions: first in connection with 1956, which "was the year of popular revolt in Eastern Europe," and then in connection with Romania's defiance of Soviet power, when Stillman openly questions Moscow's willingness to flex muscle again, like it did in 1956.[57] The article carries four photos, with one coming from the Revolution, the famous "Ruszkik haza" [Russians go home] shop-window shot.

With no significant change in message, subsequent country profiles on Hungary could add but little to the themes developed between 1961 and 1966. In 1969 and 1974 the paper reported that Hungary was "nervously building ties to [the] West," and in 1972 open praise for Kádár was printed again, with the usual street joke for starters, and a photo in the middle.[58] In these, the Revolution remains a simple reference point for the time when Kádár came to power and when things began to change for the better. A personal, intimate account of a visit to Budapest was printed from the exiled Czech writer Alan Levy in 1976,[59] and in 1977 the paper published a one-page summary which amounts to a condensed guidebook to Hungary, Paul Hofmann's "What's Doing in BUDAPEST."[60] The Polish crisis of 1980–81 brought back memories of 1956 and 1968, and yielded even more street jokes. So much so, that John Darnton's special from Budapest in 1980[61] is more a collection of jokes than actual reporting. The one that stands out is the one that links Soviet interventions in Hungary, Czechoslovakia, and Afghanistan. The question is: What is the new Moscow phone number for "friendly assistance?" The answer: 56–68–79. Kádár is described toward the end of the piece as "the aging party leader installed 24 years ago during the Soviet invasion." Unlike his counterparts in other Soviet satellites, he is "genuinely popular," and "allows himself to be spoofed occasionally." Another, more serious piece published in the same year brings together reviews of Hungary, Romania, East Germany, Czechoslovakia, and Bulgaria from five different journalists, with the tell-tale title, "East Europe Measures Its Freedoms Inch by Inch."[62] The last country profiles of Hungary to mention the Revolution were both put out in 1989. "Hungary at a Glance" is a short, facts-and-figures type introduction to the country with a sketchy map, and one comment on the Revolution: "The uprising of 1956 and its brutal suppression with Soviet tanks shocked the world and were viewed as a historic turning point for the Soviet bloc."[63] The other, "Hungarians, Maestros of Ambiguity, Confront a Whole New Political Process," by R. W. Apple, Jr., is a mixture and summation of the classic country profile themes.[64] He begins with two jokes, reflects upon the upcoming referendum on the future of the country, reports the end of "bittersweet humor," and lists the challenges facing the new Hungary he sees. He senses a new "feeling of neocolonialism experienced by long-term residents" of the country, and cites an American businessman about the possibility of an American and West European "invasion" of the country (and its economic system): "It is inevitable….Two, three years, and there will be a backlash against this capitalist exploitation."

The quality of country profiles on Hungary is rather mixed, but these articles served a major purpose by developing Kádár's clearly positive image in the paper. While this has worked against the trends identified in the articles on memory in the previous chapter, country profiles do retain their importance for memory preservation, and work against strategies of forgetting inherent in them, by constantly reminding the reader of the Soviet invasion of Hungary in 1956.

Political Coverage

Political coverage one way or another related to the Hungarian Revolution of 1956 accounts for the majority (about two thirds) of the articles identified for the purposes of this paper in the *New York Times*. The following topical-chronological overview will focus primarily on new trends and key elements in *Times* reporting, and will offer observations that either confirm or go beyond the conclusions of the previous chapters. The initial (1957–60) publication of various reports and diplomatic correspondence is one such trend, and clarifying certain aspects of the history and/or interpretation of the Revolution is another. Later political coverage was more diverse in theme but, with the exception of the Prague Spring and the rise of Solidarity in Poland, added little to the general picture.

In 1957 the *New York Times* printed extensive excerpts from the UN report on "the Hungarian Uprising,"[65] and carried the full text of Vice President Nixon's report to President Eisenhower on the "Problems of Hungarian Refugee Relief."[66] Sir Leslie Munro's report on the "Hungarian Question" to the UN was printed in full in 1959.[67] The UN line was supported by extensive quotes from speeches by Henry Cabot Lodge, the US ambassador to the UN,[68] and eventually by coverage on UN General Secretary U Thant's visit to Budapest in 1963, following the end of Hungary's suspension by the organization the month before.[69]

Clarifying and interpreting the most important questions of the Revolution got a new boost when Belgrade openly criticized Budapest for the executions in 1958.[70] It was revealed as early as 1958 that Josip Broz Tito had indeed supported Soviet intervention in Hungary.[71] Also in 1958, on account of the executions of Imre Nagy and his fellow revolutionaries, the State Department issued a public statement and duly got into a heated argument with Budapest over it.[72] Khrushchev's 1959 visit to Budapest attracted special attention, and his remarks about a split in the Kremlin over Hungary were reported and discussed. Accusations were flying in both directions, and the *Times* added reports on additional trials and executions.[73] Even more importantly, the paper quoted Marshal Kliment Y. Voroshilov's comments on the Revolution:

Such foolish things have happened there. Some people have called it counterrevolution, some called it revolution. I think it was just foolishness....Perhaps it would have been possible not to give Imre Nagy such a harsh sentence because he was just a fool. Nagy never helped us, never raised his finger to help us. He was not a real Communist.[74]

Voroshilov's statement is worthy of attention because it adds, albeit inadvertently, to the mythology of the Revolution by denying Nagy's status as a real communist. Nagy as a devoted communist leading an anti-Soviet Revolution with very strong anti-communist overtones is something the *Times* could never really digest. But this myth has not been confined only to the American media. It would be revived and carried to its logical extreme by Márta Mészáros in her recent Hungarian-made film about Nagy, *A temetetlen halott* [The Unburied Man, 2004], in which she emphasizes Nagy's religious consciousness over his Communist past and present.

Kádár's positive image in the *Times* first surfaced during his 1960 visit to the US, when he attended the UN's fall session. Detailed coverage of where he went and what he did was supplemented with accounts of the protests staged against his very presence on American soil, and interestingly, with two human interest stories: one about a family reunion, the other about the release from jail of prominent Hungarian writers Gyula Háy and Tibor Déry. During the visit, the *New York Times* printed a Hungarian government statement inviting refugees to repatriate and promising them immunity from prosecution by the authorities.[75] This is rather peculiar, because one year earlier, in 1959, the paper commented on a similar statement by Kádár that it was a trap to lure refugees home and go after them in the purges.[76] This trend would continue into the 1960s with two major themes: Kádár eases terror and purges former Stalinists from power.

Church and state relations in Hungary added yet another new dimension to *New York Times* reporting and the memory of the Revolution. The attacks on the churches are well-documented.[77] The whole project was controlled by the State Bureau for Church Affairs, headed by Imre Miklós during most of the Kádár era. The added twist in the case of Hungary was, of course, Cardinal József Mindszenty, a victim of an early Stalinist show trial and one of the symbols of the Revolution. His stay at the US Legation (from 1966, Embassy) from 1956 to 1971 was a constant reminder of the Revolution for both sides. The Vatican also played an important role in East-West relations with its new diplomatic initiative towards the Iron Curtain countries. The reestablishment of diplomatic relations between the Vatican and Budapest in 1964 became front page news in the *Times*.[78] Mindszenty remained the point of reference for the paper, but the tone of the comments followed the general trend pointed out before. In 1962 he was linked to the Soviet invasion, in 1964 to the "failure of the Hungarian revolt." The attack on the churches in Hungary remained on the agenda of the *Times* during the 1960s, and acquired new significance when Billy Graham visited Hungary in 1977. His enthusiastic reports about the (relative) freedom of religion in Hungary helped convince President Jimmy Carter to agree to the return of the coronation regalia.[79]

American-Hungarian relations hit rock bottom as a result of 1956, and improvements in bilateral relations were automatically linked to the Revolution. Reports on the naturalization of 29,000 refugees in 1959[80] were followed by factual reporting on the mutual lifting of visa restrictions between 1960 and 1963.[81] The partial amnesty granted by Kádár opened the gates for better relations, and President Lyndon B. Johnson's speech on bridge building duly followed. Expectations were riding high,[82] but the *Times* tried to cool them off by printing a one-page special from Budapest by Frankel titled "East Europe Seeks 'Bridges' to the West" on November 29, 1964. Frankel recognizes the popularity of the West in the Soviet satellites, evaluates Johnson's speech, but concludes by saying,

> The history of the last 10 years suggests that United States policy will not affect the fundamental course of Eastern Europe. The most dramatic and startling things have occurred without Western intervention. But to encourage the desired trends amid the present confusion Americans will require a perception and flexibility that they have not yet demonstrated in dealings with Communist Europe. And officials here, because they are after all Communists, will not make it easy.

Frankel's insightful comments were seemingly contradicted by the raising of the level of diplomatic representation to ambassadorial in

1966, but he was vindicated by the events of August 1968. Nixon's ascension to power marked a new policy of divide and rule not only toward the Soviet Union and China, but also toward the Soviet Union and her East European satellites. From the four points in 1969 to the return of the Holy Crown and the coronation regalia and the MFN agreement in 1978, the Revolution was pushed to the background in *New York Times* reporting. Kádár seemed more and more acceptable, as time went on, and as bilateral relations improved.

Outstanding domestic Hungarian developments were discussed in some three dozen articles between 1957 and 1981. The first such piece by Handler from 1958 reported that the Hungarian government had imported US jukeboxes to boost the low morale of the country after the Revolution and the subsequent retaliation.[83] He does not go beyond stating that this is a policy of bread and circus as practiced by Kádár. An American Friends of the Captive Nations report from 1962 asserts that "Hungarians remain pro-West," but will need US help.[84] Covering a period of September 1961 to October 1962, the report correctly states that although life has become more acceptable in Hungary, the country is still a "totalitarian dictatorship." Kádár's purge of Ernő Gerő and Mátyás Rákosi from the Hungarian Socialist Workers Party (HSWP) was reported approvingly by the paper,[85] as was the partial amnesty in 1963. The earlier noted turnaround in the attitude of the paper towards the Hungarian ruler is apparent here, too: in 1963 the *Times* recorded without much comment that Kádár supposedly said, "We shall not wage war against people because of their beliefs."[86] Economic problems were reported from time to time (1964, 1966,[87] the reforms in 1968, etc.), and Khrushchev's fall triggered extensive speculation about a possible rift between Moscow and her satellites in the mid-1960s.[88]

In 1965 the paper devoted a lot of attention to Hungarian concerns over a relatively low birth rate, the "re-evaluation" of motherhood, and abortion.[89] Binder continued to build the tragic hero image of Kádár in 1969, when he discussed the rehabilitation of former interior minister and show trial victim László Rajk.[90] Rajk was actually given a state burial a couple of weeks before the Revolution in 1956, but what would have been his sixtienth birthday was used by Kádár to remind the country of his own imprisonment. Binder dutifully reports the Rajk story but devotes the final third of the piece only to Kádár's version of the events, and concludes the article by praising the Hungarian leader's brave stand in supposedly challenging Moscow on the issue.

Hungary's economic difficulties, problems with Moscow over the delivery of raw materials by the Soviet Union and the slow pace of reforms were discussed in 1972 by James Feron and Tad Szulc.[91] Clyde H. Farnsworth reported from Vienna about street demonstrations in Budapest on March 15, the anniversary of the 1848 Revolution.[92] The attitude of the demonstrators was described as "anti-Establishment," and "tough" police action was reported. The subheading of the article gives away its real significance, a theme well developed by Farnsworth: "Demonstration Is Thought First Since '56 Uprising." Three months later, an account of Secretary of State William P. Rogers's state visit to Hungary, brought back reporting to square one: Kádár is introduced as "the Communist party chief since the suppression of the 1956 uprising," and the atmosphere of the negotiations is described as "friendly" and "cordial."[93] The last important piece before 1989 was an in-depth analysis of the Hungarian economy under the front-page title "Hungary Builds Lively Economy on West's Ideas" on December 3, 1981. Based on extensive research and interviews, Paul Lewis discusses Kádár's economic strategies, the planned economy of Hungary, the progress of reforms since 1968, and the emergence of the private sector.[94] Nineteen eighty-one and 1982 of course marked Hungary's admission to the International Monetary Found (IMF) and the World Bank.

The two key political events that automatically brought back memories of, and comparisons with, the 1956 Revolution were the Prague Spring of 1968, the rise of Solidarity, and the subsequent Polish crisis of 1980–81. Reporting in 1968 began in earnest with a Binder special from Bonn on the deposed Czechoslovak leader Alexander Dubcek on March 25.[95] He applauds Czechoslovak liberalization, but quotes the Hungarian Party daily *Népszabadság's* editorial which "warned of the tragic consequences of a similar liberalization that got out of hand in Budapest in 1956 and ended with Soviet tanks crushing a full-fledged rebellion." This type of comparison would remain a theme paper, with some historical memory thrown in. A July 6 article drawing on British opinion compares 1968 to the "sellout" at Munich in 1938,[96] and warns that world public opinion will not prevent Soviet intervention; after all, it did not prevent intervention in Hungary in 1956 either.

A Sulzberger "Foreign Affairs" article on August 7 saw a revival of the Little Entente against Hungary in the Soviet bloc in the summer 1968 events.[97] This new Little Entente, he adds, is not about frontiers but "simply aims at mutual support in securing independence within the Communist system." On July 31 Hofmann reported no Soviet troop movements from Hungary, and the joint Warsaw Pact invasion was evaluated in a front-page article (on August 21) titled "Soviet Turns Back Clock" by James Reston. 1956 is used as a natural point of reference, and Reston puts forward an interesting analysis. He describes the "Soviet intervention in Hungary in 1956" as "a spasm of Stalinist aggression, taken at a time when the hard Stalinist line was strong." Prague, on the other hand, comes after a period of de-Stalinization, "not by a dictatorial leader but by the new post-Khrushchev 'collective leadership.' The struggle between those who wanted to encourage more freedom in Moscow and those who thought freedom was too dangerous...has now apparently been resolved." A report two days later recorded the fact that the Soviet Union and Hungary vetoed a UN resolution condemning the invasion of Czechoslovakia.[98] Hungary, meanwhile, remained subdued, and, not surprisingly, *Times* reporters in Budapest heard no open discussion of 1956 and 1968.[99] Kádár's support for and a last-minute visit to Dubcek was reported, but so was his conspicuous absence from public life between the invasion and early November.[100] Coverage was rounded out by a report on Czechoslovak refugees, which drew predictable parallels with the problems of the 1956 refugees.[101]

Nineteen fifty-six, 1968, 1979, and 1980 came to be inextricably mixed in *New York Times* reporting on the rise of Solidarity and the subsequent political crisis in Poland. The logical parallels were drawn: in 1956 there was a crisis in Poland, and Hungary responded to it. The Hungarian Revolution was suppressed by superior Soviet force, and similar changes were prevented in Prague by similar measures. On January 10, 1980 John Darnton analyzed East European responses to the Soviet invasion of Afghanistan in a special article from Warsaw.[102] He sees "traces of concern and anxiety" beyond the public support on the part of some of Moscow's satellites. "Military assistance" is the catchphrase, but Czech and Bulgarian papers have openly accused the CIA of meddling in Afghanistan. He reports low-key coverage in the Polish and Hungarian press, and points to the apparent lack of editorial comment.

A six-page Sunday magazine article by Leslie H. Gelb, "Beyond the Carter Doctrine,"[103] offers a critical review of America's position in the world and the author expresses serious doubts about the possibility of handling the crisis effectively. Nor does he see any possibility of rapprochement (as after 1956, 1962, and 1968) between the superpowers within a year or two of the settlement of crisis. He lists four cornerstones for future US foreign policy: (1) a military balance of power between the superpowers; (2) a clear-cut list of American preferences and a way to let the Russians know exactly where Washington stands on these issues; (3) some basic level of cooperation between Moscow and Washington even in times of crisis; and (4) the realization that "in the competition over the third world the Russians will no more accept our rules of the game than we will accept theirs." He concludes his analysis by stating that while "the options of the left and the right [in American politics] have always seemed too dangerous, the middle-ground options have never really proved satisfactory." America's real hope lies in the fact that the Soviet invasion of Afghanistan may alienate third world leaders from Moscow. Little did Gelb know in February 1980 that, within months, yet another Polish crisis would further complicate international relations.

Reporting on the rise of Solidarity drew obvious comparisons with Hungary, but only in 1980. In 1981 such comparisons were reserved for editorial comment in the paper. The first, and most comprehensive, analysis of the possible "ripple effects" of the strikes at the Lenin Shipyard in Gdansk might have on other East European countries was published on August 28.[104] Flora Lewis reported food shortages in nearly all of the Soviet satellites, and devoted about one third of the article to Hungary.

> Hungary is the only country in Eastern Europe that has devised safety valves for popular grievances, and János Kádár is the one Communist leader whom Western diplomats believe capable of winning a free election. Economic changes introduced after the 1956 revolution have given Hungary more flexibility in coping with its problems.

Lewis cites a tacit agreement "between the rulers and the ruled" in Hungary over "just how far each side can go." The "shadow of that tragedy still marks Hungary," she continues, but economic changes and the total reorganization of the HSWP have made Hungary a special case behind the Iron Curtain. This privileged position, however, depends too much on Kádár, and he is "68 years old, a heavy smoker, and is not in the best of health." She sees a paradox in the Polish and Hungarian situation: the 1956 Revolution in Hungary was sparked by protests in Poland. The Hungarian Revolution was suppressed, while Poland was allowed to go its own way. Those concessions fell by the wayside gradually in Poland, while Hungary secured some for herself. So it is "undoubtedly the memory of the disillusionment after what seemed like victory in 1956 and again in 1970…that makes the Polish workers so distrustful of the current Government's promises." Reports on disturbances in each of the neighboring socialist countries are "filtered to a minimum," so the "ripple effect of what has been going on in Poland is likely to be slow, but to provoke far reaching changes nonetheless." While Lewis's arguments are quite convincing, she too promotes the image of Kádár as an elder statesman, a sort of Iron Curtain role model. The "tacit agreement" she cites was rather one-sided, as is the case in any dictatorship.

By December, tempers were flaring in Poland, and the American presidential election had been won by Ronald Reagan. The *New York Times* showed continued interest in the Polish crisis, and Flora Lewis and Binder provided in-depth reporting and analysis from Budapest. In "Hungary's High Stakes"[105] Lewis explains the "ripple effect" again, and contends that Hungarians have everything to lose in case of a Soviet invasion in Poland. She sees similarities with the events of 1956, "when the Polish Communists threatened to face down Soviet tanks and were spared, while the Hungarians marched in support, escalated their own demands and were finally crushed by the Red Army." Hungary learned the lessons of 1956 while the Poles forgot, but Hungarians have a vested interest in letting each Soviet satellite go her own way. Binder reported from Budapest that Hungarian leaders felt uneasy over the Polish crisis but expected no problems at home. In another piece he quotes a Hungarian trade union leader saying that the Polish situation was to a degree similar to Hungary before 1956: the unions and the demands of the people were disregarded.[106] When the decision not to intervene was made in Moscow and General Wojciech Jaruzelski introduced martial law to suppress the unrest, the *Times* moved comparisons to Hungary to the editorial pages.

In 1989 the *New York Times* kept a close watch on the events in Hungary, but was no quicker to realize the sweeping nature of the changes than the George H. W. Bush administration itself. The paper followed a policy of letting Hungarians speak their minds but its tone remained skeptical. Interviews and invited articles were contrasted with remarks such as "Hungary Is Far from Democracy, and Even from Poland,"[107] and "Hungary under New Management: A Cart Pulling a Horse?"[108] Hungary was mentioned as a possible new Spain,[109] but the paper also raised the question: "Is East Europe Too Amazing for the West?"[110] Kádár's illness (and subsequent death) was reported,[111] and his reevaluation began, but the Revolution remained an uprising and a rebellion:

> Mr. Kádár, once hailed as the most liberal Communist leader in Eastern Europe had become a detriment to the party, which is embarked on political and economic change. The process includes reassessing Hungary's past, including Mr. Kádár's role in joining the Soviet suppression of the 1956 uprising after first supporting the rebellion.

The *Times* also covered the legal recognition of the opposition as well as the disbanding of the Party Militia,[112] and the year was summed up, on December 3, in a half-page chart reviewing "Eleven Months of Peaceful Revolution" in Eastern Europe. President Bush's successful trip to Budapest received due attention;[113] after all, he was the first president in office to visit Hungary. Coverage of the fallout from the "year of miracles" in Hungary was concluded by extensive reporting on the writer and translator, and 1956 hero, Árpád Göncz becoming the country's newly elected president in 1990.[114] In the *New York Times* reports of 1989 the emphasis shifted from glorifying Kádár to the actual arrival of democracy in Hungary, the real legacy of the 1956 Revolution.

A small group of articles beyond the main trends of political reporting outlined above also touched upon the memory of 1956. In 1962 General Lucius Clay completed his mission in Germany as the president's special envoy to Berlin, and Sulzberger paid him tribute in one of his "Foreign Affairs" articles.[115] Citing a face-off that took place between Soviet and American tanks in Berlin in October 1961, he praises Clay for making the Russians understand that there was no way that "we could be pushed out by fear of war." The Russians have been more adventurous "since 1956, when we failed to react in Hungary," but this was a clear message. Without citing any background information, Sulzberger implies here that there might have been some serious discussion about possibly protecting Hungary during the Revolution. Recent evidence, however, indicates that Washington had a hands-off policy. Another article feeds on the bridge-building atmosphere of 1964: Hungary and Austria settled outstanding diplomatic and economic issues during Foreign Minister Bruno Kreisky's three-day visit to Budapest.[116] The reference to the Revolution states that it "caused new bitterness and strained relations between the two countries." The brief but forgotten Polish crisis of 1970 evoked memories of 1956, and East Germany accused RFE of "fomenting discontent" in Poland.[117] The reference to 1956 is again rather casual: "During the 1956 riots in Poland and Hungary, both Radio Free Europe and the Voice of America were widely criticized by officials who felt they had incited the rioters."

Arguably the most interesting revival of the memory of the Hungarian Revolution of 1956 in political coverage happened during the presidential elections of 1976. In the best piece on the subject, Gelb openly questions President Ford's decisions to approve a Soviet-style status quo in Europe in Helsinki and to refuse to meet the exiled Soviet writer Alexander Solzhenitsyn.[118] The (in)famous Sonnenfeldt doctrine is mentioned in connection with a shift in American thinking from bridge-building to détente with Moscow, meaning American acceptance of a more "organic" relationship between the Soviet Union and her East European satellites. The argument is that the former had led to the Prague Spring and Soviet intervention, and that the latter is a better guarantee for Eastern Europe. Two more Ford mistakes are cited: (1) he stalled the appointment of a special commission to supervise the human rights agreements made in Helsinki, and (2) he made some awkward statements in one of the TV debates. He claimed that "there is no Soviet domination of Eastern Europe and there never will be under the Ford Administration," and added that "each of these countries is independent and autonomous." Gelb does not see in what way Carter's policy would be different, and how he would "tailor actions toward particular East European states." He finds especially troubling Carter's statements about "pressing Moscow on more civil rights for the East Europeans." We now know that President Carter failed to enforce his human rights ideas in Eastern Europe, but he did initiate a selective and preferential attitude towards the Eastern bloc countries. The outstanding events were of course his state visit to Poland and the return of the Holy Crown to Hungary.

The abundance and variety of references to the Hungarian Revolution in *New York Times* political reporting ranging from domestic Hungarian matters through US-Hungarian relations to presidential elections further supports the claim that the paper intended to preserve the memory of 1956 but also sought a modus vivendi with Budapest, to the last minute in 1989. This becomes even more obvious if we take a closer look at editorials, op-ed pieces, invited commentary, and letters to the editor.

EDITORIALS AND LETTERS TO THE EDITOR

Although editorial comment and letters to the editor are two clearly distinct journalistic genres, they are discussed here in one chapter because readers often felt they had to express their views of, or offer corrections about, feature articles on Hungary, political reporting and editorials mentioning the Revolution. The fact that editorials respond to political events makes the repetition of certain earlier ideas and information inevitable, but such repetitions will be kept to a minimum.

Editorials of memory in the *New York Times* first surfaced after the execution of Imre Nagy. "Savagery in Budapest" uses emotionally charged expressions like "horror," "slaughter," and "a wave of shock, revulsion and abhorrence" to describe the papers's stance on Nagy's execution.[119] Published one year later, "Hungary Three Years After," looks at the then current situation in Hungary and sees little hope of improvement.[120] The article describes the horrors of the postrevolutionary terror, and then states, "more of the same is all the Hungarian people can expect for the foreseeable future." In October 1963 the tone was markedly different. Actually, it matched the change in political reporting and country profiles, with one significant difference. The "sacrifices of 1956 were not in vain," because Kádár has moved towards general liberalization and eased the terror, but the author finds the claims that the Revolution was won exaggerated. Unlike other *New York Times* articles of the period, this piece calls the events of October–November 1956 a revolution in the very first sentence: "Seven years ago the heroic people of Budapest began the movement against tyranny which history now calls the Hungarian Revolution."[121] The last major editorial of memory before 1989 was printed in 1976 and is called "Twenty Years After."[122] The author raises the question of why we should remember, and answers in fine style:

> In the long run men are ruled by ideas more than by guns. The aims of the Hungarian Revolution were in fact partially realized even though the revolt itself was drowned in treachery and in blood. The revolution was a cry of pain from an entire people that the decade-old Stalinist oppression was unendurable.

He then adds that "the average Hungarian is not only materially far better off than he was two decades ago, but is in effect a coconspirator with his national leaders in an arrangement providing constrained liberty." The conclusion is a warning to Moscow: the Kremlin should not believe that the wounds of 1956 have healed, since the victims of "almost unbelievable Russian treachery" will always "be remembered as long as the Hungarian people value freedom." A full review of the *New York Times* coverage of the events of 1989 would go way beyond the scope of this paper, but one editorial deserves special attention. "In Hungary, a Prophet Honored" represents a return to the style of the editorials. It describes Nagy as "a Communist who scorned Stalinism as the true heresy," and calls Kádár a "willing turncoat" who served the interests of Moscow. Kádár's reforms are mentioned, but so are his attempts to suppress the memories the Revolution and Imre Nagy. The "bells of Budapest" prove that Nagy has not been forgotten, and the author expresses his hope that the echoes may be heard in Beijing, too.[123]

The largest group of editorials, some thirty of them, commented on political developments. First on the agenda was the Hungarian question in the UN and the Hungarian government's unwillingness to cooperate.[124] On October 2, 1962, on the eve of what would be remembered as the hottest moment of the Cold War, an editorial compared the Cuban situation to the "shadow of 1956," but did so with an unexpected twist.[125] The writer admits that Castro is a threat to the Western Hemisphere, but compares the proposed "unilateral" action to the Soviet invasion of Hungary. Seeing Berlin (the building of the wall) as a major crisis, the article warns against turning Cuba into "another Suez" during an election campaign. The partial amnesty in Hungary in 1963 won accolades form the paper, as did President Johnson's speech on bridge building and the diplomatic agreement between the Vatican and Hungary in 1964.[126] The general optimism of the paper is reflected in an editorial from 1965, which raises the question, "Satellites No More?"[127]

Wishful thinking was gone by the summer of 1968, but returned briefly during the early and mid-1970s.[128] The already mentioned 1976 TV debate between Ford and Carter brought about another thoughtful piece, titled "Eastern Europe Reconsidered."[129] The author remarks on the coincidence between the anniversary of the events of 1956 and the exchanges about Eastern Europe between the presidential candidates, and then recites Stalin's attempts to homogenize Eastern Europe and the East Europeans' resistance to it. He writes, "30 years after World War II, Eastern Europe presents an enormously varied political and economic landscape....In the face of such diversity, it is an error to characterize Eastern Europe by means of a simple cliché or formula." The recommended course for American foreign policy is differentiation, taking "into account in each case the particulars of that nation's situation and the limited United States potential to help these countries toward a better and more independent future." A clear difference of opinion between opinions represented by the *New York Times* staff can be detected if we compare this article with Gelb's piece on the same topic.

This diversity of opinion carried over into coverage of the events of 1989, too. In "Salami Tactics" William Safire sees "great activity without underlying action,"[130] while Anthony Lewis simply declares communism dead in "Death of a Pretense."[131] President George W. H. Bush's visit to Budapest was anticipated with enthusiasm. Interestingly, no editorial was written on the occasion of Hungary becoming a republic and turning October 23 into a national holiday in the same year. In an extensive op-ed piece in 1997, the prominent Hungarian writer Péter Nádas revisited the events of 1989 and explained his worries about the West possibly deserting the new East European democracies.[132]

A separate group of editorials compared crises behind the Iron Curtain, as time and the Cold War progressed. Predictable comparisons between 1956 and 1968 accounted for as many as four important editorials.[133] Two years later, another editorial pieced memory and comparison together. "Prague Two Years After" looks at the "normalization" of the situation, and wonders if Brezhnev would be as willing to let Gustav Husak go his own way as was Khrushchev with Kádár.[134] As has been pointed out earlier, comparison between the Hungarian crisis of 1956 and the Polish crisis of 1980–81 was also a common feature of *Times* reporting, but the topic was moved to the editorial pages in 1981. "Since Budapest" begins with a straightforward statement: the reason why people continue to "ask whether the Soviet Union will invade Poland is twenty-five years old this week. The reason is Hungary, 1956."[135] The revolt and "the treachery of the Soviet attack" are not simply things of the past: they have "defined East European politics and much East-West diplomacy for a quarter century." Moscow learned that it could maintain its control over her satellites only by force, and proved again its unwillingness to accept even Marxist reforms in 1968. The author sees hope for Poland in the rise of East European nationalisms, and in the lasting effects of détente, interestingly more than a year after détente had been declared officially dead. Although the Soviet invasion of Afghanistan was seen as yet another show of force on the part of the Kremlin, it drew no comparisons with Hungary and 1956.

A handful of articles that represent the opinions and preferences of the editors but fit none of the above categories also deserve attention. On June 19, 1958, *New York Times* Soviet expert and legal analyst Harry Schwartz reviewed the official statement of the Hungarian government regarding the execution of Imre Nagy and his associates, identified distortions in the quotes from Nagy's earlier writings, and concluded that the case simply did not stand.[136] In 1963 James Reston analyzed American policies of asylum, and expressed his dissatisfaction with the fact that the Moscow embassy turned over thirty-two Russian Christian asylum seekers to Soviet authorities while Cardinal Mindszenty was being protected in Budapest.[137] In August 1972 Milovan Djilas was invited to analyze 125 years of Marxism, and described the then present situation as "a crisis of ideology."[138] Also in 1972 an editorial looked at the influence of American programs on Hungarian television. The wittily titled article ("Comrade Flintstone") points to the Hungarians' appetite for American programs, and alludes to the great popularity of *The Flintstones*.[139] The final comment is revealing: the middle class values mocked in the series are but a "mild spoof in the United States, but [they] can only suggest wistful envy in a Soviet satellite." The Revolution is used as a reference point: "When the Russians crushed the Hungarian rising in 1956 they could hardly have foreseen that the ultimate invader of Hungary would be the bourgeois influence of television."

Letters to the editor tended to respond to reporting and editorials in the *Times*, but on some occasions they had no immediate predecessor in the paper. Over the course of the past fifty years, the *New York Times* has published about twenty such letters that somehow addressed issues connected with the Revolution. Ferenc A. Váli, noted author of one the first scholarly books about the Revolution, explained the differences between American and British interventions in the Middle East and the Soviet invasion of Hungary in 1956.[140] One year later, Béla Varga and József Kővágó explained why Béla Kovács, a prominent Smallholder and victim of the Stalinist purges, supported the new Kádár regime.[141] In March 1959 Béla K. Király described the connection that he saw between the Hungarian Revolutions of 1848–49 and 1956, and the two Russian interventions crushing them.[142] Khrushchev's visit to Budapest in December of the same year, and his widely quoted statements about disagreements in the Kremlin during the Revolution, prompted László Bartók, a former Hungarian delegate to the League of Nations, to conclude that "the brutal crushing of the revolution by the Soviet armed forces was a deliberate armed intervention in Hungary's internal affairs."[143]

In 1961 UN Commissioner Sir Leslie Munro shared his views about Hungary with the readers, and called on the UN to force the Russians to right the wrongs they had caused to the Hungarian people.[144] Responding to a statement about possible Soviet troop withdrawal from Hungary by Kádár, political activist Béla Fábián commented that "Mr. Kádár, who was imposed on Hungary by Soviet bayonets, would be most unhappy if Mr. Khrushchev were to decide to pull his troops out of Hungary, even if it takes no more than seven minutes for his bombers to fly back again."[145] In 1965, the Rev. Imre Kovács of New York protested against Binder's feature article of December 27, in which the

Times correspondent claimed that ten million Hungarians could not be wrong about Kádár.[146]

In 1968 two prominent Hungarian-born historians, Stephen Borsody and Charles Gati, offered clarifications about the comparisons offered in the *Times* about 1956 and 1968, while a certain Laszlo Thomas Kiss suggested that Kádár should display his "evolutionary" spirit lauded in the *Times* by exerting a moderating effect on Soviet bloc hawks.[147] Robert Levy, the author of an earlier cited feature article on Hungary, compared the Soviet invasions of Hungary and Czechoslovakia to the American interventions in Lebanon and the Dominican Republic.[148] Responding to a November 28, 1970 op-ed piece, Béla K. Király explained his views on "Stalin's Plan to Invade Yugoslavia" in 1949–50.[149] In late 1975 Hungary was granted a seat on the Committee on the Exercise of the Inalienable Rights of the Palestinian People, and Borsody was quick to point out the oddity of the situation.[150] Ten million Hungarians live under direct Soviet control in Hungary, and another 3.5 million in the neighboring Socialist countries, and they cannot represent themselves legally, or in a way that would attract Western attention. His point is that the Palestinians would "be in possession of their inalienable rights well before the Hungarians in the Soviet orbit." History proved him wrong!

Responding to an October 25, 1976 editorial already cited, Borsody explained the effects of the Revolution on the Soviet bloc and concluded that Imre Nagy was actually a martyr of Eurocommunism as well.[151] Duke economist Thomas H. Naylor listed "Hungary's Lessons for Gorbachev" during the early stages of Perestroika in 1986.[152] He claims that Gorbachev should watch Hungary closely, and sees the emergence of a new breed of Soviet managers who are pragmatists rather than ideologists. In 1994 Béla Lipták, an ex-freedom fighter and Hungarian-American activist, sided with the newly elected Socialist Party Premier of Hungary, Gyula Horn.[153] Lipták claims that despite his earlier exploits he should be given the benefit of the doubt, which he had earned the hard way by splitting open the Iron Curtain while Soviet troops were still stationed in Hungary. Finally, the RFE revelations of 1996 triggered a debate in the paper. Two letters addressed the issue, both contesting the claims of the *New York Times* that RFE played a key role in inciting the Revolution.[154]

Editorials and letters to the editor were the chief outlets for the editorial staff and Hungarian émigrés respectively to express their opinions about issues related to the Revolution and its memory. Although responding to political events, editorials often used stern language (and the word revolution) and condemned the Kádár regime. In this regard, these articles match articles on memory and serve to balance the pro-Kádár tone of the country profiles. The letters are important because they represent the only form of fully traceable direct feedback to the paper by 1956 refugees and Hungarian-American political activists.

HUMAN INTEREST STORIES AND CARDINAL MINDSZENTY

Coloring its already impressive contribution to memory, the *New York Times* published a number of human interest stories related to the Hungarian Revolution of 1956. The two biggest, and most significant, stories were the refugees and Cardinal Mindszenty. Additional coverage includes the story of Philharmonia Hungarica as well as dozens of individual cases.

The Hungarian freedom fighter became a new icon overnight during the Revolution. The fact that these people were usually young, often good-looking, also helped. Their arrival in the United States, their stay in Camp Kilmer, entry into American life and the freedom awards they won were all covered extensively by American papers. The *New York Times* database shows 218 hits (144 for 1957 alone) for *Hungarian refugees* between January 1, 1957, and December 31, 1959, while for the period since January 1, 1960, we have 333 hits. This indicates a trend to cover the refugees as news items (arrival of the refugees, UN hearings, American decisions about resettlement, etc.), and not necessarily as part of the process of remembering or reminding. The following survey, therefore, focuses on individual cases and memory in later coverage of the refugees.

Americans quickly grasped the significance of highly trained and educated refugees at Camp Kilmer. Ford Motor Company President Leo Beebe and Cardinal Francis Joseph Spellman both spoke highly of the talent suddenly available.[155] In 1958 the paper reported that a US

Court of Appeals granted Hungarian refugees safeguards against deportation without hearings.[156] 1959 brought about a turn towards reporting on individual stories. On June 3 revolutionary commander Béla Király received his doctoral degree in history from Columbia University, and on June 14 economist Béla A. Balassa was reported to have received three degrees from Yale.[157] Scientists in exile continued to be a popular topic, and the National Science Foundation concluded in 1962 that the professional contributions of the 2,000 Hungarian refugee scientists and engineers "have been almost entirely favorable."[158] In 1964 Stacy V. Jones contributed a lengthy write-up of Antal Csicsátka, the man who invented FM stereo.[159]

The extent of the emotional (and material) support for the refugees was made clear by an amusing story: in Utah, in April 1957, a Hungarian refugee "was ousted from a school painting job because he smoked…at home," but parents on the local school board sided with him despite state laws against smoking, promised him new jobs, and filed an official protest with the school.[160] Family reunions and disappointed refugees returning to Hungary were also covered in the paper.[161] Reporting continued along the same lines, and the *Times* announced in 1962 that "Andau Book Figure Becomes U.S. Citizen."[162] Four years later the story of Joseph Balogh attracted some attention. He was born in Bridgeport, CT, served in the Hungarian army in World War II, and became a Communist. He gave up his Party membership after the 1956 Revolution, and fled to England, where he sought American citizenship, which he was denied.[163] Also in 1966, Maria Judith Remenyi was crowned Miss America at the age of twenty-one.[164] A physics major in California, she came from a refugee family. In 1972 former banquet manager-turned-New Jersey private club owner Julius Szakolczay and cosmetics guru Susan Winkler were profiled.[165] In 1975 William K. Stevens reported from Cleveland on the successful assimilation of the refugees.[166] The last such individual story covered by the *New York Times* was George Varga's return to Hungary in 1990 as General Electric director to buy up the Hungarian company Tungsram.[167]

In the world of music the biggest story was the defection of a large group of classical musicians who later formed the Philharmonia Hungarica, an 80-piece orchestra under Antal Rozsnyai and later Antal Doráti. A 1964 review of one of their concerts at Carnegie Hall tells parts of their early history, and describes the orchestra in the following words: "Like any orchestra formed under its set of circumstances, the Philharmonia Hungarica is as much symbol as anything else. Its members fled Hungary during the uprising in 1956....Audiences in the West cheered their gallantry, their determination to carry on as representatives in exile."[168] The two outstanding stories covered by the *Times* in the world of sports were the defection of three Hungarians at the Tokyo Olympic Games and the adventures of Alex Iby, horse rider, riding instructor, and stable owner.[169] The *Times* also covered the professional career of Hungarian boxing idol Laci (László) Papp,[170] and carried regular references to Hungarian coaches and trainers with the American Olympic teams.

In 1960 a group of former Hungarian boy scouts visited Senegal, and their leader, Edward Chaszar, warned young Africans against the Soviet menace: "We came to tell Scouts in Africa what happens to scouting when communism takes over the Government." Chaszar and his companions, all 1956 refugees, distributed copies of a booklet on "The Crushing of Hungarian Scouting" in nine African countries.[171] A more tragic human interest story dates back to April 29, 1964, when four young black criminals held up a store in Harlem, and stabbed its owners, both 1956 refugees.[172]

The prominent Smallholder Béla Kovács, the Protestant Bishop-turned-Communist Foreign Minister János Péter, and former Communist Party leaders Mátyás Rákosi and Ernő Gerő were all profiled extensively in the *New York Times* between 1957 and 1962.[173] This trend, however, was soon abandoned, with one notable exception, David Binder's tribute to György Lukács, "the Marxist critic and philosopher, on his 80th birthday."[174]

The biggest individual human interest story printed in the *Times* is that of Cardinal József Mindszenty, who has been mentioned in more than a thousand articles since 1945. His name combined with 1956 brings up 125 hits in the database. His early troubles with the Communists were reported in December 1945, and his show trial also received extensive coverage.[175] His speech on November 3, 1956, became especially memorable and made it into every American documentary on the topic. What made him a primary topic for the *New York Times* was, of course, his decision to seek asylum at the American Legation in Budapest in early November 1956. He became inextricably linked with the Revolution in the paper and in memory. Mindszenty articles cover all types of articles discussed in this paper from country profiles and political reporting through editorials and letters to the editor to book reviews and obituaries. Besides speculation on the future of the cardinal, these added little to actual news coverage, but served as a constant reminder. Next, the most interesting Mindszenty articles are reviewed briefly.

The cardinal's mother was allowed to visit her son on occasion, and her death was reported form Vienna in 1960.[176] Mindszenty's departure from the legation (and as of 1966, the embassy) was seen as one of the key issues in American-Hungarian relations. An agreement was reported as imminent in 1961 and then in 1963,[177] but serious negotiations were initiated only after Johnson's bridge-building speech and the diplomatic accord between Hungary and the Vatican.[178] The cardinal's departure from Budapest was front-page news on September 29, 1971,[179] and was followed up with a series of articles about him. He was warmly welcomed by Hungarians in America two years later, and his death in May 1975 was also reported.[180] In 1991 he too was reburied in Hungary, and Pope John Paul II began his official visit to Hungary with a tribute to Mindszenty.[181] With minor modifications, the cardinal was always referred to as someone who had stayed at the American diplomatic mission from the time of the collapse of the Revolution. Choices of words include revolt, rebellion, and uprising, with frequent references to the role of the Soviet Army. The only consistently avoided term is *revolution* after 1964, and as late as 1991 it still wasn't used.

OBITUARIES, REVIEWS, AND POLITICAL ADVERTISEMENTS

Obituaries served as a reminder of the Revolution on a scale larger than one would expect. Freedom fighters and refugees were remembered, but so were high-ranking Hungarian Party officials and prominent Americans who had something to do with Hungary in 1956. The first to be remembered, after Imre Nagy, of course, was Béla Kovács (1959). Pál Kéri, a journalist and a prominent participant in the October Revolution in 1918, passed away in 1960. He was remembered for his contributions to émigré newspapers after 1956. Archbishop József Grősz of Kalocsa, and former Hungarian President (and also a Smallholder) Zoltán Tildy, both died in 1961. In 1966 political activist, lawyer and former MP Béla Fábián was commended in a lengthy obituary. He had an eventful life, and actively participated in anti-Khrushchev and anti-Kádár demonstrations after the Revolution. György (George) Pálóczy-Horváth, a noted journalist living in London, was remembered in 1973 for his open support for Imre Nagy. In 1990, two prominent Hungarians living in America were praised posthumously for their support of the refugees: Professor Géza Charles Paikert and Smallholder, physician and anti-Nazi resister Tibor Hám. József Kővágó, the mayor of Budapest during the Revolution, died in the US in 1996, while other revolutionary heroes György Krassó (1991) and Miklós Vásárhelyi (2001) died in Hungary. Fencing trainer and saber world champion Charles de Pesthy died in 1971, and architect László Miskolczy passed away in 1974.

The prominent Social Democrat Árpád Szakastits (1965) was listed as president of Hungary between 1948 and 1950, and as a politician released from jail just before the Revolution. Top Hungarian Communists General Mihály Farkas (1965), István Dobi (1968), Mátyás Rákosi (1971), Ernő Gerő (1980), Kádár (1989), Károly Grósz (1996) and András Hegedűs (1996) were all given extensive obituaries, often with pictures.

Americans remembered in connection with the Revolution included three diplomats, an army official and two news reporters, as well as a prominent human rights lawyer and a disenchanted Communist Party official. Elim O'Shaughnessy (1966) was chargé d'affaires in Hungary from November 1964 to September 1966. Edward Thomas Wailes (1969), a former assistant secretary of state and the American minister to Hungary in 1956, died at the age of sixty-six in 1969. The Hungarian-born John Pauker (1991) led an eventful life according to his obituary. He was raised in New York, became a poet and joined the Office of War Information during World War II. In 1956 he covered the Revolution for Voice of America and later became presidential speech writer and USIS official. C. Rodney Smith (1999) of the Army Corps of Engineers served as director of RFE after the Revolution. *New York Times* correspondent John MacCormack (1958) and

James M. J. Pringle (1970) were both remembered for their reporting from Budapest during the Revolution. Luis Kutner (1993) was a founding member of Amnesty International and defended the Fascist poet Ezra Pound. He also represented Cardinal Mindszenty during the negotiations that led to his eventual departure from Budapest. George Charney (1975) was New York State Communist Party chairman until he resigned in 1958, in part in protest against "the bloody suppression of the liberal Communist regime in Hungary."

Adding an unexpected dimension to the memory of the Revolution, the *New York Times'* obituary of French philosopher Jean Paul Sartre in 1980 highlighted his break with Soviet communism following 1956.[182] He had worked with French communists in the anti-Nazi resistance movement, but "[his] support lasted until the Hungarian uprising of 1956 and the intervention by Russian troops. 'The French Communist Party supported the invasion of Hungary, so I broke with it,' he explained." All in all, obituaries carried a political message not in their choice of words but in their choice of topic.

During the past half century the *Times* carried reviews of some two dozen books related to the Revolution. Most of these were published immediately after 1956. The first in line was László Beke's *A Student's Diary* (1957), which largely contributed to the glorification of the freedom fighters, just like the book written under a pseudonym, *Boy on the Rooftop* (1958).[183] Also in 1958 *Escape from Fear* was reviewed rather favorably.[184] In 1959 *Child of Communism*, Tibor Méray's *Thirteen Days That Shook the Kremlin*, American journalist Barrett McGurn's *Decade in Europe*, and a spy story, *Praying for an Assassin* (twice), were all reviewed.[185] In 1960 *Anna Teller* was introduced to the *Times* readers, together with Leslie Bain's *The Reluctant Satellites*.[186] Bain, educated in Hungary, offers an eyewitness account of Eastern Europe, and voices strong criticism of American diplomacy and of the role of RFE in the Revolution. In 1966, *In Praise of Older Women*, a deeply honest love story, hit the shelves and was promptly received by the *Times*.[187] David Pryce-Jones's *The Stranger's View* of 1968 was published just before the joint Warsaw Pact invasion of Czechoslovakia.[188] Harvard Soviet expert Adam Ulam reviewed a book on the bluffs of Soviet foreign policy in 1981,[189] and his Princeton counterpart, A. James McAdams, analyzed Charles Gati's *Hungary and the Soviet Bloc* in 1986.[190] Meanwhile, the Hungarian government published its own white book on the trial of Imre Nagy in 1958 and another one on *Hungarian-American Relations, 1918–1960*, which were promptly covered by the *New York Times*.[191] As may be expected, 1989 marked reduced interest on the part of the *New York Times* in such books.

The *New York Times* database has yielded a set of seemingly unrelated reviews, some of which deserve attention. Former Communist dignitaries now living in the West met for a conference at the University of South Carolina in September 1969. The report lists three proposed books on their discussions.[192] Also in 1969 Tad Szulc, a Czech-born *Times* correspondent for Eastern Europe, reviewed three books on the Prague Spring, and mentioned "the Soviet intervention in Hungary in 1956."[193] Ursula K. LeGuin's *Orsinian Tales* bore thinly veiled references to Hungary and the Revolution, as was pointed out by Gerald Jonas in 1976.[194] In 1989 Joyce Carol Oates remembered the world of her parents in a wonderfully written Sunday magazine article[195] and brought up memories of the Revolution, too. A 1989 report from the Frankfurt Book Fair looks at the new freedom of publishing long banned books after the repeal of censorship in Eastern Europe.[196] These reviews go a long way to show how the Revolution has became part of memory over the years.

The audio-visual media has devoted less attention to the memory of the Revolution than the print media. A thorough library catalogue search of the New York area universities and of the Library of Congress yielded one play and two films about the Revolution. Television memories are more abundant, but the network archives are fairly difficult to access. Since 1957 the *Times* has reviewed the play and the film, and carried two articles on television memory.

In 1961 Howard Taubman penned an extensive review of Robert Ardry's *Shadow of Heroes*, the only known English language play about the Revolution.[197] It was staged by Warner Le Roy, and premiered at the York Playhouse on December 5. It is a dramatic, documentary-like reenactment of the major turning points of Hungarian history between 1944 and 1956, and features such characters as Nagy, Kádár, the Rajks, Gerő, Rákosi, and the head of the secret police, Gábor Péter. According to Taubman, the play "assembles facts of recent history and arranges them in an indictment of murderers of freedom." Ardry offers a sympathetic portrayal Kádár:

The man who came to power in 1956 as the Soviet tanks smashed the rebellion is revealed with a measure of understanding. With a touch of sympathy Mr. Ardry recounts the jail sentence Kádár served and the crippling injury visited on his hand. But the contempt for the little man is intensified by giving the character human credibility.

Interestingly, the better-known American filmic representation of the Revolution, Anatole Litvak's *The Journey* (1959), also refrained from telling the story in black and white, as good versus evil. Its hero is a Russian officer played by Yul Brynner, who has a human touch. The film was so successful that the *Times* reviewed it twice in 1959.[198] Meanwhile, CBS was applauded by the *Times* for broadcasting and rebroadcasting documentaries on Hungary in evening prime time in 1958 and again in 1961. In 1958, *Hungary: Return of the Terror* recalled the execution of Imre Nagy, and featured József Kővágó and Béla K. Király as invited guests. In 1961 CBS rebroadcast *Revolt in Hungary* on October 22 and then aired a new feature, *Hungary Today*, on October 29.[199] Subsequent television commemorations of the Revolution (e.g. in 1976 and 1986) were ignored by the *New York Times*.

The last group of *Times* contributions to memory, some two dozen paid political advertisements, represent the intention of the paper's patrons to remind the readers of the Revolution. Some of these are quite outspokenly anti-Soviet, others call for support for the refugees, while still others use the tragic fate of the Revolution to highlight contemporary political issues from the Middle East to the Prague Spring.[200]

CHOICE OF WORDS

In the detailed analysis of *New York Times* contributions to the memory of the 1956 Hungarian Revolution a lot has been said about choice of words representing editorial policies. A statistical look at what words *Times* editors and correspondents used to describe the Revolution reveal a striking variety in usage. Historical events usually have one identifier: we never call the American Revolution the American Uprising, nor the French Revolution the Paris Rebellion. *New York Times* editors in their editorial comments willingly admitted that the proper name of the events of October–November 1956 in Hungary was "*the Hungarian Revolution*,"[201] but they themselves, as well as their correspondents over the years, have used a variety of other words. These include *revolution, revolt, uprising, rebellion*, and *rising*. Of these, rising can only be interpreted as an interchangeable term for *uprising*. The word *rebellion* sounds condescending, while the others were used as synonyms. But before taking a detailed look at these choices of words we must review Communist Hungarian and émigré Hungarian usage.

As has been indicated in the section on the political coverage of 1989, the situation in Hungary was no simpler. Before 1989, the Revolution was a *counterrevolution*, or the *October events*. Then in 1989 it became a *popular uprising*, by the middle of the year it was a *revolution*, and by the end of the year it became a national holiday, too. Since the Revolution is a key point of reference in contemporary Hungarian politics today, different political parties with different orientations use different words to describe and remember it; however, the "politically correct" word is *Revolution*. As regards additional Communist choices of words, we must briefly look at *counterrevolution* and *martyr*. The word *counterrevolution* was first used by Hungarian aristocrats and conservatives who opposed the 1918 and 1919 revolutions in Hungary. It became associated with fascism only during the early Cold War, when American foreign policy was also described as "fascist American geopolitics." It simply does not fit classic Marxism-Leninism in the sense the various post-1945 Communist regimes have used it, because the founders never expected the people themselves to rebel against the system. This is the very contradiction that repeated Polish crises (1956, 1970 and 1980–81) brought home to different generations. Even more disturbing is the Communist use (and abuse) of the deeply religious term *martyr* to describe people who met a violent death in service of an atheistic ideology.

Hungarian émigrés also had some problems with terminology. *Revolution* was, of course, the uncontested and exclusive word of choice for Hungarians living in the West. But they also misused the word *martyr* when they applied it to Imre Nagy (and the two others who were executed together with him in 1958)[202] and to Cardinal Mindszenty alike.

As regards the *New York Times*, of the 1,944 articles that include both *Hungary* and *1956*, over one thousand carry both revolt (1171) and uprising (1048), while revolution gets 944 hits, rising 234, and rebellion 230. When used in the same article, revolution and revolt combine for 92 hits, and revolution and uprising for 93. At the same time, rebellion combines with revolution for 21, with revolt for 32, and with uprising for 40 hits. These statistics clearly indicate that there is no one single denominator for the Revolution in English, memory has simply failed to create one. The *New York Times* regularly used these words as interchangeable synonyms without meaning harm or insult, but, as has been emphasized, certain words failed to show up in certain types of articles after the mid-sixties. The one exception is the relatively large number of hits for rebellion; and it is fair to say that journalists who used the word rebellion were unlikely to use any of the more complimentary words. This inconsistency of usage, which was conscious editorial policy, has earned the paper the criticism of Hungarian political activists. Treachery, for example, was the word of choice to describe Soviet action between 1956 and 1958 in the *New York Times*, but András Pogány, a prominent leader among the '56ers, mistakenly claims that the word disappeared from the paper by 1976, when it was reintroduced in an anniversary editorial.[203] The database returns six hits for Soviet, treachery and Hungary between January 1, 1959, and December 31, 1976, and only twelve if we expand the search to include 1957 and 1958. Of the twelve, however, five are editorials, one each from 1957, 1958, 1959, 1968, and 1976. A sixth one is a long retrospective piece on account of the execution of Imre Nagy, which, incidentally, uses rising, revolt and rebellion to describe the Revolution, and freedom fighters, rebels and insurgents to describe the participants.[204]

The main purpose of naming all the journalists who contributed the preservation of the memory of the Revolution was to demonstrate the prestige the *New York Times* attributed to the matter. The list is more than impressive: it includes a dozen Pulitzer Prize winning journalists representing three generations of the best talents in the world of American journalism. Regardless of choice of words, or personal preferences thereof, the *Times* provided invaluable service to memory preservation. Databases similar to that of the *New York Times* are available for the *Wall Street Journal* (full), the *Washington Post* (up to 1990), the *Chica-*

go *Tribune* and the *Los Angeles Times* (both up to 1985). While these papers tended to take a more open anti-Kádár stand, their combined output of related articles amounts to less than that of the *New York Times* alone. For the record, with the same keywords (*Hungary* and *1956*) and the same time period when available, the *Wall Street Journal* has 179 hits, the *Washington Post* 760, the *Chicago Tribune* 427, and the *Los Angeles Times* 557. Rebellion returns one, revolution 25, uprising and revolt 29 each in the *Journal*. In the *LA Times* revolution and revolt return 90 matches each, uprising brings up 92, and rebellion 10 hits. In the *Post*, revolution, revolt, uprising and rebellion score 222, 207, 258 and 43 matches respectively. As regards the *Tribune*, which is often hailed as the leading conservative press organ in the United States, the figures are similarly low. Excluding repetitions from different editions from the same issue of the paper and accidental matches, the 427 hits are reduced to about 250. Revolution returns 216 hits, uprising 211, while riot and rebellion come in at 69 and 67 respectively. Revolt was used 118 times in this context. Here, Kádár gets 537 mentions, but only 39 link him to 1956. For Nagy and Mindszenty, similar figures are 90 and 22 and 200 and 26 respectively. Soviet and treachery combine for 44 hits, but for only one (a Méray book review in 1957) if we include Hungary, too. For the sake of accuracy, for the search terms Hungary and 1956, the *New York Times* archive returns 1,440 hits for 1957–1985 (the scope available for the two papers with the shortest time span), while the *Wall Street Journal* database lists 81 matches, and the *Post* 618. It follows from the above that the *New York Times* devoted space and quality journalism to the memory of the 1956 Hungarian Revolution on a scale that matched the combined output of all four of the other "big five" dailies.

To some degree it is fair to say that the *New York Times* as a trend-setter in the American media and in world public opinion is partly responsible for having no single identifier in English to describe the Revolution. But looking at what has been said and written about the Revolution in English for English and American audiences, it is difficult not to see the influence of radio and television, too. Many Americans old enough to remember the events describe the Hungarian Revolution as their first major TV or radio memory. On radio, one of the most memorable events was Ambassador Lodge's nationally broadcast speech in the UN in December 1956, in which he called for the withdrawal of Soviet troops from Hungary. The founding television memory is the CBS documentary narrated by a young Walter Cronkite, *Revolt in Hungary*, from 1958. Both Lodge and Cronkite used the words revolt, uprising and revolution as synonyms. These audio-visual memories, which do function as reminders when rebroadcast (1961, 1986, etc.), have added to the variety in the choice of words used to describe the Hungarian Revolution of 1956.

That notwithstanding, the overall reluctance to use the word revolution by the *New York Times* is still striking. There seem to be two possible explanations for this. One is provided by Michael H. Hunt in his seminal work on ideology and American foreign policy: revolution for Americans had come to mean trouble, chaos and disorder by the beginning of the twentieth century and the Soviet abuse of the word and the idea has contributed to its negative connotation. Hunt actually goes as far as to state that revolution (with the exception of the sacred "American Revolution") is considered something un-American, a bad word for both the people and decision makers.[205] The other answer is more simple, but requires verification from the editors of the *New York Times*. When *Times* editors made the choice of accepting Kádár as a necessary evil and extending to him some support, they did not want to provoke the Hungarian government by calling what it consistently called a counterrevolution a revolution. This editorial policy was a balancing act between Kádár's Hungary and the politically active 1956 Hungarian refugees in the United States; and, however inadvertently, it contributed to memory preservation.

NOTES

1. In Hungary the "big five" currently are the *New York Times*, hereafter cited as *NYT*, the *Washington Post*, *USA Today*, the *Wall Street Journal* and the *International Herald Tribune*. The New York Public Library database lists the *Times*, the *Post*, and the *Wall Street Journal* in its "big five," together with the *Chicago Tribune* and the *Los Angeles Times*.

2. Ferenc Kőszeg, "Hungary Doesn't Deserve Model Communist Image," *Wall Street Journal*, Jun 18, 1986; and James Feron, "Kádár Appears

Stronger Than Ever in Stable, Affluent Hungary," *NYT*, December 7, 1972. In the *Times* Timothy Foote's 1966 article discussed below in the chapter on memory is the only exception

3. Lisa Larsen, "Hungary, Twenty Months After," *NYT*, June 22, 1958. A two-page piece in the Sunday magazine section, the subsequent quote is from the first page of the article. Page two consists of two half-page photos with captions.

4. "Rally Here Cites Hungary Revolt. U. S. Aid to Subject People Proposed—MacCormack of *Times* Honored," *NYT*, October 21, 1958.

5. "Hungarian Rising Still Stirs Reds. Party Officials Admit Errors of Rákosi, but Are Bitter About Revolt Itself," *NYT,* December 4, 1958.

6. The "official" version was: János Berecz, *Ellenforradalom tollal és fegyverrel* (Budapest: Kossuth Kiadó, 1969). It was republished in 1981, and 1986. Also in English, Berecz, *Counter-Revolution in Hungary: Words and Weapons* (Budapest: Akadémiai Kiadó, 1986).

7. *Time* selected the Hungarian Freedom Fighter as its man of the year for 1956, and the cover was reprinted by *Szivárvány* [Rainbow], a Chicago based literary and political quarterly for the thirtieth anniversary in 1986.

8. William J. Jorden, "Budapest Revolt Is Marked by U. S. State Department Honors rebels of '56 and Assails Soviet Suppression," *NYT*, October 23, 1959.

9. "U. S. Assails Soviet on Hungary Uprising," October 23, 1960.

10. The paper covered the visit between November 30, and December 3, 1959. The quote and the reference to disagreements come from the last article: "Khrushchev Cites '56 Kremlin Split on Hungarian Move. Says Some of His Colleagues Opposed Decision to Use Troops to Quell Revolt."

11. "The Thirteen Days of the Hungarian Revolt," *NYT*, December 6, 1959.

12. "Hungarian Exiles Mark '56 Revolt. Men Who Played Key Roles in Drama Widely Scattered—Some Still in Prison," *NYT*, October 24, 1960, and "Danube Wreath Marks revolt," *NYT*, November 5, 1961.

13. "Recent History in Stamps," *NYT*, September 23, 1961.

14. "Troubles Beset Hungarian Reds. Regime Seeks More Soviet Help in Economic Plight," *NYT*, November 5, 1961. Attached to this article is a short piece on the picketing: "Pickets Here Mark Revolt."

15. "Socialists Deplore U. S. Role," *NYT*, May 9, 1965.

16. "Nixon Recalls Hungary," *NYT*, April 11, 1965.

17. "'56 Hungarian Rising Marked at Carnegie," *NYT*, October 24, 1966.

18. "Hungary Marks Crushing of '56 Revolt for First Time," *NYT*, November 5, 1966.

19. "Dwight David Eisenhower: A Leader in War and Peace," *NYT*, March 29, 1969; and Richard H. Rovere, "Eisenhower Revisited—A Political Genius? A Brilliant Man?" *NYT*, February 7, 1971.

20. David Binder, "Embatled Radio Free Europe Defends Role," *NYT*, March 15, 1971.

21. This is as far as RFE employees or journalists would go in discussing the role of the CIA and RFE in the events of 1956. The issue was revived during the mid-1990s and will be discussed further, when our chronological survey takes us there. For one notable example see, George R. Urban, *Radio Free Europe and the Pursuit of Democracy: My War within the Cold War* (New Haven, CT: Yale University Press, 1998).

22. Henry Kamm, "The Station That Fulbright Wants to Shut Down," *NYT*, March 26, 1972.

23. "Hungary Marks '56 Revolt," *NYT*, November 5, 1968.

24. Charles Gati, "In Hungary. It's Now a Question of Making Best of It," *NYT*, December 4.

25. For a detailed account, albeit only in Hungarian, see András Pogány, "A Magyar Szabadságharcos Szövetség rövid története" [A short history of the World Federation of Hungarian Freedom Fighters], in *Október útján a szabad világban*...[Along the Path of October in the Free World...] (Munich: Herp, 1984), pp. 284–344, esp. pp. 335–44.

26. Charles Fenyvesi, "Hungary 20 Years Later. A Veteran of the 1956 Uprising Finds the Dream of Freedom Has Died—Replaced by Peace, Prosperity and a Bad Odor," *NYT*, October 17, 1976.

27. During the course of Hungarian history no leader has been able to forge and sustain national unity in a multiparty system. The various forces in the Revolution put forward very different, often conflicting, political, economic and social programs. The unity of purpose existed to the degree that most people wanted to end Stalinist terror, Soviet troops out of Hungary, and multiparty elections. On the various major forces at play, see György Litván, "Az 1956-os forradalom eszméi és irányzatai" [The ideas and trends of the 1956 revolution] in *Októberek üzenete. Válogatott történeti írások* [The Message of Octobers. Selected Historical Writings] (Budapest: Osiris, 1996), pp. 347–56.

28. Béla K. Király, "Budapest, 20 Years Ago," *NYT*, October 23, 1976.

29. Malcolm W. Browne, "20th Anniversary of '56 Uprising Is Nearly Unnoticed in Hungary." *NYT*, October, 29, 1976. The figure of 60,000 returnees is grossly overstated. The real number is 10,000. Browne must have had the information from the Hungarian government.

30. David Binder, "'56 East European Plan of the C.I.A. Is Described.

Ex-Aide Says Units Were Trained to Return for Risings Spurred by Disclosure of Khrushchev Talks," *NYT*, November 30, 1976.

31. For details see: Tibor Glant, *A Szent Korona amerikai kalandja, 1945–1978* [The American Adventure of the Holy Crown, 1945–1978] (Debrecen: Kossuth Egyetemi Kiadó, 1997); and "American-Hungarian Relations and the Return of the Holy Crown," in *Hungary's Historical Legacies. Studies in Honor of Steven Béla Várdy*, ed. Dennis P. Hupchick and R. William Weisberger (Boluder, CO: East European Monographs, Atlantic Research and Publications, 2000), pp. 168–186.

32. Stephen G. Esrati, "Listening to the World," *NYT*, January 19, 1978.

33. Michael T. Kaufman, "Some Hungarians Remember 1956, Some Forget," *NYT*, October 24, 1986. The report is from Budapest.

34. Michael T. Kaufman, "The Hungarians, Gingerly, Recall Day in '56 When It All Changed," *NYT*, November 5, 1986. Berecz was no historian; he was a chief Party ideologue. See note 6.

35. Michael T. Kaufman, "Poles Take Note of Hungary's Revolt," *NYT*, November 10, 1986.

36. Priscilla Van Tassel, "Colleges Offering Hungarian Courses," *NYT*, November 2, 1986.

37. "Hungary, in Turnabout, Declares '56 Rebellion a Popular Uprising," *NYT*, January 29, 1989; "Party in Hungary Signals Division," *NYT*, February 5, 1989; "The Lasting Pain of '56: Can the Past Be Reburied?" *NYT*, February 8, 1989; "Hungary Prints a Liberal Soviet View of 1956," *NYT*, February 11, 1989; "Hungary's Party Compromises on View of Uprising," *NYT*, February 12, 1989; and "Hungarian Radio Broadcasts Long-Banned Revolt Speech," *NYT*, May 7, 1989; This article includes the revelations by Ormos.

38. Henry Kamm, "Hungarians to Honor '56 Uprising Leader With Huge Funeral," *NYT*, June 13, 1989; "Hungarian Who Led '56 Revolt Is Buried as a Hero," *NYT*, June 17, 1989; and "Supreme Court in Hungary Declares Nagy Was Innocent," *NYT*, July 7, 1989.

39. Henry Kamm, "Hungarians Mourn the Passing of Kádár. Thousands Pay Surprise Visit to the Coffin of Ex-Leader," *NYT*, July 14, 1989.

40. Serge Schmemann, " New Hungary...," *NYT*, October 24, 1989.

41. Henry Kamm, "Eastern Europe's Historians, Now Free, Face New Burden," *NYT*, March 24, 1991; Jane Perlez, "Archives Confirm False Hope Fed Hungary Revolt," *NYT*, September 28, 1996; and Jane Perlez, "Hungary Reluctant to Give Up Secrets of Its Past," *NYT*, September 6, 1997.

42. Celestine Bohlen, "Hungarians Debate How Far Back to Go to Right Old Wrongs," *NYT*, April 15, 1991; Bohlen, "Victims of Hungary's Past Press for an Accounting, but With Little Success," *NYT*, August 4, 1991; Judith

Ingram, "Coming Trials That May Try the Hungarian Soul," (from Moson-magyaróvár, the scene of one of the worst communist massacres in 1956), November 13, 1991; Jane Perlez, "Hungarian Arrests Set Off debate: Should '56 Oppressors Be Punished?" *NYT*, April 3, 1994; and Jane Perlez, "A Look Back at '56 Revolt as Hungary Holds Trial," *NYT*, September 19, 1999.

43. "Yeltsin Gives Hungary Soviet Files on Revolt," November 12, 1992.

44. Jane Perlez, "Tapes May Reveal If U.S. Urged On the '56 Hungarian Revolt," *NYT*, October 23, 1995, and Jane Perlez, "Thawing Out Cold War History," *NYT*, October 6, 1996.

45. Harvey Ararton, "Raw Emotion and Spilled Blood of '56," *NYT*, July 21, 1996.

46. M. S. Handler, "Defiance in Hungary. Many Intellectuals 'Emigrate Spiritually' to Evade Communist Regime's Control," *NYT*, November 4, 1961.

47. Howard Taubman, "Hungarian Arts Gain in Freedom. Pressures on Red Regime Show Direct Results," *NYT*, June 30, 1962. Taubman wrote the *Times* review of the only play in English on the Revolution in 1961. For details see the section on reviews below, and note 197.

48. "Hungarians Find Curbs Are Easing. Attacks on Church Reduced—Police Powers Cut," *NYT*, September 27, 1962. Western newspapers were, of course, not freely available on the street, and especially not for ordinary Hungarians.

49. Max Frankel, "Strain Still Bars U.S.—Hungary Link. Diplomats' Desire for Thaw Stalls on Unsettled Issues Persisting since Revolt," *NYT*, September 9, 1963.

50. Max Frankel, "A Land of Euphemism. Hungarains Speak of 'October Events' When They Mean Khrushchev's Ouster," *NYT*, November 28, 1964.

51. David Binder "10,000,000 Hungarians Can't Be Wrong," *NYT*, December 27, 1964. It is interesting to note that, as has been pointed out above in note 34, the same argument about not knowing exactly what happened during the early days of November 1956 was echoed in 1986. This is one of the lesser-known myths of the Revolution in the West.

52. David Binder, "Pleasantly Pampered Hungary," *NYT*, March 14, 1965.

53. C. L. Sulzberger, "Foreign Affairs: Not Titoist or Polycentrist," *NYT*, July 16, 1965.

54. C. L. Sulzberger, "Foreign Affairs: Hungary between Two Symbols," *NYT*, July 18, 1965.

55. One way to demonstrate the trend setting role and worldwide influence of the *New York Times* is to look at the articles contributed by Ferenc Váli and François Fejtö to Tamás Aczél ed., *Ten Years After. The Hungarian Revo-*

lution in the Perspective of History (New York: Holt, Rinehart and Winston, 1966). Váli challenges the positive image of the Kádár regime, while Fejtö analyzes "de-Stalinization" and "de-satellization."

56. "A Thaw in East Europe's 'Ice Age.'" The term probably comes from the title of a very successful novel about pre-1956 Hungary: Tamás Aczél, *The Ice Age* (New York: Simon and Schuster, 1965).

57. The Romanian theme would be developed further, but with a well-know twist. Binder praised Ceausescu as a "fortright [*sic*] Romanian with [an] independent spirit." The thesis was that while Kádár followed Moscow's line in foreign affairs and brought about domestic liberalization, Ceausescu pursued an independent foreign policy but had serious problems with "alleged discrimination" against minorities. For details, see Edmund Stillman, "Fortright Rumanian With Independent Spirit," *NYT*, April 14, 1978. Soviet troops were withdrawn for good from Romania in 1958.

58. Paul Hofmann, "Hungary Nervously Building Ties to West," *NYT*, November 29, 1969; Malcolm W. Browne, "Hungary Moves Cautiously in Making Western Friends," *NYT*, June 29, 1974; and James Feron, "Kádár Appears Stronger Than Ever in Stable, Affluent Hungary," *NYT*, December 7, 1972.

59. Alan Levy, "Along the Danube to Budapest: The Iron Curtain Revisited," *NYT*, April 4, 1976.

60. Paul Hofmann, "What's Doing in Budapest," *NYT*, August 7, 1977.

61. John Darnton, "Hungary Wields One Weapon Against Moscow: Humor," *NYT*, April 26, 1980.

62. "East European Measures Its Freedom Inch by Inch," *NYT*, December 21, 1980. The section on Hungary comes from Flora Lewis.

63. "Hungary at a Glance," *NYT*, May 15, 1989.

64. R. W. Apple, "Hungarians, Maestros of Ambiguity," *NYT*, November 21, 1989.

65. June 21, 1957. Nearly two full pages were devoted to the report.

66. January 2, 1957.

67. November 28, 1959.

68. Thomas J. Hamilton, "Lodge Denounces Nagy's Execution," *NYT*, June 18, 1958; Lindesay Parrott, "Reign of Terror in Hungary Laid to Soviet by U.S.," *NYT*, December 12, 1958; and Edward C. Burks, "Lodge Holds Out Hope to Hungary. Gets Big Receptions From Chicago Minorities as He Speaks on Freedom," *NYT*, October 24, 1960.

69. "Report to U.N. Says Kádár Eases Rule," *NYT*, September 28, 1962; "Thant Accepts Invitation to Make Visit to Hungary," *NYT*, December 5, 1962; Paul Underwood, "Budapest Regime Welcomes Thant," *NYT*, July 2,

1963; and Thomas J. Hamilton, "U.N. and Hungary. Opposition to the Kádár Regime Seems Ended as Credentials Are Accepted," *NYT*, July 7, 1963.

70. Elie Abel, "Belgrade Assails Budapest on Nagy. Says Hungarian Contention Yugoslav Embassy Aided in Revolt Is Baseless," *NYT*, June 24, 1958.

71. "Tito Said to Back Soviet on Hungary. Visitor to Belgrade Reports Split in Yugoslav Party at Time of 1956 Revolt," *NYT*, September 19, 1958.

72. "U.S. Says Hungary Must Heed Pacts to Achieve Amity. Note to Budapest Charges Moscow, Not Washington, Interferes in Affairs," *NYT*, November 22, 1958. The full text of the State Department note was printed on the same day. About a dozen denouncements of the executions were printed by the *Times*.

73. "Hungarian Boys of 14 Face Trial in Uprising," *NYT*, January 15, 1958; "Hungary accused of Killing Youths. B.B.C. Says 150 Teen-Agers Were Executed Last Year for Joining '56 Uprising," *NYT*, January 31, 1958; "U.S. Urges Hungary to Reveal Fate of 24," *NYT*, March 14; and Dana Adams Smith, "U.S. Reports Trials Of Former Rebels Grow in Hungary," *NYT*, July 11, 1958.

74. "Voroshilov Asserts Nagy Was a 'Fool,'" *NYT*, August 14, 1958.

75. Homer Bighart, "Street Is Closed to Guard Kádár. But Few Pickets Show Up to Demonstrate Against Hungarian Communist," *NYT*, September 20, 1960; Homer Bighart, "Kádár Emerges After 28 Hours. Hungarian Quits Residence for Trip to U. N. Session—Drive Is Uneventful," *NYT*, September 21, 1960; "Kádár Tours City from Tip to Top. Hungarian Leader Stays in Manhattan as Ordered—He is 'Impressed,'" *NYT*, September 26, 1960; "Soviet Arms Plan Praised by Kádár. Hungarian Red Also Hails Khrushchev—Opponents Quit Hall as He Speaks,"*NYT*, October 4, 1960; and Sam Pope Brewer, "Kádár Sees U.S. Losing U.N. Sway. Says, in Interview, Recent Assembly Votes Show Drop in American Influence,"*NYT*, October 12, 1960. The report on Háy and Déry dates from April 1, 1960: "Hungary Frees Authors Jailed after '56 Revolt."

76. Lawrence Fellows, "Amnesty' Called Trap in Hungary. Regime Accused of Seizing Thousands of Exiles Who Were Lured Home," *NYT*, April 6, 1959.

77. "Hungary Ousts Clerics. Bishop Among Those Who Have Been Removed," *NYT*, January 23, 1968; "Hungary Reported Jailing 7 Priests," *NYT*, July 9, 1965; and Paul Hofmann, "Church in Eastern Europe: Toleration and Tension," *NYT*, December 25, 1969.

78. "Vatican and Hungary Sign Accord on Church Rights," *NYT*, September 16, 1964.

79. Glant, "Holy Crown," p. 177; for more details see Glant, *Szent Korona*, pp. 79–80.

80. "105,000 Naturalized. U. S. Total for '59 Is Below Those of '58 and '57," *NYT*, December 25, 1959.

81. "Hungary Visa Ban Ends. U.S. Permits Travel to Nation After Curb of Four Years," April 30, 1960; and "Hungary Lists Visa Terms for Visits by '56 Refugees," *NYT*, August 15, 1963.

82. Max Frankel, "Renewal of U.S. Tie to Hungary Studied as Kádár Eases Curbs," *NYT*, March 23, 1963; and Frankel, "Johnson Speech an Offer to East. Capital Sees It as Spur to Splits with Moscow," *NYT*, May 24, 1964; on the amnesty: "Hungary Decrees a Wide Amnesty. It Includes 1956 Prisoners—Church Ties 'Normalized,'" *NYT*, March 22, 1963.

83. "Budapest Imports Gaiety in a Jukebox," *NYT*, November 19, 1958.

84. "Hungarians Remain Pro West But Need Hope, Report Declares," *NYT*, November 30, 1962. The AFCN was one of many American organizations that kept the memory of the Revolution alive in the highest political circles. Its leaders included Adolf A. Berle, Jr., a former assistant secretary of state.

85. Seymour Topping, "Hungarian Chief Ousts 25 in Purge of Pro Stalinists," *NYT*, August 20, 1962. "Sketches of Purge Figures," from the same date carry pictures and short bios of Rákosi and Gerő.

86. "Kádár Rules Out 'War' on Beliefs," *NYT*, July 3, 1963. Of course, he never did give up the ideological fight.

87. Max Frankel, "Economic Problems Spur Debate in Hungary on Policies of Conciliation," *NYT*, November 26, 1964; and "Price Rises Pares Kádár's Backing. Hungarians, Turning Bitter, Also Face Travel Curbs," *NYT*, February 8, 1966.

88. Paul Underwood, "East Europe Stirring. Hungary's Bid for Relations With U.S. Indicates Liberalizing Influence Emerging in Bloc," *NYT*, May 19, 1963; Anatole Shub, "Moscow's Satellites In and Out of Orbit. Change and Growing Diversity, an Observer Finds, Mark the East European Bloc Today," *New York Times Magazine*, March 15, 1964; and David Halberstam, "Disunity Grows in Eastern Europe," *NYT*, January 24, 1965.

89. David Halberstam, "Hungarian Plan (Unofficial): One-Child Families," *NYT*, August 21, 1968; David Binder, "Budapest: Motherhood Re-evaluated," *NYT*, October 9, 1965; and Binder, "East Bloc Frets Over Birth Rate. Sharp Decline Is Expected to Hurt Economic Plans," *NYT*, October 23, 1965.

90. "Hungary Reviews '49 Purge of Rajk. Probes Background of Trial of Key Victim of Stalin," *NYT*, June 22, 1969.

91. James Feron, "Hungarians Are Realizing Reforms, but Slowly," *NYT*, January 15, 1972; and Tad Szulc, "Soviet, Hungary in Serious Split. Dispute on Economic Links Disclosed by Budapest," *NYT*, April 9, 1972.

92. "Visitors Report Hungary Protest," *NYT*, April 12, 1972.

93. Raymond H. Anderson, "Friendliness Marks Rogers Discussions in Budapest," *NYT*, July 8, 1972.

94. This is a good example of the double standards employed by the paper. In the late Kádár era it became acceptable that people had to have two or three jobs to make a decent living. These are not "Western ideas," but strategies of survival. It is worth noting that the *Wall Street Journal* was more critical of the Hungarian economy: Ferenc Kőszeg "Hungary Doesn't Deserve Model Communist Image," *Wall Street Journal*, June 18, 1986.

95. "Dubcek's Challenge. Reforms by Czech Chief Could Shake The Bastions of Communist Orthodoxy," *NYT*, March 25, 1968.

96. Anthony Lewis, "Echoes of Munich. Czech Crisis Recalls 1938 Sellout, But Situation Is Seen as Different," *NYT*, July 6, 1968.

97. "A New Little Entente," *NYT*, August 7, 1968.

98. Drew Middleton, "Security Council Balked In Condemnation Effort," *NYT*, August 23, 1968.

99. Israel Shenker, "Budapest Appears to Be Calm; Press Remains Loyal to Soviet," *NYT*, August 24, 1968; and Alvin Shuster, "Hungary Uneasy on Invasion Role. Kádár Is Silent and Press Is Restrained on Prague," *NYT*, September 20, 1968.

100. Jonathan Randal, "Kádár Reappears on Hungary Scene. Silent Since Czech Invasion, He Affirms Reform Plans," *NYT*, November 4, 1968.

101. Thomas J. Hamilton,"Czech Refugee Flow to U.S. to Start," *NYT*, October 24, 1968. He reports on preparations modeled on 1956–57 and Camp Kilmer.

102. "Eastern Europe Has Mixed Reaction to Afghan Move," *NYT*, January, 10, 1980.

103. Leslie H. Gelb, "Beyond the carter Doctrine," *NYT*, February 10, 1980.

104. Flora Lewis, "Ripple From Poland: Eastern Europeans Will Feel It," *NYT*, August 28, 1981.

105. Flora Lewis, "Hungary's High States," *NYT*, December 19, 1980.

106. David Binder, "Hungarians Uneasy Over Polish Events. Leading Officials Say Labor Unrest Is Worrisome but Feel Certain Their Country Is Immune," *NYT*, December 21, 1980; and Binder, "Pre-1956 Hungary Likened to Poland. Budapest Trade Union Official Sees Similar Disregard by the Party for the Needs of Workers," *NYT*, December 23, 1980.

107. Henry Kamm, "Hungary Is Far from Democracy," *NYT*, July 10, 1989.

108. Henry Kamm, "Hungary Under New Management," *NYT*, February 13, 1989.

109. James M. Markham, "There's a Demand for Instruction in Democracy," *NYT*, April 16, 1989. The writer wonders whether Hungary can perform a democratic turn like Spain did in the 1970s. Interestingly, the *Nation* in 1938 also compared Hungary to Spain, but in a totally reversed context: "Hungary—The Spain of the East," May 28, 1938.

110. Craig R. Whitney, "Is Europe Too Amazing for the West?" *NYT*, October 29, 1989.

111. "Kádár Ill, Loses Party Posts," *NYT*, May 9, 1989.

112. "Hungary Legalizes Opposition Groups. Non-Communist Parties to Be Recognized—Legislators Ban Workplace Cells," *NYT*, October 20, 1989; and "Hungary to Disband Party Militia," *NYT*, October 21, 1989. The latter also reported the rehabilitation of show trial victims and people sentenced for revolutionary activity after 1956.

113. Maureen Dowd, "East Europe Visit Challenges Bush. He Seeks to Stress Democracy Without Offending Hosts in Poland and Hungary," *NYT*, July 9, 1989; and Henry Kamm, "Bush Extends Support to Hungary And Offers Modest Ecnomic Aid," *NYT*, July 13, 1989.

114. Steven Greenhouse, "Top Hungarian Parties Agree to Elect Dissident Writer to Presidency," *NYT*, May 3, 1990; and Glenn Collins, "A Writer Moves Up, This Time In Hungary," *NYT*, May 19, 1990.

115. C. H. Sulzberger, "A Remarkable Feat as Proconsul," *NYT*, April 28, 1962.

116. "Hungary Settles Austria Dispute. Will Pay for Properties—Hopes to Spur Trade," *NYT*, November 1, 1964.

117. "East Germany Accuses Radio Free Europe of Fomenting Discontent in Poland," *NYT*, December 19, 1970.

118. Leslie H. Gelb, "East Europe Is Made an Issue in Campaign," *NYT*, October 26, 1976. Note Gelb's earlier cited piece on the Carter doctrine. See note 103 for details.

119. "Savagery in Budapest," *NYT*, June 18, 1958.

120. "Hungary Three Years After," *NYT*, December 12, 1959.

121. "Hungary Seven Years After," *NYT*, October 21, 1963.

122. "Hungary Twenry Years After," *NYT*, October 25, 1976.

123. "In Hungary, a Prophet Honored," *NYT*, June 16, 1989. The reference to Beijing is a reference to the Tienamen Square massacre on June 4, 1989.

124. "The U. N. and Hungary," *NYT*, June 23, 1958; and "Report on Hungary," *NYT*, November 28, 1959. The latter comments on Sir Leslie Munro's report to the organization. Munro was prevented from entering Hungary, so he had to base his report on official Hungarian news releases.

125. "Shadow of 1956?" *NYT*, October 2, 1962.

126. "Restore Relations With Hungary?" *NYT*, May 14, 1963; "Building Bridges," *NYT*, May 26, 1964; "Evolution in Hungary," *NYT*, May 27, 1964; and "Hungary and the Vatican," *NYT*, September 19, 1964.

127. "Satelites No More," *NYT*, July 24, 1965.

128. "Green Light for Kádár," *NYT*, December 18, 1972. The piece looks at economic reforms, but refers to Kádár as the man who "ruthlessly betrayed the 1956 rising against Soviet tyranny." Meanwhile, "Mr. Gromyko's Character" (July 5, 1973) looks at the Soviet position at the Helsinki Conference.

129. "Eastern Europe Reconsidered," *NYT*, October 12, 1976.

130. William Safire, "Salami Tactics," *NYT*, May 4, 1989.

131. Anthony Lewis, "Death of a Pretense," *NYT*, June 11, 1989.

132. Péter Nádas, "Democracy without Borders," *NYT*, September 28, 1989.

133. "Fractured East Europe," *NYT*, March 23, 1968; "Communist Ferment," *NYT*, April 27, 1968; "Soviet Invasion," *NYT*, August 21, 1968; and "Compromise in Moscow?" *NYT*, August 27, 1968.

134. "Prague Two Years After," *NYT*, August 20, 1970.

135. "Since Budapest," *NYT*, November 5, 1981.

136. Harry Schwartz, "Conflicts Noted in Anti-Nagy Case. Evidence Indicates Budapest Text Twisted Statements of Ex-Premier and Aide," *NYT*, June, 19, 1958.

137. James Reston, "The Principle of Asylum in U.S. History," *NYT*, January 4, 1963.

138. Milovan Djilas, "Realizing Marx's Vision," *NYT*, August 2, 1972.

139. "Comrade Flintstone," *NYT*, January 18, 1972.

140. Ferenc A. Váli, "Defining Intervention. Differences Between Troop Landings in Hungary and Mideast Discussed," *NYT*, August 6, 1958.

141. Kovács was a member of Nagy's cabinet during the Revolution, but joined the Kádár regime in early 1959. He was reported dead in June, and Varga and Kővágó responded to this article: "Tribute to Bela Kovacs. He Was Symbol of Hungarians' Desire for Freedom, It Is Said," *NYT*, June 25, 1959.

142. Untitled, *NYT*, May 15, 1959.

143. "Soviet Move in Hungary. Implications of Khrushchev Version of Crushing of Revolt Discussed," *NYT*, December 13, 1959. Note in the quote that Bartók used the word revolution, of course.

144. "Hungary's Fate Recalled. Discussion of Question by the Next General Assembly Awaited," *NYT*, May 6, 1961.

145. "Kádár's Statement. Remarks on Withdrawal of Soviet Troops Called Misleading," *NYT*, June 5, 1961. The original report citing Kádár was printed on May 25.

146. Reverend Imre Kovács, "Kádár's Hungary," *NYT*, January 24, 1965. Binder's piece is discussed in detail among the country profiles on Hungary. See note 51.

147. Stephen Borsody, "East Europe's Peace," *NYT*, March 31, 1968; Charles Gati, "Limits on Czech Goals," *NYT*, April 16, 1968; and Laszlo Thomas Kiss, "Kádár's Role," *NYT*, July 30, 1968.

148. Robert Levy, "Big Power Intervention," *NYT*, September 2, 1968. His piece on Hungary was printed in 1976. See note 59.

149. Béla K. Király, "Stalin's Plan to Invade Yugoslavia," *NYT*, December 11, 1970.

150. Stephen Borsody, "Hungary at the U.N.: The Red Badge of Courage," *NYT*, March 15, 1976.

151. Stephen Borsody, "Hungary: A Revolution's Legacies," *NYT*, October 26, 1976. This editorial is discussed above. See note 122.

152. Thomas H. Naylor, "Hungary's Lessons for Gorbachev," *NYT*, January 11, 1986.

153. Béla Lipták, "Even Ex-Communists Can Be Patriots," *NYT*, August 19, 1994. Horn was foreign minister when the Hungarian government decided to open the border with Austria for East German tourists in 1989.

154. Eva M. Thury, "U.S. Misled Hungarians in 1956 Revolt," *NYT*, October 3, 1996; and Kevin Klose (of RFE), "Radio Programs Gave Hungary 'Gift of Truth,'" *NYT*, November 9, 1996. Thury responded to a Perlez article (notes 41 and 44), while Klose reacted to a November 2, editorial about the same issue.

155. "Refugee Talents Held Gain for U.S. President's Group Hails Skills of Arrivals—Spellman Visits Kilmer," Jan. 12, 1957.

156. Edward Ranzal, "Hungarian Refugees Win Constitutional Safeguards. Appeals Court Rules That Even Though Aliens Have No Visas They Cannot Be Deported Without Hearings," *NYT*, November 7, 1958.

157. "Budapest Revolt Hero Gets Columbia Degree," *NYT*, June 3, 1959; and "Hungarian Fugitive Gets 3 Honors at Yale," *NYT*, June 14, 1959.

158. "Hungary Exlies Aid U.S. Science. 2,000 Refugees of '56 Are Lauded for Contributions," *NYT,* October 28, 1962.

159. "G. E. Stereo-FM System Patented. Hungarian Engineer, Who Fled in 1956, Is the Inventor," *NYT*, February 29, 1964.

160. "Refugee Loses Job Because He Smokes," *NYT*, April 19, 1960.

161. "17 Hungarians Leave. Refugees From Revolt Elect to Leave U.S.—Job Lack Cited," June 11, 1958; Anna Petersen, "26 Who Fled Reds Will Be Reunited. Mother, 68, to Arrive Here Today as Last in Family to Escape From Hungary," *NYT*, August 28, 1958; and Sam Pope Brewer, "Anxious Couple

Get Kádár's Ear. Hungarian Leader Says He Will Consider Case of Their 7-Year-Old," NYT, September 22, 1960. This was during Kádár's first visit to the US. See the section on political coverage and note 75.

162. "Andau Book Figure Becomes Citizen," *NYT*, July 24, 1962. The reference is to James A. Michener, *The Bridge at Andau* (New York: Random House, 1957).

163. Untitled, *NYT*, January 9, 1966.

164. "Title of Miss U.S.A. Won By Hungarian Refugee, 21," *NYT*, May 22, 1966. No photo is included.

165. Harry Forgeron, "He Mixes Work and Play," *NYT*, December 3, 1972; and "She's Making Her Mark in the World of Cosmetics," *NYT*, December 6, 1972.

166. William K. Stevens, "Hungarians Reflect on Transition. Rebel 'Fifty-Sixers' See Self-Reliance as Prime Value. Most Have Become Americanized and Have Prospered," *NYT*, May 24, 1975.

167. Steven Greenhouse, "Running on Fast-Forward in Budapest. George Varga fled Hungary in 1956. Now he's back, transforming G.E.'s new light-bulb company," *NYT*, December 16, 1990.

168. Thomas Archer, "Born of Revolution. New Orchestra, Now Touring America, Is Composed of Hungarian Refugees," *NYT*, October 4, 1959; and Harold C. Schonberg, "Hungarians at Carnegie Hall. Miltiades Caridis Leads Exiles' Philharmonia," *NYT*, January 13, 1964. The review was rather negative: "Indeed, there even was some out-of-tune playing, and in several sections the musicians sounded very hard pressed to play the notes as written." Interestingly, the two sons of one of the leaders of the orchestra founded an experimental progressive jazz group, Think, in Germany, and issued the album *Variety* in 1973. It is one of the most collectible German rock records.

169. "3 Hungarians Defect At Olympics to U.S.," *NYT*, October 24, 1964; and "Iby, Hungarian Rider, Cleared Many Obstacles to Get Stable," *NYT*, April 14, 1968.

170. Robert Daley, "A Boxer Goes West. Iron Curtain Lifts for Papp of Hungary, Offering a Vista of Fame ad Fortune," *NYT*, May 29, 1962. The reference to the Revolution here is simply a temporal one: he was the first Hungarian athlete to be allowed to compete professionally after the Revolution.

171. "Hungarian Exile Warns Africans. Jerseyan Heads Ex-Leaders of Scouts Relating 1956 'Crushing' by Reds," *NYT*, September 11, 1960. Ede Chaszar was an émigré leader and the author of a study on the Hungarian minority in Romania.

172. Franklin Whitehouse, "6 Youths Found Guilty in Harlem Holdup-Murder," *NYT*, July 18, 1965; and "Life Terms Given 4 Harlem Slayers. 2

Other Youths in Store Killing Sent to Bellevue," *NYT,* September 9, 1965. This was a big story in 1964 and 1965 with a lot of Hungarians living in Harlem. The couple in question were Margit and Frank Sugar, owners of the Eve and Pete Clothing Store on West 125th Street.

173. On Kovács see the section on letters to the editor (note 141), on Rákosi and Gerő see political coverage on Kádár's purges in the HSWP in 1962 (note 85). "Reds' Cleric-Diplomat, János Péter," December 9, 1959.

174. David Binder, "Hungarians Hail Lukács at 80; Scholar Leads Red Progressives. Professor, Forced to Recant in Stalin Era, Stresses Humanism in Marx," *NYT,* April 19, 1965. Lukács was a member of Imre Nagy's cabinet in 1956. This is arguably the best, and the least provocative, among Binder's articles.

175. Even a film (*The Prisoner* [1955]) starring Sir Alec Guinness was made about his show trial.

176. "Mindszenty's Mother Dies," *NYT,* February 6, 1960.

177. "Pardon for Mindszenty Hinted; Hungary Seeks Talk With U.S.," *NYT,* December 5, 1961; and "Agreement to Permit Mindszenty To Leave Hungary Is Reported," *NYT,* May 16, 1963. In the 1963 article the reference is to "the 1956 Hungarian revolution."

178. Max Frankel, "U.S. and Hungary to Open Talks Aimed at Better Relations," *NYT,* November 27, 1964. In this piece, the Revolution is called "revolt" and "uprising."

179. "Mindszenty Leaves Hungary, Goes to Rome," *NYT,* September 29, 1971.

180. John T. McQuiston, "Hungarians Greet Mindszenty Here," *NYT,* September 29, 1973; and Albin Krebs, "Cardinal Mindszenty Dies As an Exile in Vienna at 83," *NYT,* May 7, 1975. In the former, the Revolution is referred to as an "uprising" and a "counterrevolution" (an obvious typo), in the latter as "the abortive Hungarian uprising."

181. Celestine Bohlen, "Hungarian cardinal Is Reburied in Homeland as 'Red Star' Is Extingusihed," *NYT,* May 5, 1991; and Stephen Kinzer, "Pope Begins Hungary Visit With Tribute to Mindszenty," *NYT,* August 17, 1991.

182. Alden Whitman, "Jean Paul Sartre, 74, Dies in Paris," *NYT,* April 16, 1980.

183. "Books—Authors," *NYT,* March 19, 1957 for the Beke book; and Henry C. Wolfe, "Young Fighters in Freedom's Cause," *NYT,* September 7, 1958.

184. Hal Lehrman, "Strangers in the House," *NYT,* March 16, 1958.

185. Harry Schwartz, "New Class Nightmare," *NYT,* March 15, 1959; Louis Fischer, "Before Darkest Night, the Light of a False Dawn in Budapest," *NYT* July 5, 1959; Herbert Mitgang, "Reporter At Large," *NYT,* June 7,

1959. The two reviews of the spy story: Wirt Williams, "The Assignment Was Murder," *NYT*, May 31, 1959; and Orville Prescott, in "Books of the Times," *NYT*, July 24, 1959.

186. Herbert Mitgang, "Big Mama From Hungary," *NYT*, September 4, 1960; and A. M. Rosenthal, "The Most Anti-Communist People on Earth," *NYT*, July 31, 1960, respectively.

187. Eliot Fremont-Smith, "A Valentine for Adults Only," *NYT*, February 14, 1966.

188. Burke Wilkinson, "Caught in Double Jeopardy," *NYT*, June 23, 1968.

189. Adam Vlam, "Soviet Diplomacy: Bluffing," *NYT*, June 28, 1981.

190. A. James McAdams, "Moscow, Often a Captive," *NYT*, December 14, 1986.

191. "Budapest Publishes Book on Nagy Trial," *NYT*, August 9, 1958; and "Hungary Issues Book. Bids for Improved Relations and Coexistence with U.S.," *NYT*, October 25, 1960.

192. "Ex-Reds Exchange Details on Party. 3 Books to Be Produced by Conference of Scholars," *NYT*, September 14, 1969.

193. Tad Szulc, *NYT*, "Prague Spring," May 4, 1969.

194. Gerald Jonas, "Orsinian Tales," *NYT*, November 28, 1976.

195. Joyce Carol Oates, "My Father, My Fiction," *NYT*, March 19, 1989.

196. Ferdinand Protzman, "At the Book Fair, a Hot Story Is the Take-overs," *NYT*, October 16, 1989.

197. Howard Taubman, "Shadow of Heroes' Opens," *NYT*, December 6, 1981.

198. Bosley Crowther, "A Border Incident in Hungary," *NYT*, February 20, 1959; and Crowther, "Cold War Cavalier. Mr. Brynner a Surprise in 'The Journey,'" *NYT*, March 1, 1959. The other movie has long been forgotten. It is *The Beast of Budapest* (1958), directed by Harmon Jones and produced by Archie Mayo. It is a love story of a Communist woman and the son of a liberal professor, set against, in part, archival footage of the Revolution. www. answers.com/topic/ the-beast-of-budapest (access date July 24, 2006).

199. Val Adams, "Report on Hungary Offered by C. B. S.," June 21, 1958; and "News of Television and Radio—Hungary," *NYT*, October 15, 1961.

200. For example: "Sanctions Against Israel? Sanctions Against Russia. Sanctions Against India," *NYT*, February 12, 1957, protested against the Soviet invasion of Hungary; "National Communism and Popular Revolt in Eastern Europe," *NYT*, April 28, 1957, advertised a book by Paul Zinner; and "Double Talk at World H. Q.," *NYT*, December 20, 1976, was an anti-UN ad.

201. "Hungary Seven Years After" from 1963. For details check the section on editorials and note 121.

202. One example is the 1986 commemorative plaque on Somerset Street in New Brunswick, NJ.

203. Pogány, "Szabadságharcos Szövetség," p. 342. While this is a minor correction, it raises the issue of perception. Such criticism for the *New York Times*, regardless of its truth value, was self-induced. The paper earned it with it is openly pro-Kádár stand. On the other hand, this was a conscious choice on the part of the editors.

204. "Nagy Was Leader in Historic Rising. Named Premier After Start of Fighting, He Sought to Gain Soviet Withdrawal," *NYT*, June 17, 1958.

205. Michael H. Hunt, *Ideology and US Foreign Policy* (New Haven: Yale University Press, 1987). See especially Chapter 4: "The Perils of Revolution." Interestingly, he does not discuss 1956.

DIPLOMATIC MEMOIRS

INTRODUCTION

The political memory of the Hungarian Revolution of 1956 played an important role in the Cold War. As it is pointed out in the essay on Nixon and memory, the vice president introduced the concept of "the mortal blow to Communism" into the American political discourse by making it one of the central themes in his public relations campaign at the turn of 1956 and 1957. The print and electronic media used the Revolution as a recurrent point of reference, especially on anniversaries and at times of other crises behind the Iron Curtain. The politically active Hungarian immigrants of 1956 background also worked hard to preserve the memory of the Revolution and to remind the free world of it. The United States refused to talk to Kádár until amnesty was granted at least to some of the participants, and the fact that József Cardinal Mindszenty, Hungary's highest-ranking Catholic dignitary, found refuge in the American legation complicated bilateral relations and political memory even further.

It is easy to see why and how American diplomats played a key part in shaping American perceptions of Hungary and of the Revolution. Their conduct at the time of the anniversaries, their public statements and their political memoirs were primary sources of political remembrance. Edward T. Wailes, the new American minister to Hungary in 1956, reached his post two days before the Soviet crackdown in Hungary. He refused to present his credentials, and left his post on July 26, 1957. For the next ten years, the United States was represented in Hungary only by temporary chargé d'affaires. During the tenure of the last one, Richard W. Tims, relations between the two countries were raised to the ambassadorial level, officially on November 28, 1966. The first American ambassador to Hungary was Martin J. Hillenbrand, and he was succeeded by seven others during the Kádár years. Four of the eight ambassadors published memoirs or books that carry references to their personal experiences during their tenure in Hungary. All four were published after the fall of Communism, and all but one were written with these political changes in mind. This essay looks at these four volumes.

Martin J. Hillenbrand

Hillenbrand was born in Youngstown, Ohio, in 1915 and served in the diplomatic corps between 1939 and 1976. He held posts in Burma, India, Mozambique and France; and was United States ambassador to Hungary and Germany. Between his two ambassadorial tours of duty, he was assistant secretary of state for European affairs under William P. Rogers in the first Nixon administration. Afterwards, he joined various important organizations, including the Council on Foreign Relations. He wrote four books, including his memoirs in 1998, and died in 2005. He became the first American ambassador to Hungary: he was appointed on September 13, 1967, and presented his credentials in Budapest on October 30 of the same year. When a new president is sworn in, all appointed Foreign Service officials are required to offer their resignation, which, in the case of Hillenbrand and President Nixon, was accepted in the spring of 1969. He was replaced by Alfred Puhan.[1]

When Hillenbrand penned his memoirs in 1998, he had the benefit of hindsight provided by the year of miracles, 1989, and the total collapse of the Soviet empire. He frankly admits "that we in the West did not really know how intrinsically weak the malfunctioning Communist economies really were." He also comments on the Western inability to realize "the psychological readiness for change in Eastern Europe." In trying to answer the "puzzling question why, when confronted with massive street demonstrations and other signs of popular discontent, Communist regimes...collapsed without any real attempt to use the security and military forces under their control to break up these demonstrations by violence," his best answer comes from his own experience in Hungary: "the waning of ideological fervor in Communist systems." The Communist systems, according to Hillenbrand, were about securing "the privileges and prerequisites that the exercise of power brought with it."[2]

Twenty-three pages of Hillenbrand's four hundred-page memoir deal with his service in Hungary. In 1967, US-Hungarian relations were nothing short of paradoxical: the United States had not had an accredited minister in Hungary since 1956, but diplomatic relations had just been raised to the ambassadorial level. The ambassador's final meeting with President Johnson gets special attention in the book. Hillenbrand recalls that most of their conversation was about Vietnam, but Johnson also asked him about Hungary and Cardinal Mindszenty.[3]

The jump from temporary chargé d'affaires to ambassador was a challenge to both sides, and, combined with Cardinal Mindszenty's threats to walk out of the American Embassy, made Hillenbrand's arrival quite eventful. David Binder reported from Budapest on October 18 that the cardinal suggested that he was considering leaving the embassy, and it took all the staff to persuade him not to. It would have been rather awkward for the United States, Hillenbrand comments, if one of the living symbols of the 1956 Revolution were to be arrested outside the American Embassy just as the first ambassador was arriving. They then developed a working relationship including long conversation about Hungary.[4]

It is only after describing his initial encounter and contacts with the cardinal that Hillenbrand tells about the presentation of his credentials and the key politicians he met. His first meeting with Kádár left him with "mixed feelings." The physical description reads as follows: "My first impression was of a florid, slightly puffy-faced individual of solid proportions but not fat." His very next remark is connected to the Revolution: "this was not a man at ease with history. He did not specifically refer to the events of 1956, but his rather lengthy opening remarks seemed to be an elaborate indirect justification of his action in coming back with the Soviet tanks that crushed the Hungarian Freedom Fighters." Other topics for discussion included the state of American-Hungarian relations, Mindszenty, and "the recent shooting of a Hungarian attempting to escape over the Austrian frontier." His mixed feelings were due to the fact that Kádár "was more personally sympathetic than I had expected, yet as a Communist party boss he represented a system that was basically repugnant to democratic values." Hillenbrand's impression was that Kádár traded off compliance with Soviet goals in foreign policy for domestic reforms, and cites the joint Warsaw Pact intervention against Czechoslovakia as an example.[5]

The first American ambassador to Hungary also witnessed the launching of NEM, the new economic mechanism, a Kádár-style government reform package to somehow make the economy work by combining elements of a market economy with a centrally controlled one. He correctly states that the reform package implemented on January 1, 1968 had its ups and downs, "depending on whether the Communist Party boss, János Kádár, gave them a green light or withdrew his favor." He points to the heavy legacy Hungary was facing in 1998 of the largely futile attempt to drive a Communist state towards a market-oriented economy.[6]

Before dealing with the most important issues of his ambassadorship, Hillenbrand comments on wiretapping and continuous eavesdropping on conversations carried on in the Chancery, the embassy building: "Most of our staff lived with this reality of constant surveillance in good style, but a few found it beyond their capacity to adjust and had to be transferred out before their normal tours." The only place where they could carry on a conversation without Hungarians listening in was in the electronically sealed safe room in the embassy.[7]

Hillenbrand's wife was an art lover, and they brought to Budapest a sizeable collection of contemporary American art. While politicians and intellectuals had to be cleared by the Ministry of the Interior before going to an embassy reception, musicians, ballet dancers and opera singers were more freely available. Thus, parties were "lively," and Hungarian guests appreciated the chance to consume food and drinks "not normally available" to them.[8]

After dealing with Soviet-Chinese relations and the "internal Communist tug-of war" over it, he returns to Mindszenty for a three-page subchapter, "Life with the Cardinal." The main concern for all American chiefs of mission in Budapest was the actual health risk involved in providing safe have for an elderly churchman. Mindszenty was born in 1892, and hospitalization would have meant the end of his stay at the embassy: "Once in official Hungarian hands, he would never be allowed to return to American diplomatic refuge." Their relationship became more intimate as time passed by, and the only thing that irritated the cardinal was "the sight of Stalin's statue [in fact it was a Soviet war memorial] in Freedom Square" right outside his window. Hillenbrand reiterates that, contrary to rumors spread by Hungarian Communist officials and other diplomats in Budapest, he never was a burden on the embassy staff. The cardinal provided religious mass for the embassy staff every Sunday.[9]

Another major event one expects to read about in Hillenbrand's memoirs is the Prague Spring. Accordingly, he describes Kádár's perennial dilemma about domestic reforms and unconditional support for Moscow's foreign policy against domestic reforms in other Soviet bloc countries. This was a pressing issue with the economic reforms (NEM) launched in the same year in Hungary. Displaying considerable honesty, Hillenbrand does not claim to have understood the dynamics of the situation, but he recites a characteristic, Kádár-era joke: "What are the five armies doing in Czechoslovakia?" And the answer is, "They are trying to find the fellow who invited them."[10]

Hillenbrand offers factual insights into the conduct of American-Hungarian relations. His chief negotiating partner was Deputy Foreign Minister Béla Szilágyi, and they had a set list of topics for discussion. One pressing issue was the exchange rate for American social security beneficiaries in Hungary: several thousand American-Hungarians returned to Hungary, they received their checks in the mail, and this represented cheap access to hard currency for the government. Another issue, this time pushed by the Hungarians, was the export of canned ham to the United States. The Hungarian diplomat János Radványi defected to the States, and this became a matter of hurt pride for the Kádár regime. He recalls the organized protests outside the embassy against the Vietnam War and points to the fact that Hungarian government warnings about timing were always miraculously accurate. The stones thrown at the building always shattered the windows only on the ground floor, and the Hungarian government always footed the bill for the repairs.[11] In his final comments on Hungary he again returns to the collapse of the Soviet bloc, and attributes it to the elite's lack of belief in the system on the one hand, and to Western inability to see the real weaknesses of the socialist economies because of the "cooked official statistics." In Hillenbrand's own words from 1998: "Phony statistics taken for granted as reliable led to a whole host of faulty judgments about the economic potential and competitiveness with the West of the centrally planned economies."[12]

ALFRED PUHAN

Alfred Puhan was born in Marienburg, Prussia, in 1913. The family moved to the United States in 1925 and he served in the US Army in the war. After a stint with Voice of America, Puhan entered the Foreign Service. His first encounter with Hungary came not with his ambassadorial appointment but during his tour at the American Embassy in Vienna. He worked for the political section of the embassy until the State Treaty, and was asked to stay on by Ambassador Llewellyn Thompson. Puhan agreed, and was on hand when the refugee crisis struck after the Hungarian Revolution. He was assigned as escort officer to Vice President Nixon during his visit to Austria in late December 1956. He then worked in Washington, and was appointed to become Hillenbrand's successor in 1969. His appointment took place on May 1, he presented his credentials in Budapest on June 16, and left his post on July 9, 1973. In 1977 he testified in Congress in favor of returning the Holy Crown to Hungary, and after retirement he worked for various business firms. He wrote his memoirs sometime in the eighties, but the book was published only in 1990, after the changes of 1989.[13]

Puhan's connections with Hungary in 1956 are described in a total of five pages, while his ambassadorial experiences are covered in fifty, more than one fifth of the whole book. He devotes special attention to Cardinal Mindszenty not only in the text but also in the title of his memoirs: *The Cardinal in the Chancery and Other Recollections*.[14]

The Austrian State Treaty in 1955 brought about sweeping changes in the life of ordinary Austrians and American diplomats in Vienna alike. Puhan was asked, as has been mentioned above, to stay on as political counselor for Ambassador Thompson, which then was the third highest post in the embassy.[15] He recalls the excitement with which the embassy staff viewed the Revolution, but also points out Ambassador Thompson's "highly skeptical" report to Washington. Thirteen days of freedom then were cut short by the Soviet attack on November 4, and the flow of refugees began. He speaks of more than a quarter of a million refugees in Austria, and tells some amusing stories about those hectic days. On one occasion a group of refugees showed up at the embassy demanding guns to be able to fight the Soviets, and he needed all his skills to dissuade them.[16] However, much of Puhan's account of 1956 revolves around Nixon's visit to Austria. The vice president arrived on December 19, and Puhan was "not too happy with the appointment," because Nixon was involved in the "McCarthy witch-hunts [*sic*]." But Nixon proved to be a pleasant surprise and a good listener, and organized such a busy schedule that Ambassador Thompson could not catch up with him.[17]

Puhan writes extensively about Nixon's trip to the Burgenland, which he mistakenly associates with the vice president's last day in Austria. Burgenland Governor Johann Wagner invited Nixon for lunch, and delivered a spontaneous, highly anti-Communist toast at the meal. Nixon responded without written remarks, and Puhan had to translate on the fly. In his reply Governor Wagner, who spoke some English, complimented Puhan for delivering the best of the three speeches heard. Nixon, according to Puhan, never found out what the governor had said on that occasion.[18] This was a successful encounter, and Puhan was offered the Budapest post when Nixon became president and Hillenbrand was recalled to Washington to the European desk.

Alfred Puhan served in Budapest for four years, and was somewhat disappointed when his resignation was accepted in 1973, following Nixon's reelection. Puhan attributes his appointment to the positive impressions he had made on Nixon in 1956 and 1969. In March 1969, he briefed the president, Secretary of State William P. Rogers and National Security Advisor Henry Kissinger for ten hours before Nixon's first European trip. His appointment was then confirmed and Rogers himself swore him in, in front of more than two hundred guests including the Hungarian ambassador to Washington, János Nagy. *Newsweek* applauded his appointment, and he left for Budapest with great enthusiasm.[19]

US-Hungarian relations were in a bad shape with a lot of room for improvement when Puhan arrived in Budapest. He presented his credentials to President Pál Losonczi, threw his first Fourth of July party, and the two countries agreed on four major issues to settle.[20] Relations temporarily froze when American astronauts involved in the Apollo program were turned down by the Hungarian government because they were not offered to the Soviet Union as well, but the Hungarian Ministry of Foreign Affairs made a major gesture by unilaterally lifting all restrictions on Puhan's movements. He tells the story of how he bailed out Kitty Hoffman, an American woman who caused a fatal car accident in Hungary, and his 1971 visit to Marienburg, which he called a dream come true. By then, of course, it had become Malbork, a Polish town. He writes extensively about visitors ranging from Liz Taylor to Congressman Charles J. Vanik, who was also involved in the return of the Holy Crown.[21]

Judging from the attention he devotes to detail, Puhan felt his greatest success was the peaceful and safe departure of Cardinal Mindszenty from the embassy in 1971. He gives an insider's account of life with the Cardinal, the diplomatic background of departure, and the tug of war over the manuscript of Mindszenty's memoirs. Puhan eventually drove the manuscript to Vienna himself, and the Cardinal left the embassy on September 28, nearly fifteen years after he had entered the building, and less than a month before the fifteenth anniversary of the Revolution. Puhan believes that the "departure of the cardinal from our embassy removed the last and most important stumbling block to improving our relations with Hungary."[22] He then reports on Secretary of State Rogers's visit to Budapest, but does not list the agreements that were signed.[23] Eventually, his resignation was accepted in 1973, but his replacement, Richard F. Pedersen, did not arrive until the end of September, so the Puhans said farewell to Budapest with their fifth Fourth of July party and reception.

Alfred Puhan played an important role in the normalization of American-Hungarian relations, and the stories he tells are quite entertaining, but his memory failed him repeatedly. As it is discussed in the essay on Nixon's trip to Austria, he visited the Burgenland on December 20, and left for Germany from Salzburg on the 22nd. Puhan also had difficulties remembering the Stalinist Hungarian dictator, Mátyás Rákosi's name: he becomes Rákoczi and Rákocsi. Puhan mistakenly claims that in 1956 the Americans had an atomic bomb but the Soviets did not. Nor was Puhan the first Western ambassador received by Kádár.[24] As we have seen, Hillenbrand was received by the Hungarian dictator in 1967. These are technical details, but they highlight one of the key problems with political memoirs: their unreliability.

Puhan was succeeded by Richard F. Pedersen (1973–75) and Eugene V. MCAuliffe (1975–76) during Nixon's second term and Gerald Ford's tenure. American-Hungarian relations continued to improve after the claims settlement and consular agreement (both in 1973) had been signed. The two countries worked together in preparation for the European Security Conference in Helsinki (1975) and Hungary was invited to supervise the armistice in Vietnam (1973–75). The election of Jimmy Carter meant that the Democrats would return to the White House, and his choice for ambassador to Budapest was Philip M. Kaiser.

PHILIP M. KAISER

Kaiser was born in Brooklyn in 1913, and was one of ten children. He graduated from the University of Madison, Wisconsin, and went on to work in the Department of Labor in the Truman administration. In the fifties he was special assistant to Governor W. Averell Harriman of New York, and then served as United States Ambassador to Senegal and Mauritania, between 1961 and 1964. Afterwards, he moved to London, where he worked for the embassy first, and then for Democrats Abroad. He was Secretary of State Cyrus Vance's choice for Hungary, Carter approved, and he was appointed on July 7, 1977. Kaiser presented his credentials in Budapest on August 4, and left his post on March 9, 1980. He was transferred to Vienna, where he served until Reagan took office and he was forced to resign his post. Since 1981 Kaiser has worked for various international firms and was a member of the Council for Foreign Relations. He lives in retirement in Washington, D. C.[25]

Although Philip M. Kaiser's most significant contribution to American-Hungarian relations was the return of the coronation regalia and the MFN agreement (both in 1978), his memoirs from 1992 carry interesting comments about Hungary and the memory of the 1956 Revolution. His pro-Kádár statements must be viewed in light of the dramatic improvements in American-Hungarian relations between 1969 and his arrival. Unlike Hillenbrand and Puhan, Kaiser was not being constantly reminded of the Revolution by the presence of Cardinal Mindszenty in the embassy. Nor did he have Puhan's first-hand experience with the refugees. In other words, this is the first memoir which is motivated not by wanting to remember the Revolution but by wanting to accept the Soviet-sponsored Hungarian political elite at face value. In *Journeying Far and Wide*, Kaiser devotes forty pages (about one eighth of the whole book) to his mission to Hungary.[26]

Kaiser's first choice was Yugoslavia, but the outgoing secretary of state, Henry Kissinger, insisted that Lawrence Eagleburger be sent there. Kaiser was asked if he would take Budapest instead. He accepted the offer because he saw "real possibilities for creative American diplomacy" there.[27] "By 1977 Hungary had become the most liberal country in Soviet-dominated Eastern Europe," he claims, and Kádár played an all-important part in this process. His evaluation of Kádár shows a marked change from those offered by his predecessors. Hillenbrand and Puhan expressed serious reservations about Kádár and his role in and since 1956, but much of this feeling was gone by 1977. Kaiser describes Kádár's conduct in 1956 as "perfidious" and not treacherous: "Kádár shamelessly emerged as Moscow's stooge. Later, as the new head of the Hungarian regime, he directed a draconian policy of repression, disbanding free institutions that had emerged during the revolution and imprisoning or executing supporters of the uprising." As regards the secret trial and execution of Imre Nagy, Kaiser exonerates Kádár of direct responsibility: "When Nagy… and his top colleagues had received asylum in the Yugoslav embassy, Kádár did nothing to prevent Soviet military intelligence from kidnapping and exiling them to Romania. Nor did he try to deter the Russians from executing Nagy." Kádár later turned hate into acceptance, and by 1977 "it was generally agreed that he would be overwhelmingly elected president in a free democratic contest." He remarks that his impression was confirmed by Hungarian exiles who returned to Hungary during the seventies. Kaiser attributes this "extraordinary reversal" to the economic reforms of NEM, and to the easing of "political, religious, and intellectual restraints." With the reforms initiated in 1968, Hungary "was challenging Soviet gospel that a completely controlled economy was the sole road to economic and social salvation."[28]

This is the summation of the carefully constructed positive image of Kádár that comes through in the reporting of the *New York Times* as well. And yet, as it is pointed out in the essay on the *Times* and memory,

Kádár has never been portrayed as pure evil not even at the very beginning of his reign. As time passed by and Kádár stayed in power, emphasis naturally shifted to his success as a survivor and constructor of a Soviet-dominated Hungary that was more liberal and generally more acceptable than the other East European satellites of Moscow. We now know that the Soviets did not insist on Nagy's execution, nor on how he should be humiliated in death. If in 1977 Hungary had been given the chance of a free election preceded by open discussion of Kádár's role in the suppression of and the retaliation following the Revolution, if the secrets of Plot 301—where Nagy was buried anonymously—had been revealed and the destructive effects of Kádár's rule on the Hungarian society and economy had been discussed freely, he surely would not have been elected. What Kaiser encountered in 1977, however, was a Socialist "miracle," a regime with no opposition with political humor tolerated, and a leader would not tolerate a conventional cult of personality.[29]

Kaiser's evaluation quoted above demonstrates that the Carter White House wanted to see Hungary in a better light than its predecessors. In its own list of preferences, Washington elevated Budapest to the level of Bucharest and Warsaw, as the stated goal of the Carter administration was to improve relations with countries behind the Iron Curtain that were willing to act independently of the Soviet Union. This was a continuation of Nixon's divide and rule policy, and in such context a positive image of Kádár was a prerequisite. The return of the coronation regalia and a bilateral trade agreement (the MFN treaty) were unilateral American gestures to test Budapest's willingness to act alone, without Soviet consent.[30]

The rest of Kaiser's account revolves around the return of the Holy Crown. He recalls the resistance of the Hungarian-American communities against Carter's decision on the grounds that the return "would legitimate the Kádár government."[31] As part of the emerging compromise over the return, Washington insisted on a people to people formula which had no room for Kádár to be present at the ceremony: "I was to tell the Hungarian government that President Carter would be politically embarrassed if Kádár were present at the ceremony celebrating the Crown's homecoming." He calls Kádár's acquiescence a "remarkable gesture." He then gives a three-page, itemized account of their meeting in which they discussed this American request.[32]

Kaiser concludes his chapter on Hungary with a short account of the changes in 1989. According to the ambassador, Hungary's economic miracle turned into disaster by the mid-1980s, and led to collapse in the absence of transition to a market-oriented economy. Economic troubles brought back the reform Communists (he names Rezső Nyers and Imre Pozsgay), who ousted Kádár in 1988. The "counterrevolution" of 1956 became a revolution, Nagy was reburied, and the Communist Party, "on its own initiative," legalized the establishment of other parties and "voluntarily [gave] up its monopoly role." In September, the Hungarian government opened the borders for East Germans to cross into Austria, and in October the Hungarian Socialist Workers' Party reorganized itself as the Hungarian Socialist Party.[33] A new election law was drafted, and Hungary held its first free elections in almost fifty years in March 1990. Kaiser was an international observer in this election. He concludes his account with an anecdote about an elderly victim of 1956: the man was imprisoned after the Revolution and his brother was executed. "With tears in his eyes he concluded, 'I never believed I would live to see a free election in Hungary.'"[34]

Kaiser's summary of the year of miracles also reflects his bias towards Kádár inasmuch as he attributes the coming of the reform Communists to Kádár's liberalism and tolerance of difference of opinion.[35] It goes without saying that the concept of the Communist Party initiating change towards a multiparty system voluntarily does not hold water. The economic miracle described by Kaiser was operated not primarily by the economic reforms of 1968 but, more importantly, by the Hungarians' ingenuity and desire to survive by creating a black market economy to provide supply for demand. Unlike Hillenbrand and Puhan, who were emotionally attached to the memory of the Revolution and had to deal with one of its last Mohicans, Cardinal Mindszenty, in person, Kaiser's preferences lay with the Kádár regime. His most important achievement in government service was the return of the Holy Crown, but this issue had been unduly ignored in other, earlier memoirs of the Carter administration.[36] This, in turn, explains the attention the ambassador pays to the matter and why he presents the Communist Party and Kádár himself as forerunners and initiators of the sweeping changes of 1989.

The Reagan years were marked by confrontation and negotiation between the two superpowers. Kaiser was replaced by Harry E. Bergold, Jr. (1980–83). He was succeeded by the first and only American ambassador to Hungary with a Hungarian background, Nicholas M. Salgo (1983–86). Unfortunately, neither Bergold nor Salgo published any recollections. Salgo was replaced by Mark Palmer in 1986.

ROBIE MARCUS HOOKER PALMER

Palmer was born in Ann Arbor, Michigan in 1941, graduated from Yale in 1963, and began his career with the print and electronic media. He joined the foreign service in 1964, and had various stints in New Delhi, Moscow, and Belgrade. In between these missions, he served in various capacities in the State Department, and wrote speeches for six presidents and six secretaries of state. Following his tour in Budapest (1986–90), Palmer became a successful businessman and advocate of democratic institutions. He is vice chairman of Freedom House and lives in Washington, D. C. He published *Breaking the Real Axis of Evil* in 2003. The book is a guide to bringing about democracy and ousting dictators, and his recollections about Hungary are tied to the various items on this agenda. Palmer was the most visible ambassador Washington has ever sent to Hungary; he even marched with the opposition on March 15, 1989. Palmer was appointed on July 24, and presented his credentials on December 8, 1986. He left his post on January 31, 1990. His successor, Charles H. Thomas, was appointed on June 27, and presented his credentials on July 2 of the same year.[37]

In his book on how to get rid of early twenty first-century dictators, Palmer seems most comfortable with the role of chiefs of missions in dictatorships. An ambassador to a dictatorship, Palmer claims, must be politically active even if he risks personal attacks or calls for his resignation. He recalls Foreign Minister Gyula Horn's complaints to Secretary of State James Baker about him, and then his personal triumph when opposition leaders (including his friend, Viktor Orbán) came to run Hungary within a short while.[38] Ambassadors and NGOs must provide democrats in a dictatorship with strategy. Representatives of democracies in a dictatorship must listen to the demands of local democrats, because they feed off each other: "Their perspective on their struggle, through no fault of their own, is truncated. In 1986 I saw Hungarian democrats unable to think tactically much beyond getting their passports returned."[39]

Palmer's most detailed recollections of his tour in Hungary are included in chapter six, "Embassies as Freedom Houses, Ambassadors as Freedom Fighters." As regards sending messages on arrival, "prior to meeting the representatives of the dictators or the dictator himself, the ambassador can meet with the democrats." He regrets that his much publicized meeting with László Rajk and János Kiss in the Gellért Hotel took place after and not before he presented his credentials in Budapest. His comment on the meeting is quite frank: "I told Kiss and Rajk I considered that I was accredited to them and to the Hungarian people and asked what I could do to help. Their request—restoration of their passports—was exceedingly modest, and we immediately satisfied it. We then began a dialogue about much larger objectives."[40]

Palmer maintains that an ambassador must try to become one of the most popular persons among the oppressed citizens. He claims that a 1992 poll in Hungary still listed him among the ten most popular people in the country, and he quotes a July 29, 1989 *Washington Post* article extensively: "Palmer, a youthful live-wire type who operates out of a building that looks like the campaign headquarters of a maverick, is something of a cult figure. He represents the democratic government that Hungarians can almost taste for themselves."[41] An ambassador in a dictatorship can even march with the people, as Palmer did in March 1989: "Hungarians in all walks of life encouraged me to play an active role in their society in a host of different ways. They even selected me to chair the Miss Hungary contest live on national television. I was invited to join them in the streets to march for freedom in March 1989, and the reaction was enormously positive when I did so along with many of my embassy staff."[42]

An ambassador must develop direct contacts with the dictator himself, too. In the subchapter titled "Waltzing a Dictator on the Danube," Palmer recites his interactions with Károly Grósz. The comment with which he introduces Grosz sounds more like Hillenbrand than Kaiser: "A year after I arrived in Budapest, János Kádár, the dictator in power since the slaughter of 1956, gave way to a somewhat younger, though still hard-nosed, dictator, General Secretary Károly Grósz. Others in the

Communist leadership included Prime Minister Miklós Németh, Foreign Minister Gyula Horn, and economic czar Rezső Nyers."[43] Palmer took Grósz on an extended tour of the United States in 1988, as a result of which his "will to fight was sapped. He and I developed a relationship that I believed played a modest but helpful role in assuring a peaceful transition when sufficient pressure had been mounted." Grósz asked him to "intervene with Fidesz…to stop demonstrations and pressures" because he was afraid of being lynched. While stating that he was opposed to violence, Palmer refused to comply, and elevated Orbán to "the most prominent position during President George [H. W.] Bush's 1989 visit to Hungary."[44] Palmer claims he noticed that some members of the People's Militia were not only openly anti-Semitic but they also felt that the opposition was led by the Jews. He warned the government and the head of the militia that firing into the crowd on March 15 might injure many Americans, including the ambassador. Palmer claims that he also advised various members of the Communist elite on possible transition to post-Communist life and on business opportunities: "Many communists have done well under democracy. Some have been elected to political office, some have made more or less legitimate money in business. Most have not ended up being lynched, as they feared."[45]

Palmer's unorthodox treatment of his memories as ambassador culminates in the subchapter "Ambassador in Budapest," in which lets newspaper articles and photographs tell his story. His reasoning is equally surprising, entertaining, and unhistorical:

> I allow the rest of the story of the American embassy's efforts during those years to be told by journalists who covered it. From helping Mickey Mouse and Ronald McDonald to break through the Iron Curtain, to founding the first business school in the communist world, to bearing witness at Imre Nagy's reburial, to marching in the streets, I hope the pictures and articles shown…will give some flavor of how much fun, how exhilarating, and of course occasionally how tough it can be to help others gain their freedom. Staid, conventional ambassadors in despotisms are missing the best moment in their lives.[46]

It follows from the above that, according to Palmer, anything goes against a dictatorship. An ambassador can be undiplomatic; he can, and should, march against the regime and meet leaders of the opposition openly. It is easy to see why he gave so many headaches to Secretary of State James Baker.

Judging Palmer's book by his comments on Hungary would be doing injustice to a book which is not a political memoir but a political program proposal on how to solve one of the most pressing problems of the post-Cold War world. In 2002–2003, when he wrote it, the chief concern for the United States was what President Bush described as the Axis of Evil. Palmer tries to achieve two things. Firstly, he tries to extend public discussion to include all dictatorships, and names all forty-five of the surviving ones, including Saddam Hussein of Iraq. There is no qualified judgment here: someone is either a dictator, or not, and Palmer urges action against all of them. Secondly, he justifies intervention (not necessarily military intervention) as a moral duty, and promotes a Woodrow Wilson-style mission to spread democracy and to "oust the world's last dictators by 2025." It is in this broader framework that Palmer recalls his Hungarian adventures, and in connection only with some, but not all of his arguments. Although he was one of the most popular and most visible ambassadors in Hungary, one gets the impression by reading the relevant parts of his book that he almost single-handedly ended Communism in Hungary. Palmer wants to remember his own contributions, and the role he played (or claims he played) in the termination of Communism finds additional justification in emphasizing the dark side of the Hungarian dictatorship. In such context, his choice of words about Kádár and the Revolution, "the massacre of 1956," is quite natural and logical.

CONCLUSION

By way of conclusion we may say that the four American ambassadors who gave an account of their tenure in Budapest during the Kádár years wrote very different books. Hillenbrand and Puhan were emotionally attached to the Revolution and its visible symbol in the embassy, Cardinal Mindszenty, while Kaiser was clearly pro-Kádár, and Palmer used the Revolution and its suppression to highlight the dictatorial nature of the system he helped to bring down. Whereas wiretapping is a major concern for Hillenbrand and

Puhan (which is the logical and natural approach), Kaiser avoids it (since it does not fit his image of the Kádár regime) and Palmer ignores it. One common feature, however, is that all four books were published after 1989, so all four authors had to comment on the change of regime, too. In this regard, Hillenbrand's main goal is to somehow explain why the actual collapse of the Soviet bloc happened, and why without armed resistance by the outgoing elites. Puhan's book was in print during the events of 1989, so he could only insert a comment in an "Author's Note" on page 1: "This book was written before the momentous changes in the face of Europe. If my chapters on Germany and Hungary have been overtaken by the events, it should be remembered that scarcely anyone in 1988 and 1989 expected the Berlin Wall to crumble so quickly, or that Hungary would be allowed to have free democratic elections in 1990." This lack of hindsight might have worked to the benefit of Puhan's recollections, but his inconsistent memory renders his statements and anecdotes subject to doubt. As has been pointed out, Kaiser, in self-justification, connected the changes to Kádár's policy of liberalization, while Palmer claimed a larger than life role for himself in the events, without explaining the causes or nature of changes (1989) in Hungary. It is also important to reiterate that Palmer's book is not a political memoir, while the other three all are.

These four books, although different in style, content, and scope of attention paid to Hungary, remain important records of how American political memory has treated the Hungarian Revolution of 1956. They were chosen over other, more tangible manifestations of political memory (e.g. presidential proclamations or Congressional resolutions) in order to highlight different approaches to, and different strategies of, remembering. These recollections represent a surprisingly wide scale of opinions, ranging from all-out rejection (Palmer) to qualified, yet semi-enthusiastic support (Kaiser) for Kádár, who, nonetheless, was always identified as the villain of 1956.

NOTES

1. Biographical information was drawn from: http://politicalgraveyard. com/bio/hilla-hillhouse.html and from Hillenbrand's memoirs discussed here. All heads of mission to Hungary with dates of appointment, arrival, and departure are listed on the State Department website at: http://www.state.gov/ r/pa/ho/po/com/10880.htm (access date for both sites: 9/25/2006).

2. Martin J. Hillenbrand, *Fragments of Our Time. Memoirs of a Diplomat* (Athens, GA and London: University of Georgia Press, 1998), pp. 374–75.

3. Ibid., pp. 245–46.

4. Ibid., pp. 246–48.

5. Ibid., pp. 251–53.

6. Ibid., p. 251.

7. Ibid., p. 253. Hillenbrand then revisits this issue in his final remarks on Hungary, on p. 263.

8. Ibid., pp. 253–54 and 265–66.

9. Ibid., pp. 256–58. All quotes are from p. 256.

10. Ibid., pp. 258–60. The joke is on p. 260 and deals with the Soviet justification for the invasion.

11. Ibid., pp. 260–62. He mistakenly identifies Szilágyi as István, not Béla.

12. Ibid., pp. 263–65. The two quotes are from p. 264 and 265 in that order.

13. Biographical information was drawn from http://politicalgraveyard. com/bio/pugsley-puntley.html, and Puhan's memoirs discussed here.

14. Alfred Puhan, *The Cardinal in the Chancery and Other Recollections* (New York: Vantage Press, 1990).

15. Ibid., p. 97.

16. Ibid., pp. 102–03.

17. Ibid., pp. 103–04.

18. Ibid., pp. 104–06.

19. Ibid., pp. 169–71. For the briefing see p. 169, for the appointment and swearing in, see pp. 170–71.

20. Ibid., pp. 176–77.

21. Ibid., pp. 177–79 (on the astronauts), p. 179 (on lifting restrictions on his movements), pp. 181–82 on Hoffman, pp. 183–84 (on his visit to Poland), and p. 184 and 216 (on visitors).

22. Ibid., pp. 185–215. The quote is from p. 215.

23. Ibid., pp. 215–16. During the Rogers visit the two countries signed

a consular and a scientific agreement. In 1973 a claims settlement ended disputes over damages and debts going back to the time of World War I.

24. Ibid., p. 104 (on Nixon), p. 175 and 188 (on the misspelling of Rákosi's name), p. 106 (on the bomb), and p. 215 (on being the first Western ambassador to be received by Kádár).

25. Biographical information was drawn from http://politicalgraveyard-com/bio/kabzinski-kanczuzewski.html, from Kaiser's memoirs, and from an interview with the ambassador (Washington. D. C., May 31, 2001).

26. Philip M. Kaiser, *Journeying Far and Wide. A Political and Diplomatic Memoir* (New York: Charles Scribner's Sons, 1992). The chapter on Hungary is "Carter's Ambassador to Communist-Controlled Hungary," pp. 265–99.

27. Ibid., p. 266.

28. Ibid., pp. 266–69.

29. Ibid., p. 287. The Hungarian dictator became a benevolent uncle figure by the 1980s, but this is simply a different version of the personality cult of a dictator

30. Tibor Glant, "American-Hungarian Relations and the Return of the Holy Crown," in *Hungary's Historical Legacies. Studies in Honor of Steven Béla Várdy,* ed. Dennis P. Hupchick and R. William Weisberger (Boulder, CO: East European Monographs, 2000), pp. 168–86.

31. Ibid., p. 273.

32. Ibid., pp. 287–90. Both quotes are from p. 287.

33. Ibid., pp. 297–99. The two quotes are from p. 298.

34. Ibid., pp. 297–99.

35. Ibid., p. 269, and again on p. 298.

36. This applies to the memoirs of President Carter and his wife, Secretary of State Cyrus Vance, and White House Chief of Staff Hamilton Jordan. The national security adviser devoted half a page to the crown. See Zbigniew Brzezinski, *Power and Principle. Memoirs of the National Security Adviser, 1977–1981* (New York: Farrar, Straus, Giroux, 1985), p. 299.

37. Biographical information was drawn from http://politicalgraveyard. com/bio/palmer.html and from Palmer's book described here.

38. Mark Palmer, *Breaking the Real Axis of Evil: How to Oust the World's Last Dictators by 2025* (Lanham, MD: Rowman & Littlefield Publishers, Inc., 2003), pp. 24–25.

39. Ibid., pp. 58–59. The quote is from p. 58.

40. Ibid., pp. 94–95.

41. Ibid., p. 96.

42. Ibid., p. 99.

43. Ibid., p. 103. Palmer is the only one of the four ambassadors who pays no attention to the original, Hungarian way of spelling names. In quotes from his book his spelling is used (without [*sic*]), while in my own comments I use the correct spelling.

44. Ibid., pp. 103–04. The two quotes are from p. 103 and 104 in that order.

45. Ibid., p. 104.

46. Ibid., p. 139.

AMERICAN COLLEGE HISTORY TEXTBOOKS ON THE HUNGARIAN REVOLUTION OF 1956:
(A Selective, Preliminary Overview)

INTRODUCTION

One important way to look at the academic memory of the Hungarian Revolution and War of Independence of 1956 in the United States is to survey the various types of history textbooks used at American colleges and universities. These textbooks define the memories of generations of students and their immediate families. This essay can offer only a preliminary overview, since a full survey would take an expert research team and about a year, with full cooperation from the publishers. Six types of history textbooks have been selected for the purposes of this preliminary survey: (1) Western Civilization, (2) twentieth-century world history, (3) twentieth-century European history, (4) Russian and Soviet history, (5) American foreign policy in the Cold War, and (6) East and Central European history in the twentieth century and/or after 1945. The main selection criteria for this survey revolve around my attempt to represent as many of the major textbook publishers as possible, to analyze texts that are used in several programs around the United States, and to look at different editions of some of these publications, especially if these display shifting attitudes towards the Hungarian Revolution. Some of the books discussed in categories 4, 5, and 6 are not textbooks in the strict sense of the word, but they have all been adopted in various higher education courses in the United States during past ten years. I have narrowed the list, somewhat arbitrarily, by looking at not more than six textbooks per category, and by choosing texts (especially in the sixth category) that represent different attitudes toward the Hungarian Revolution of October–November 1956.

Even a cursory look at American college and university textbooks makes it abundantly clear that the Revolution is the usual focal point of all their discussions in connection with Hungary. In other words, if and when American college history textbooks mention Hungary, they almost always do so in connection with the 1956 Revolution. This demonstrates beyond a reasonable doubt that the Hungarian Revolution and War of Independence against Soviet domination is indeed seen as a formative event of the twentieth century. Yet the quality of the comments in each of the six categories is surprisingly mixed, and the contested nature of the collective Hungarian memory of the Revolution[1] that continues to mar contemporary Hungarian politics in 2006 has found its way into some American textbooks, too. The six categories were set up in such a way as to present an ever-narrowing focus on Eastern Europe under Soviet rule.

WESTERN CIVILIZATION TEXTBOOKS

Histories of Western civilization tend to offer sweeping overviews with limited attention to detail, and they often do so in multi-volume publications. With such broad focus it is quite natural that the Hungarian Revolution gets limited attention. Most textbooks in this category devote less than one page to 1956, and the complementing photographs usually take up more space than the actual discussion of the Revolution.

Western Civilization: The Continuing Experiment has multiple, three-volume editions and a brief, two-volume version.[2] The 1994 first edition looks at the postwar dilemmas of the Soviet bloc and discusses the East Berlin uprising before de-Stalinization. The subchapter on de-Stalinization carries a timeline and sections from Khrushchev's secret speech. The analysis begins with the effects of the speech, but then takes an interesting turn, when the authors claim that the rise of Imre Nagy and Władysław Gomułka was due to the fact that in "the face of the East German uprising of 1953, the Soviets backed off from hard-line Stalinism." They interpret the Polish October as "changes within the system," while the events in Hungary turned out to be "changes that would undermine the system itself." This is why Gomułka was acceptable to Moscow, and Nagy was not. In Hungary, they claim, "reformers led by the moderate communist Nagy took advantage of the liberalizing atmosphere by mid-1956 to begin making dramatic changes." The next paragraph sums up the nature of these changes with the following words:

> The Hungarians dismantled their collective farms and moved toward a multiparty system and democratic coalition government. Then they called for Soviet troops to withdraw, enabling Hungary to exit the Warsaw Pact and become neutral....So when a democratic coalition government was set up by November, the Soviets finally used tanks to crush the Hungarian reform movement.

This is the only reference to the two Soviet interventions against Hungary 1956. No names are given, and no personal or political dilemmas are described. Following a reference to the refugees and postrevolutionary retribution, the authors state that despite the intervention, the old Stalinist ways were not reintroduced in Eastern Europe. Kádár is mentioned as "the new Hungarian leader" only here, and as the man who collectivized agriculture but decentralized the economy. "There was eventually an amnesty for political prisoners, as well as considerable liberalization in cultural life," and Hungary enjoyed "freer contact with the West than the other satellites." Only Kádár's year of birth is given, the authors surely missed his death in 1989.

The brief edition came out in 1999, and replicated the above comments almost word for word. The Khrushchev speech is omitted, and a photo of the October 23 demonstration is inserted instead. The caption is almost as long as the discussion of the Revolution itself, but it at least does carry an accurate reference to the nature of the events. The march depicted in the picture is described as the initiation of "the revolutionary phase of the movement for change in communist Hungary."[3] The third edition of the original text from 2002 again echoes the first edition with changes only at the end. The reference to Kádár is introduced with a new comment here: "So after 1956 the satellites were granted greater leeway, and showed greater diversity, than had previously seemed possible. And from the sentence on Kádár the reference to the amnesty was removed.[4] By using powerful expressions like "movement for change" and "march," the authors imply similarities between the Hungarian Revolution of 1956 and the American Civil Rights Movements of the 1960s.

In the fifth edition of *A History of Western Society* (1995),[5] the Hungarian Revolution is again treated in the context of de-Stalinization and reform in the Soviet bloc. "De-Stalinization stimulated rebelliousness in the eastern European satellites. Having suffered in silence under Stalin, communist reformers and the masses were quickly emboldened to seek much greater liberty and national independence." Gomułka could negotiate "greater autonomy for Poland while calming anti-Soviet sentiments," but "Hungary experienced a real and tragic revolution." It was led by the workers and the students (described here as "the classic urban revolutionaries"), and brought to power "a liberal Communist reformer, Imre Nagy." Soviet troops were "forced to leave the country," but when Hungary exited the Warsaw Pact, the Soviets returned: "As in 1849, Soviet leaders answered by invading Hungary with a large army, and once again crushed a national, democratic revolution." Hungarians fought to the very end in the hope of American military aid in fulfillment of "earlier propaganda promises," but no help came. This was a bitter lesson for the satellites: they had to live within the Soviet orbit and trade limited domestic reform for support of Soviet foreign policy. For the eighth edition in 2006[6] the section on the Revolution was made shorter by omitting the references to 1849, and to unfulfilled American propaganda promises. Two paragraphs became one, totaling about 140 words.

Another standard Western civilization textbook, *The Western Heritage*, had is brief, fourth edition published in 2005.[7] It is a teacher's guide, and, as such, carries condensed, single-paragraph summaries of the various topics. In the case of the Khrushchev era, the two pages have six paragraphs. Three deal with the "The Three Crises of 1956": Suez, Poland, and Hungary. The section on Hungary totals eighty words, and calls the events an "uprising" in its title. In response to the street fighting, the "Hungarian Communist Party appointed a new ministry headed by former premier Imre Nagy," who "was a communist but wanted Soviet troops withdrawn from Hungary," and wanted to take the country out of the Warsaw Pact. "This was totally unacceptable to the Soviets, who invaded, deposed (and subsequently executed) Nagy, and made János Kádár (1912–1989) premier. In the second volume of the ninth edition (2007)[8] the only significant additions are a timeline (describing the Revolution as an "uprising") and excerpts from Khrushchev's secret speech that take up more space (more than three quarters of a page) than the discussion of the three crises. In an attempt to improve on the content of the previous editions, the authors claim that Nagy "went much further in his demands than Gomułka and directly appealed for political support from noncommunist groups in Hungary." They also realized (or were reminded) that it was not the Soviets but the Kádár regime that executed Nagy in 1958, and modified the text accordingly.

The current editions of three other standard Western civilization textbooks display similar problems. The sixth edition of *Western Civilization* by Jackson Spielvogel (2006) treats the Polish and Hungarian crises and the Prague Spring to a half-page subchapter titled "Upheaval in Eastern Europe."[9] The usual timeline calls the Hungarian Revolution a "revolt," and two pictures show Khrushchev in Yugoslavia in 1955 and a Soviet tank in Prague in 1968. The Revolution is discussed in a rather superficial, single paragraph of some 230 words. "Intense debates" among Hungarian communists "resulted in the ouster of the ruling Stalinist and the selection of Imry [*sic*] Nagy (1896–1958) as the new Hungarian leader." Anti-Soviet sentiments, the terror of the "Stalinist secret police," and economic difficulties combined to make "the situation ripe for revolt." In response, to "quell the rising rebellion, Nagy declared Hungary a free nation on November 1, 1956. He promised free elections," and this suggested the end of Communism in Hungary. Khrushchev could not "allow a member of the Communist flock to fly the coop," so he decided to intervene. "The Soviets reestablished control over the country, and János Kádár (1912–1989), a reform-minded cabinet minister, replaced Nagy and worked with the Soviets to crush the revolt" and "saved many of Nagy's economic reforms."

The ninth edition of The *Western Experience* (2007)[10] also devotes more space to a photo than to analysis. Soviet tanks in the streets of Budapest take up almost half of a page, but the caption calls the Revolution an "uprising." Summaries of the East German uprising and the Polish October are followed by a short paragraph (ca. 130 words) on Hungary, in which the events are described as "risings," "riots," and "revolution." The Soviets seemingly accepted Hungary's desire for more autonomy, but returned with force when Nagy declared Hungary neutral. "The Soviet leaders pressured, threatened, and finally sent their army to crush the revolution….Rebel radio stations pleaded for the Western aid that many Hungarians expected. None came. Hungary suffered a heavy-handed, repressive Soviet occupation." Nagy was executed, "yet his successor, János Kádár [*sic*], slowly led the country on a more national course."

The second edition of *The West: Encounters & Transformations* (2007)[11] advertises itself with the question, "What does chocolate have to do with the study of history?" Lacking similar creativity in looking at the Soviet Union, the authors sum up the period from the end of the war to the death of Brezhnev in two pages. The entry on 1956 in the timeline included here reads, in part: "Hungarian Revolution crushed by Soviet forces." The satellites get more attention than the Soviet Union, and the subchapter on "Diversity and Dissent in Eastern Europe" is further divided into "1956 and After" and "The Prague Spring." De-Stalinization and Khrushchev's secret speech are cited as the immediate causes of the events in Poland and Hungary. Unlike Gomułka, Nagy "proved unable to resist demands for a break with the Soviet Union." Four days after Hungary announced her withdrawal from the Warsaw Pact, Khrushchev sent in Soviet troops to crush Hungarian resistance. "Nagy was executed in 1958," and "as many as 20,000 Hungarians may have died." They go on to say that the "repression of the Hungarian revolt defined the limits of de-Stalinization in eastern Europe:" no satellite country would be allowed to leave the bloc. Hungary after 1956 "became the most liberal country in the Eastern bloc under Nagy's successor, János Kádár (1912–1989), a reformist communist who…encouraged debate within the Communist Party, loosened censorship on film studios and publishers, and permitted private business ventures."

Western civilization textbooks carry the odd photograph and one or two-paragraph references to the Hungarian Revolution and some of the key figures involved. They usually describe the events in Hungary in the broader context of the Suez crisis and de-Stalinization, and some comment on the West's failure to meet propaganda promises. They all correctly draw the conclusion that Hungary's tragedy was her attempt to leave the Soviet sphere of influence. However, the overall quality of the passages cited above is quite poor. Jumbled chronology and confusion about terminology tend to be the primary problems here. It must also be noticed that Kádár's controversial conduct during October and November 1956 is hardly mentioned, and he is often described as a liberal, which he never was. Hungarian casualties are overstated (the current estimate is 2700), but the interactions within the Eastern bloc are ignored. Most of these accounts also carry some annoying factual mistakes which should be corrected. In some cases the attempt is there, but the results are not.

TEXTBOOKS ON TWENTIETH CENTURY WORLD HISTORY

Histories of the world in the twentieth century are fewer in number than Western civilization textbooks, but they have a narrower focus and one expects more detailed, and more accurate, treatments of the Hungarian Revolution. I have selected three such texts for review, and again included two different editions of one of them for comparison.

William Keylor's *The Twentieth-Century World* (1992)[12] begins with de-Stalinization, and then sums up the Polish October in one page. Hungary gets a page and a half, and Suez is discussed separately. Whereas Gomułka, "this shrewd Polish patriot," successfully protected domestic reforms at the expense of continued support for Soviet foreign policy in the Warsaw Pact, Imre Nagy was not so "prudent, and not so fortunate." Communism "never succeeded in enlisting mass support" in Hungary, and Khrushchev's secret speech in which he denounced the cult of Stalin in February 1956, and the events in Poland "inspired a popular insurrection in Hungary." Nagy "formed a coalition government which, for the first time since the advent of the Cold War, included non-Communist elements." Nagy declared free elections (in fact this was a general demand by early November but not voiced by Nagy), and also secured from the Kremlin promises to evacuate Soviet forces from Hungary. "But as Soviet troops streamed out of Budapest on November 1, Nagy took an extraordinarily provocative step" and "announced Hungary's withdrawal from the Warsaw Pact." The new, "politically independent and militarily neutral Hungary was evidently too much for the Soviet leadership to entertain," because it could have set a "dangerous precedent." The Soviet Union intervened, and "inaugurated a reign of terror that undid all that had been accomplished during the previous month: The Nagy regime was forcibly replaced by a puppet government under János Kádár [*sic*], whose authority rested entirely on the presence of Soviet troops." Suez gets its only mention here, as a "tempting opportunity" provided by the West for the Soviet Union to act against Hungary without fear of American intervention, "despite all of the talk on Western transmitters pledging support for the anti-Soviet resistance."

Daniel Brower's *The World in the Twentieth Century: The Age of Global War and Revolution and The World in the Twentieth Century: From Empires to Nations* appear to be similar enough to be treated as different versions of the same text.[13] In the former (3rd ed., 1996), the Revolution is discussed in the subchapter on the Soviet empire. The first page and a half recalls the rise and fall of Khrushchev, but mentions Hungary only in connection with 1956. The actual paragraph (ca. 200 words) on Hungary is very much like the ones we have seen in Western civilization textbooks: short, no names, jumbled chronology, and sweeping conclusions. Students and workers led the "mass uprising" against "all forms of Stalinism," and "one of their first acts was to destroy a giant forty-foot statue of Stalin in the middle of the city" of Budapest. Though only a few units and individual soldiers joined the revolutionaries, it is claimed that the Hungarian army and the Hungarian Communists joined the "uprising" and the new leaders "quickly introduced a series of reforms to restore civil and political liberties, and declared their intention to make Hungary a free, neutral state." The Soviets could not tolerate this, and they "intervened to repress the Hungarian uprising and imposed on the country leaders loyal to the Soviet Union. Hungary lost its attempt at independence."

In his other text (6th ed., 2005) Brower follows the same line of argument, but this time he presents Khrushchev as a misunderstood tragic hero, a victim of the system he could not reform because his "colleagues were not prepared to undermine the privileges that they enjoyed or the stability of their one-party dictatorship." The factual tone of the previous edition is replaced by an exoneration of Soviet tyranny in a most peculiar way. Brower's interpretation has amazingly little to do with historical facts, and is quoted here extensively to support my judgment. Brower correctly claims that Khrushchev and his successors kept the satellites in orbit by force if needed, but what comes next is oversimplification:

> They recognized the urgency of ending the terrorist system…and the policies of economic exploitation that Stalin had put in place there. They altered the terms of trade between the Soviet Union and the satellite countries to allow improvements in the peoples' miserable living conditions. They made concessions to the deep-seated longings of these peoples (as well as Soviet peoples) to develop the cultural and historical traditions of their nations. But they were prepared to use military force to prevent these countries from freeing themselves from Soviet domination.

In 1956 Hungary mounted one such challenge, and "Soviet leaders acted quickly and forcefully to quell revolution," when "illegal demonstrations by…students and workers, protesting political and economic oppression, quickly turned into a mass uprising against Stalinism." The rest of the paragraph is a word-for-word repetition of Brower's former text, with the addition of one half-sentence at the end: "Hungarians lost their chance for national independence, but not their hostility to communist rule." This is the only textbook I have seen where a later edition shows such deterioration in the academic quality of the presentation. Especially disturbing is the author's decision to call demonstrations against a repressive, totalitarian dictatorship "illegal," because it represents a dubious value judgment.

William Duiker provides a more balanced, but equally superficial, account in the third edition (2005) of his *Twentieth-Century World History*.[14] Duiker's starting point is that the fifties began "with the world teetering on the edge of a nuclear holocaust," but, "as the decade drew to a close, a measure of sanity crept into the Cold War." Yet, Khrushchev's calls for "peaceful coexistence" did not allow for toleration of dissent in the Soviet bloc. The first signs of dissent emerged in East Germany in 1953 and then in Poland in 1956. Mátyás Rákosi is mentioned here as the "local 'Little Stalin,'" who was too brutal even by Soviet standards. When "student-led popular riots broke out" in October, Rákosi "was forced to resign and was replaced by Imre Nagy (1896–1958), a 'national Communist,'" who tried to toe the line between the demands of the people and the expectations of Moscow. Nagy, unlike Gomułka, "was unable to contain the zeal of leading members of the protest movement." When he promised free elections, which surely would have ended Communist rule in Hungary, Moscow decided to intervene. Soviet troops returned to Budapest, and "installed a new government under the more pliant party leader János Kádár," who "rescinded many of Nagy's measures." Meanwhile, "Nagy sought refuge in the Yugoslav Embassy. A few weeks later, he left the embassy under promise of safety but was quickly arrested, convicted of treason, and executed." Duiker then explains why many expected the United States to intervene on behalf of the Hungarians (rollbackt propaganda and the radios), and why Washington decided not to (for fear of a nuclear holocaust). But Moscow realized that concessions were needed to maintain control over her satellites, and even "Kádár, derisively labeled the 'butcher of Budapest,' managed to preserve many of Imre Nagy's re-forms to allow a measure of capitalist incentive and freedom of expression in Hungary."

Histories of the world in the twentieth century devote more attention to the Hungarian Revolution of 1956 than textbooks on Western civilization. This is logical, since these books have to work with a narrower time frame, but one would expect better academic quality as a result. All three textbooks presented here have their shortcomings. Keylor's otherwise very solid work offers a romantic image of Nagy the nationalist revolutionary, which he might have been, and presents him as the prime mover of the events, which he certainly was not. The only explanation I have for the changes in the Brower texts between 1996 and 2005 is that he was trying to put forward a provocative new interpretation. But he does so with disregard for the basic Western consensus over the interpretation of totalitarian regimes; such loose interpretations of hard facts might soon lead to exonerations of Fascist/Nazi regimes, too. Duiker also pays little attention to detail and chronology, but, to his credit, provides an international context for interpretation.

TEXTBOOKS ON EUROPEAN HISTORY IN THE TWENTIETH CENTURY

Five textbooks from five major publishers on the history of Europe in the twentieth century have been selected for review for the purposes of the present essay. These texts provide more comprehensive insights than Western civilization or twentieth-century world history textbooks, and reflect more specific interest on the part of their respective authors. The symbolic destruction of the giant statue of Stalin, for example, gets additional attention via pictorial representation in three of the five books.

The second edition of Robert Wegs' *Europe Since 1945* (1984) is included here because of its surprisingly high academic quality for a book more than twenty years old.[15] Following summaries of Khrushchev's policy of de-Stalinization and the Polish October, Wegs devotes a four-page subchapter to "The Hungarian Revolution." He offers a narrative account of the power struggle between Nagy and Rákosi, and explains the basic differences between their attitudes towards the collectivization of agriculture and the development of heavy industry in Hungary. Nagy's first tenure as premier is described correctly as the relaxation of economic, political, and intellectual controls. Wegs mentions the Writers Union and the Petőfi Circle as sources of opposition to Rákosi, especially after his return to power following Soviet Prime Minister Georgy Malenkov's fall in early 1955. Khrushchev's secret speech shook up the bloc again, and anti-Rákosi sentiments were riding high in Hungary. He, in turn, tired to crush his opposition, but Soviet leaders removed him and appointed Gerő as the new prime minister. The author puts forward his first hypothetical claim here, when he postulates that Soviet support for Nagy at this point "might have prevented the radical revolution that was to follow."

One symbolic step towards revolution was the rehabilitation and reburial of László Rajk, a Communist minister of the interior, who fell victim to Rákosi's purges in the late 1940s. Wegs recalls the demonstrations of October 23 and Gerő's decision to ask for Soviet intervention. The first Soviet intervention was met not only by force in Budapest but by the mushrooming of anti-Soviet workers' and students' councils in the countryside. And when the Hungarian army sided with the rebels, Moscow decided to give Nagy a try. Nagy permitted the reestablishment of the major political parties that had been destroyed before 1949, and, under pressure, reformed his government to include non-Communist members as well. Khrushchev saw this as a sign of Hungary wanting to leave the bloc and intervened by force after securing Tito's support against the "fascist counterrevolution." Meanwhile, Kádár became the new premier and Party leader, and invited the Soviets back in to crush resistance. Wegs then compares Hungary and Poland in the early 1960s and indicates that the Hungarians might be the true winners of 1956: "Kádár removed the Stalinists from the party and concentrated on promoting economic development and raising the standard of living. Yet the Hungarian people never accepted Kádár fully; the memory of 1956 continued to rankle." The subchapter ends with an explanation of why and how Khrushchev's position weakened in the Party after the intervention in Hungary.

The third edition of Roland Stromberg's *Europe in the Twentieth Century* from 1992[16] is a more traditional account. In a five-page subchapter on "The Semi-Thaw in the Cold War, 1954–1956" Stromberg discusses Western concerns in the 1950s ranging from NATO expansion through rearming Germany for Cold War purposes to the Austrian State Treaty. The Soviet response was the creation of the Warsaw Pact and rapprochement with Yugoslavia after Stalin's death. The Soviet suppression of the East German uprising in 1953 made it abundantly clear that de-Stalinization had its limits, but Khrushchev's secret speech at the 20th Party Congress triggered a "Polish uprising," and "Hungary exploded in revolution." The next one page (the shortest treatment in the five texts discussed here) is a sympathetic but superficial, and, at times, inaccurate account of the Revolution. Hungary was forced into World War II on Hitler's side and suffered heavy losses and Russian occupation. "The only resistance Hungarians could offer to a tough Communist dictatorship was to rally around Roman Catholic Cardinal Mindszenty, who was arrested and condemned to life imprisonment in 1948."

Between 1949 and 1953, Rákosi introduced a Stalinist program and collectivized agriculture. During the power struggle following the death of Stalin, Nagy became prime minister but was removed from office in 1955, when Rákosi returned. In July he was replaced by Gerő, "evidently to appease Tito." But the Hungarians wanted "the popular

Communist professor, Nagy," back. Although a committed Communist, Nagy "believed that real communism was not Stalinism: it should be democratic and free. He had released political prisoners, offered freedom of expression and religion, and slowed down the pace of collectivization and industrialization." Then, on October 23, "the secret police brutally broke up a meeting of students and writers." A "spontaneous revolution" followed, and Soviet troops were driven out of Budapest. Nagy was reinstated as premier, political prisoners were released from jail, and Mindszenty was freed. In Stromberg's own words, "It was an intoxicating moment, a truly remarkable example of popular revolution." The Kremlin was "deeply embarrassed and perplexed," but decided to intervene. "They crushed the revolution and arrested and shot Nagy." Hungarians appealed for help to the West and the United Nations in vain, because both were preoccupied with the Suez crisis. At the same time, the Soviet intervention brought on a moral crisis for Western communism: "the country which claimed to represent world revolution" was now repressing a revolution.

The fifth edition of *The End of the European Era, 1890 to the Present* (2002)[17] devotes six pages and two photographs to the Revolution and its immediate context. The two-page introduction sums up the problems of collectivization and industrialization in Hungary and the power struggle in the Kremlin and between Rákosi and Nagy. Appointed in the summer of 1956, Gerő "was expected to steer a middle line between Rákosi's Stalinism and Nagy's new course." The failure of this "controlled transition" was due largely to external conditions. Khrushchev's attempt to appease Tito brought about a joint communiqué on June 20, 1956, according to which "the ways of socialist development vary in different countries and conditions," and this diversity contributes to the success of building socialism. Poland won concessions along these lines, and Hungary tired to follow suit. What follows is a concise and reliable account of the Revolution, with a good exposition on how it escalated and the dilemmas Nagy had to face.

The authors freely use "revolt" as a synonym for revolution, but mistakenly claim, like all the other texts cited so far, that the Soviet invasion on November 4 was a response to Nagy's declaration of Hungary's exit from the Warsaw Pact. 200,000 Hungarians fled the country, 20,000 were imprisoned, and 2,000 were executed (the actual number is 230) by the new regime of János Kádár, installed by the Soviet army. But, following the brutal repression of the Revolution, Kádár took "a somewhat surprising course." While he thoroughly collectivized agriculture, the administration of agriculture and industry were decentralized, and Kádár "encouraged a limited degree of free enterprise." Hungary could "develop closer intellectual ties with the West than any other satellite country" following the "broad amnesty" issued "at the end of 1960" (in fact in 1963) and the relaxation of state control over literary and intellectual life.

In a long chapter on "De-Stalinization and Destabilization," in *Twentieth Century Europe: Politics, Society, Culture* (2004),[18] Spencer Di Scala offers a detailed and reliable summary of the effects of Stalin's death, the subsequent power struggle in the Kremlin, and its effects on the East European satellites of the Soviet Union. He mentions strikes in Bulgaria and Czechoslovakia in May 1953, then discusses the East German uprising at length. In a one-page analysis of Khrushchev's secret speech, Di Scala postulates that the Soviet leader followed up his rhetoric with action: forced labor camps were closed, the influence of the secret police was reduced, and some intellectual discourse was allowed. He partly contradicts his earlier statements by saying that Boris Pasternak's novel, *Dr. Zhivago,* was published only in the West, but supports his argument by invoking the Soviet publication of Alexander Solzhenitsyn's *One Day in the Life of Ivan Denisovich.* As a result, the Kremlin "barely managed to prevent the Polish disorders" of 1956 "from escalating into revolution." The Polish October "demonstrated that the poor economic conditions caused by Communist policies could combine powerfully with national pride and rich cultural heritage to destabilize the Soviet Empire."

A reliable summary of Hungary's road to revolution includes an interesting take on the fall of Rákosi. According to Di Scala, it was a combination of the relaxation of international tensions through the emergence of the non-aligned nations and the Austrian State Treaty on the one hand, and of Tito's dislike of Rákosi on the other. The author's account of the Revolution itself is brief and generally acceptable, but still could benefit from further clarification. He begins with Rákosi's deposition in July, and continues with the October 6 demonstrations without identifying it as Rajk's reburial. As a result of the October 23 demonstrations and the subsequent street fighting, the Kremlin "allowed

Nagy to return to power as Premier, but, unlike Gomułka, Nagy failed to resolve the situation." His reluctance to act prompted the leaders of the spontaneously emerging revolutionary councils in the country to force Nagy's hand. In response, he transformed his government and announced multiparty elections. The Soviets agreed to withdraw their troops, but insisted that "Hungary must remain a Socialist state." The Soviet Union could not allow Hungary to leave the bloc, and the invasion began on November 4. The one sentence that requires major rewriting reads, "The Red Army killed about 3,000 fighters and executed about 2,500 Hungarians after the revolution, including Nagy." The rapid collapse of Communist rule in Hungary proved that "Soviet domination and poor economic conditions" were the keys to the fragility of the Soviet system. Khrushchev had to reconcile the diversity of the Soviet bloc with the unity of its purpose, and could only do so by the use of force as the last resort.

The fourth edition of Robert Paxton's *Europe in the Twentieth Century* (2005) devotes two pages of text and two half-page photographs to "Eastern Europe: Thaw and Rebellion, 1953–1956."[19] Paxton first points out the contradictions between the nature and conduct of socialist economies under Stalin and the desires of the people. He concludes that the Soviet dictator's death "and the experiments of his successors released volatile responses in Eastern Europe," and continues with the May 1953 Czechoslovak strikes and the East German uprising. Paxon introduces the discussion of the Hungarian Revolution by stating that "Hungarian Premier Imre Nagy (1953–1955) went furthest in the quest for a more relaxed, more national variant of socialism within the Soviet bloc." Nagy's reforms were cut short by Malenkov's fall in Moscow and his removal from office by Rákosi and the old Stalinists in Budapest. Khrushchev's secret speech unleashed "even more threatening Eastern European reactions." Paxton states that "Polish de-Stalinization was carried through peacefully; in Hungary, de-Stalinization led to insurrection followed by harsh repression." He mistakenly puts the October 23 demonstration to October 20 (probably a typo, but an awkward one nonetheless). "Events might have been channeled into something parallel to the Polish compromise, but shots were fired and the demonstrations became uncontrollable." Paxton also mentions the destruction of the Stalin statue in Budapest, and includes a photograph for added emphasis. The countryside responded to the events in the capital, and Nagy announced the withdrawal of Soviet troops and the restoration of the multiparty system on October 29 and 30 respectively. Following the declaration of Hungary's neutrality and exit from the Warsaw Pact, the Soviets returned by force. "A deeply wounded Hungary was restored to firm Communist rule under János Kádár. Nagy and other leaders of the Hungarian 'New Course' were subsequently put to death." Paxton concludes that the fate of Hungary clearly demonstrated two things. On the one hand, room to move within the Soviet bloc was rather limited and did not include any challenge to Soviet rule. The lack of American or United Nations intervention showed, on the other hand, that changes behind the Iron Curtain "would have to come by internal evolution."

Three of the five texts covered in this subchapter carry photographs of the destruction of the giant statue of Stalin in Budapest, and, although this goes beyond the scope of the present essay, we must pause briefly here to take a look at how they represent the actual events and how they supplement the arguments put forward in these textbooks. The choice of image is obvious: it drives home forcefully the people's desire to destroy (and deface) the whole system by the destruction of the physical image of its leader, Stalin. The Keystone Press Agency photo in the Wegs book (p. 130) is easily the most powerful one because it forcefully drives home the absurd and macabre nature of the situation. It shows Stalin's jovially smiling head placed on the ground between streetcar rails at an intersection; he looks at the sky, while people are walking by as if the head was not there. In *The End of the European Era* we see a different approach through two images presented side-by-side (p. 406). The first picture shows the process of toppling the statue (with Stalin at 45 degrees), while the second one is a shot from below of the boots (which the revolutionaries could not remove from the pedestal) with the national flag stuck in one of them. For one of two images for the chapter, Paxton chose a picture (p. 528) of the statue already on the ground but still in one piece, with people standing around it, and with graffiti on it saying "pimp" and "toilet." If used carefully, classroom discussions of these photographs can help students understand the psychology of the region and the events.

Four of the five textbooks discussed here include fairly reliable and extensive accounts of the Hungarian Revolution of 1956, but not without some apparently typical mistakes. The most common mistakes include statements regarding the sequence of events and to the Soviets executing Nagy. Stromberg's *Europe in the Twentieth Century* is the odd one out; it looks more like a Western civilization or twentieth-century world history textbook than a European history. The author apparently has a romantic attachment to the Revolution, which may be commendable, but he failed to make a genuine attempt to separate political myths from reality. It must be emphasized that attention to detail combined with the introduction of more and more of the people involved in the various decisions make these books reliable classroom resources. Coverage of East-West relations and of Soviet-Yugoslav rapprochement in the early fifties provide the necessary background for discussion. In most cases, the narrowing of the focus of these works to Europe in the twentieth century goes hand in hand with considerable improvement in the quality of the discussion of the Hungarian Revolution, too.

The next logical step is to narrow the focus even further and look at East European histories, but before we do that we must review some representative textbooks on Russian history and American foreign policy in the Cold War. After all, the international context of the Revolution was the Cold War, and any survey would be incomplete without a glance at some of these textbooks.

RUSSIAN AND SOVIET HISTORY TEXTBOOKS

Interest in Russian and Soviet history has been on the decline since the end of the Cold War, and this is reflected both in the number of Russian history courses at American universities and in the decreasing number of Russian/Soviet history textbooks. Four such books have been selected to represent four major publishers. What these textbooks share besides a common subject is that all four were published after the Cold War had ended.

The second edition of Martin McCauley's *The Soviet Union, 1971–1991*, was published in 1993. The author follows a chronological line both in the book and within the chapters. The relevant sections are found in the subchapter "1955–57"[20] in the chapter on "The Khrushchev Era." McCauley describes Khrushchev's foreign policy initiatives in detail. He opened toward China and Yugoslavia, approved the Austrian State Treaty and the subsequent evacuation of the country, and visited India, Burma, and Afghanistan, too. The author then details Khrushchev's secret speech and offers a number of explanations why the Soviet leader delivered it. It is after all this that he mentions Hungary, and does so in connection with what he calls "the first phase of destalinization [*sic*]." Developments in Poland and Hungary in October 1956 forced Khrushchev to slow down. In the East European countries, where the socialist revolutions were brought about not by local Lenins but by the invading Red Army in 1944–1945, "the ice of legitimacy was very thin," and "it cracked in Poland but broke in Hungary." The single most important consideration for Moscow was whether the unquestioned leadership of the Party was being challenged or not. In Poland it was not, but "the Poles stood their ground and won greater control over their internal affairs while promising to support Soviet foreign and defence (British specially in a quote) policies. In Hungary Imre Nagy's new government sough to take the country out of the Warsaw Pact and the party lost its dominating role." By way of conclusion McCauley postulates that the Soviet invasion made it clear once and for all that the Kremlin "would tolerate no new Titos in eastern Europe." All in all, this is a convincing argument with the discussion of the Revolution nicely fitted into the author's train of thought.

The fourth edition of *A History of Russia, the Soviet Union, and Beyond* (1993)[21] also treats "The Khrushchev Era, 1953–1964" in a separate chapter. It opens with a reference to the post-Stalin power struggle and to "revolts in Poland and Hungary" which "loosened Soviet control over the satellites." A lengthy exposition on politics and the economy is followed by the subchapter on foreign policy, and it is here that the authors discuss the Hungarian Revolution. After outlining the main goals of Soviet foreign policy for the 1950s, the authors explain Khrushchev's "pilgrimage to Belgrade" and his attempts to appease Tito. Other issues discussed include the Austrian State Treaty and the Geneva Conference (1955). Meanwhile, in Eastern Europe the relaxation of Soviet controls combined with Khrushchev's secret speech caused crises in the bloc. The authors mention only the 1953 East German uprising and the June 1956 Polish crisis before explaining what happened in Hungary. There, students and intellectuals "demanded drastic political reforms. Prime Minister Imre Nagy failed to halt Stalinist Hungary's rapid disintegration. After a revolt in Budapest (October 23), Nagy announced that Hungary would leave the Warsaw Pact, become a neutral country, and restore a multiparty system." The army joined the "insurgents," and Hungary asked for Western help. Kádár was "hastily named the new first secretary of the Hungarian Party," and he invited Soviet troops in to crush the "rebels." The presentation of the sequence of events in Hungary may be faulty, the conclusion is convincing: "The Soviet response in Hungary showed that the USSR would act militarily within its sphere of interest whenever Communist rule was threatened, a move that demonstrated anew the existence of Communist control in eastern Europe based not on consent but on Soviet bayonets." The only other mention the Revolution gets in this textbook is in connection with the loosening of domestic controls over culture: the "Hungarian Revolution profoundly affected Soviet university students. In Leningrad alone, some 2,000 were disciplined or expelled for condemning Soviet armed intervention in Hungary. They formed a number of political and literary groups that produced *samizdat* journals." The inclusion of the spontaneous, domestic Soviet response to the events is an excellent idea.

In *A Vision Unfulfilled* (1996))[22] John Thompson devotes more attention to the Revolution than the previous two texts combined: a bit more than one page. The focus is again, and justifiably, on the changes Khrushchev initiated in the Soviet system. He concludes that both Khrushchev's foreign and national security policy brought mixed results. The Soviet leader could not prevent the rearmament of West Germany, but Soviet-Yugoslav relations were normalized. A reduction in the size of the army went hand-in-hand with the beefing up the nuclear arsenal and active support for anti-Western governments and political forces in the Third World. But again, he "failed to prevent an attack on Egypt by France, Great Britain, and Israel in November 1956." Establishing no connection between Suez, Poland, and Hungary, he switches to Eastern Europe. A brief review of the Polish October is followed by Thompson's account of the Revolution. Intellectuals wanting change "found a sympathetic hearing among reform-minded Communists and democratic leaders from the presocialist [*sic*] era. But antisocialist and anti-Soviet sentiments among Catholics and nationalists created a volatile political brew." Hard-line Stalinists lost control in the "October 23 antigovernment riots," and, together with the Soviet ambassador, Yuri Andropov, asked for Soviet intervention against the "counterrevolution." Two Soviet Presidium members were sent to Budapest on October 24, and their report convinced the Kremlin that concessions were needed. The Soviets "seemed prepared to negotiate on October 30," but the next day Andropov again demanded intervention and Mashal Georgy Zhukov was instructed to "plan military action against the Hungarian revolution." Nagy's decision to withdraw from the Warsaw Pact convinced Khrushchev that intervention was inevitable, and on November 4 "sixty thousand Soviet troops moved into Hungary and bloodily suppressed the revolution." The Soviets then "installed a subservient orthodox regime under János Kádár [*sic*]. Subsequent reprisals saw three hundred revolutionaries executed and more than ten thousand imprisoned." Thompson's accurate and logical conclusion is in line with those of the other historians discussed above: The West was taken by surprise and was preoccupied with the Suez crisis in October–November 1956. Direct support was considered too risky, so they "settled for aiding Hungarian refugees" instead, and condemned the Soviet invasion in the United Nations. In the West, many Communists left the movement, while the suppression of the Revolution "accelerated some Soviet intellectuals' disenchantment with the regime." Word-of-mouth told a story other than Moscow's official interpretation. "Protests erupted and hard questions cropped up in Party meetings."

The fourth and final text considered here, *A History of Russia: Peoples, Legends, Events, Forces Since 1800* (2004), also treats the Revolution in the context of Khrushchev's policies.[23] The one-page subchapter titled "Imperial Arena: The Bloc" opens with a short exposition on the post-Stalin thaw within the bloc between 1953 and 1955 and continues with a brief account of the Polish October. As regards Hungary, the authors state that a harsher regime met with "more vigorous" resistance. The situation was so bad the Kremlin intervened and appointed Gerő, whom the authors surprisingly call "a moderate." This failed to solve the problems, and "students and other restless forces took to the streets on October 22, 1956, and were fired on by the police." Nagy came to power, and "declared Hungary neutral, withdrew from the Warsaw Pact, and enacted democratic reforms ending the power of police, party, and censors." An unidentified workers' councilman is quoted next, who stated that they wanted a genuinely Hungarian version of socialism. In response, "Russian tanks rolled through the streets of Budapest and other towns, ripping up bodies as well as the aspirations of Hungarian anticommunists, who were falsely accused by Moscow of being fascist hirelings." Communists in the West were appalled by Soviet action and left the movement, while Khrushchev made it clear that membership in the bloc was meant to be for life.

The four Russian history textbooks surveyed here have many features in common. They, quite naturally, discuss the Hungarian Revolution as part of the Khrushchev era, and, even in terms of foreign policy, their focus is on the bloc and Soviet-Yugoslav relations. Suez is mentioned here only as a sideshow to the developments in Eastern Europe after Stalin's death. The familiar problems of jumbled chronology and factual mistakes also show up in these texts. Since the Hungarian Revolution was a defining moment in the history of the Soviet empire, one would expect detailed and accurate coverage in Russian history textbooks. As has been pointed out, this is not the case: accounts range from one paragraph to one page in textbooks of three to eight hundred pages, and the narrative on the Revolution in the second and fourth texts needs some rewriting.

TEXTBOOKS ON AMERICAN FOREIGN POLICY IN THE COLD WAR

Three textbooks and two monographs generally used in Cold War history courses have been selected for this category to cover a wide variety of interpretations. These texts usually discuss the Revolution in the broader context of Soviet-American confrontation, together with the Suez crisis. The second monograph included looks at United States policies towards Eastern Europe, and represents a logical transition to the last category, East European history textbooks.

One traditional, consensus-school history of American foreign policy is Thomas Bailey's *A Diplomatic History of the American People*. Its eighth edition from 1969 is included here to serve as the reference point for subsequent texts written after the Cold War had ended.[24] The subchapter on "Hungarian Horrors" begins with a look at Khrushchev's speech on de-Stalinization, but with an original twist: "Even a donkey can kick a dead lion, and Khrushchev denounced his former chief as a ruthless and bloody bungler." As regards Soviet-Yugoslav rapprochement and the joint declaration on different roads to socialism, Bailey is equally critical: "Russian leaders came crawling to Tito, whom they had long denounced as a 'fascist hireling,' and signed a pact in June, 1956, proclaiming that there were 'differing roads to socialism.'" De-Stalinization led to "bloody riots" in Poznan, but the "Poles finally gained some semblance of autonomy in October, 1956, when they managed to elect their own Communist Party chief in defiance of strong pressure from Moscow."

Meanwhile, demonstrations in Hungary "quickly flared into a large-scale revolt among a people whose passion for liberty was traditional. Carried away by the heady champagne of freedom, the Hungarians boldly renounced the Warsaw Pact." This was too much for the Kremlin: "Treacherously massing a formidable array of tanks near Budapest, they slaughtered hundreds of the rebels and installed a puppet regime subservient to Moscow." His evaluation of the American position is quite outspoken from an historian not known for his critical remarks about American foreign policy: "The American people were stirred to their depths by the Hungarian uprising, as they had been in 1849, when the Russian Cossaks had crushed Kossuth." Americans sent medical aid and provided safe haven for a lot of refugees, but military help was out of the question. "The United States could do nothing except perhaps to threaten Moscow with atomic warfare—and that might touch off World War III. Cruel though the conclusion was, the policy makers in Washington deemed it better that a rebellion should die rather than a world should perish." The United Nations, the United States, and Russia all "lost face" as a result.

Besides his entertaining language, Bailey also features a *Washington Post* cartoon from 1956, which serves as a link between the accounts on Hungary and Suez. In the cartoon, a big, fat, grinning Soviet soldier is wiping blood off his sword with a dead civilian lying on his face behind him. There is a flag with a broken pole in front of him, on the ground. It reads, "Free Hungary." And the caption is, "I'll be glad to restore peace to the Middle East, too." Bailey also establishes this connection with the last sentence of the subchapter on the Revolution: "But bleeding Hungary still lay in chains, while the contemporaneous British-French-Israeli attack on Egypt weakened the moral position of the Western world."

The seventh revised edition of Stephen Ambrose's *Rise to Globalism* (1993) devotes two pages and two additional comments to the Hungarian crisis and treats it as a sideshow to Suez.[25] Ambrose begins the ninth chapter, "From Hungary and Suez to Cuba" with a categorical statement: "The overwhelming first impression of American foreign policy from 1956 to 1961 was one of unrelieved failure. America's inability to do anything at all to aid Hungary's rebels made a mockery of the Republican calls for liberation." This promising start is then followed by a four-page exposition on the Suez crisis. New developments in Eastern Europe, according to the author, "complicated everything." Khrushchev's speech on de-Stalinization resulted in riots and compromise in Poland, which "won substantial independence and set an example for the other satellites."

Ambrose's opening statement on Hungary must be quoted in its entirety, because it may easily be misread, and because it reflects unfavorably on the author's vision of history: "The excitement spread to Hungary, before the war the most Fascist of the East European states and the one where Stalin's imposition of Communism had been most alien." This is shockingly unhistorical: degrees of fascism are difficult to measure, but, more importantly, Hungarian resistance to Stalinism was fuelled not by the country's tragic past involvement with fascism but by what the Soviet system and its local servants stood for during the 1950s. Student demonstrators on October 23 demanded the replacement of "Stalinist puppets" with Nagy. Khrushchev gave in, but the Hungarians went on to demand Soviet withdrawal and "the creation of an anti-Communist political party." Khrushchev gave in again, and on October 31 Nagy announced Hungary's withdrawal from the Warsaw Pact. The Soviet response was invasion, and "Russian tanks crushed the Hungarian rebels who fought back with Molotov cocktails." Hungarians asked for American help on the radio, but no help came. "There never would be American troops. Eisenhower did not even consider giving military support to the Hungarians," as he would never risk

World War III for Eastern Europe. Concerning the lessons of the two crises, Ambrose writes, "American politicians learned to stop their irresponsible prattling about liberation. The Russians learned just how strong a force nationalism was in Eastern Europe."

The sixth edition of Walter LaFeber's *America, Russia, and the Cold War* (1991) also presents the Revolution in the context of the Suez crisis.[26] His account is somewhat like Ambrose's, but LaFeber offers more accurate detail and comment: "On October 23 students moved into the streets to demand that long-time Stalinist Ernö Gerö [*sic*] be replaced with Imre Nagy. When the secret police attempted to put down the protests, workers joined the students. One huge demonstration destroyed a gigantic statue of Stalin in central Budapest." The Soviets gave in, and Hungarians upped the ante. They now demanded Soviet troop withdrawal and "the creation of a political party in opposition to the communists." Soviet withdrawal began on October 28, but the Kremlin changed its mind on October 31, when Nagy "announced Hungary's withdrawal from the Warsaw Pact." In fact the declaration came on November 1. The Soviet army "crushed the Hungarian uprising" just as the Anglo-French attack was launched in the Middle East. "Having smashed the Hungarian rebellion, Khrushchev entered the Middle East scene," but could not get much out of it. In LaFeber's evaluation, Eisenhower emerged "from the winter crises with increased powers and prestige." Khrushchev, on the other hand, clearly failed: "Despite his triumphant proclamation that Dulles's failure to interfere in the Hungarian uprising had proven the hollowness of 'liberation,' the fiasco of Khrushchev's policies in Eastern Europe and his inability to take advantage of the power vacuum in the Middle East immersed him in deep political trouble in Moscow."

Thomas McCormick's *America's Half-Century* (1989), the first of the two key monographs discussed here, is generally considered to be the founding text of the "world systems" interpretation of the Cold War.[27] It is included here to check whether an approach fundamentally different from those of Bailey, Ambrose, and LaFeber would offer a different view of the Hungarian Revolution. Would he call it a "revolution," or would it remain an "uprising," a "rebellion," or a "riot," like in the previous texts? McCormick treats "The Suez and Hungarian Crises, 1956" to two pages of text, with half a page discussing Hungary. His comparison of the two crises rests on the element of surprise. Whereas America's allies acted in

Egypt without notifying Washington, the Hungarian crisis proved to be "a worst-case scenario" in an instable situation created by Khrushchev's secret speech. Hungary's "road seemed to lead away from socialist economics and out of the Warsaw Pact. Encouraged by Western preoccupation with the Suez crisis, Russia resolved the Hungarian one by a swift and bloody suppression of the Hungarian dissidents. Having done so, it immediately adopted the posture of Egypt's defender by threatening the West with nuclear-armed missiles." McCormick's conclusion echoes Ambrose's opening statement: "Russia's unopposed 'pacification' of Hungary belied the empty rhetoric of the American doctrine of liberation for Eastern Europe, while Russia's rhetorical intervention in the Suez crisis enabled it to pose as the defender of Third World self-determination." Thus, the Revolution again remains a sideshow to Suez.

The most widely used text on United States-East European relations is Bennett Kovrig's *Of Walls and Bridges* (1991).[28] Kovrig is of Hungarian origin, and his focus is on Eastern Europe, so this time Suez becomes a sideshow to the Revolution. As may be expected, he treats the Revolution an extensive account, although Kovrig never forgets that his book is, first and foremost, about American foreign policy. Accordingly, a four-page synopsis of the Hungarian events is followed by a twelve-page account of American options and decisions. He begins with the Hungarian power struggle between 1953 and 1956, and argues that by the middle of October "the classic prerevolutionary [*sic*] situation was in evidence: a divided and demoralized ruling elite, a restive and outspoken intelligentsia, and an alienated population yearning for change." Following a brief review of the events of October 23, Kovrig explains the dynamics of the Revolution: "In thirteen days the revolution went through stages of armed confrontation, democratic consolidation, and final repression." He covers First Deputy Prime Minister Anastas Mikoyan and Party theoretician Mikhail Suslov's repeated trips to Budapest, the reappearance of traditional political parties and newspapers, and Mindszenty's return. "The new political consensus favored a pluralistic democracy, some form of mixed economy, and, above all, national autonomy."

Kovrig attributes Moscow's decision to intervene to a variety of factors: the Russians concluded sometime between October 29 and 31 that "Hungary was abandoning communism, the Americans had made clear they would not intervene; and the Western allies were divided over the impending military action against Egypt." Thus the Kremlin saw limited risk in intervention, and started to mobilize. Kovrig's is the first one among the texts reviewed thus far which correctly states that Nagy's decision to leave the Warsaw Pact and declare Hungary neutral was not the cause but the effect, or result, of the Soviet invasion. Kádár, Tito's choice for Hungary, "was brought back to Budapest in a Soviet armored car, and set about the thankless task of restoring Communist rule." By citing Robert Murphy, one of the doyens of American diplomacy at the time, Kovrig demonstrates that "Washington had neither advance warning nor a contingency plan for the Hungarian uprising."

These three textbooks and two monographs widely used in American Cold War history courses all treat the Hungarian Revolution in the context of the Suez crisis and East-West confrontation. Bailey's account is entertaining, his language is more emotional than that of the other texts, and he pays limited attention to detail. Ambrose and LaFeber evaluate America's participation in the two crises in totally different ways. What the two books share is a surprisingly limited scope of attention paid to the events in Hungary. In books dealing with America's role and participation in the Cold War one expects more attention to the Revolution than what we get in Western civilization textbooks. This applies to McCormick as well, who limits his comments on Hungary to an elegantly written short paragraph. Kovrig's focus is on United States policy towards Eastern Europe, and he provides a reliable and useful account of both the Revolution and the American responses to it. His book, as has been pointed out, borders on our last category, East European history textbooks.

EASTERN EUROPEAN HISTORY TEXTBOOKS

Six texts have been selected for survey in this category. In East European history texts, the closest we get to the history of the Hungarian Revolution of 1956 in undergraduate courses, one expects detailed discussion, reliable historical analysis, and attention to detail. These six books were published between 1992 and 2004, and the list of authors includes two Hungarians (but of very different backgrounds), a Pole, and several Brits. This highlights a most peculiar factor: American college history courses on East European history, if they are offered at all, tend to rely on American historians of East European backgrounds or on generally quite solid British scholarship, but not on the output of American historians. This, in turn, means that the American aspect is totally absent. I firmly believe that the British way of writing and interpreting history is fundamentally different from the American one (or ones), while historians of East European background are emotionally involved, regardless of how hard they try, and how successful they might be, in trying to remain objective.

Chronologically first in line is Joseph Held's *The Columbia History of Eastern Europe in the Twentieth Century* from 1992.[29] Held, as editor, chose the country-by-country approach, and he himself contributed a thirty-page chapter on "Hungary: 1945 to the Present." About two thirds of the chapter discusses the Communist takeover and the early Stalinist period in Hungary. The Revolution dealt with in two pages. Held recites the events of October 23, Soviet withdrawal, and the October 25 massacre in front of the Parliament Building. He inserts the following comment on the siege of the Party headquarters and the subsequent killing of its defenders: "Given the enormity of the crimes committed by the ÁVO-ÁVH, there were remarkably few incidents of this sort during the revolution." Held, indirectly, responds to the propaganda of the Kádár regime, according to which criminal elements and fascist hordes were ravaging the streets of the Hungarian capital.

Held goes on to say that the Revolution had won by October 28. Negotiations were under way about full Soviet withdrawal from Hungary, but the Hungarian delegates were arrested by the NKVD. Hungary declared her neutrality, and the Soviets attacked. The West was preoccupied with Suez, and the Russians succeeded. Nagy fled to the Yugoslav Embassy but was arrested and deported to Romania after he was "forced to leave" Tito's embassy in Budapest. "For more than a year Hungary's legal prime minister was held prisoner in a foreign country. On June 16, 1958, after a short trial, he and several of members of his government were executed. They were secretly buried in unmarked graves." Some 200,000 Hungarians fled to the West, while the Soviets hand-picked Kádár to lead the new regime. "Kádár's counterrevolutionary terror lasted well into the early 1960s. The atrocities and judicial murders were no less brutal and vicious than those in Rákosi's time." The final four pages of the chapter sum up the achievements of the Kádár era and explain how his "soft dictatorship" earned some sort of legitimacy in Soviet-dominated Hungary.

In *Eastern Europe in the Twentieth Century* (1994), Richard J. Crampton discusses the Hungarian revolution in a separate chapter, "The Upheavals of 1956: Hungary."[30] He identifies four major causes of the Revolution: "an affronted nationalism," a mistaken economic policy geared towards heavy industry, "a challenging intelligentsia," and a divided Party elite. He then treats the reader to a detailed review of the Rákosi vs. Nagy power struggle and to what he calls the "Gerő interregnum." The second half of the chapter deals with the Revolution, the dismantling of communist authority, the Soviet crackdown, and the significance of the Revolution.

His narrative account of the events of October 23–30 is very accurate, and includes such hitherto unmentioned aspects as student demonstrations in Szeged and the founding of the Hungarian University Student Alliance, the MEFESZ, as well as the role of the revolutionary councils in the countryside, from Győr to Debrecen. Crampton claims that the "destruction of communist authority" took place on October 28 and 29, when the National Guard was established and the Central Committee of the Party and the ÁVH were dissolved. He correctly notes that "Hungary had scored a great victory, but that victory was not Nagy's, nor did he control the forces that had driven out the Soviets." It was done by local commanders, including Pál Maléter, who "earned the glory and accumulated the authority. And outside the capital it was the national councils not the government ministries which exercised power." The rivalry between the Nagy government and the revolutionaries was resolved on October 30 by Soviet delegates Mikoyan and Suslov, who approved the establishment of a coalition government "as long as capitalism was not restored and Hungary did not become a base for anti-Soviet forces."

This was "the high-water mark of the revolution," and democratic life and institutions were reborn. Mindszenty was freed from captivity, political parties long banned now reemerged, and more than two dozen newspapers were published. The Kremlin could not tolerate such level of dissent, and Soviet troops began to move. Crampton states correctly that "Nagy had declared neutrality because he knew his country was being invaded." Andropov's treacherous conduct is highlighted in the author's account of the trapping of the Hungarian negotiators (most importantly of Maléter). Invasion and retaliation followed, and Kádár had to deal with postrevolutionary strikes and demonstrations as late as December 4. In conclusion, Crampton discusses the significance of the Revolution in two pages. This section is as much a dialogue with the propaganda of the Kádár regime as it is a summary of Crampton's views. "The revolution was entirely unpremeditated and spontaneous." It was "first and foremost national," but "also anti-totalitarian and pro-democracy." And unlike in 1989, there were no signs of "a desire to return to capitalism." He also challenges the key arguments of Communist propaganda regarding the true nature of the Revolution:

> And Soviet propaganda claims that the revolution was a Horthyite, fascist conspiracy were nonsense. A few right-wing groups did emerge towards the end of the revolution, some of which placed their hopes for political leadership in cardinal Mindszenty, but there were no fascists; no one raised the name of Gömbös, whilst the man whom the Soviet portrayed as a fascist, [József] Dudás, was a fanatical national communist.

Crampton also looks at Hungary's losses and changes in Communist strategy in Eastern Europe after the Revolution, and draws the familiar conclusion that United States would not challenge Moscow inside the Russian sphere of influence, and the Kremlin would not tolerate departure from the Warsaw Pact.

Another contribution from British historians, *Eastern Europe Since 1945* was first published in 1993; the third edition came out in 2003.[31] The authors, Geoffrey and Nigel Swain, are both established authorities on Soviet history and Eastern Europe after World War II, and their book is a combination of solid scholarship and unorthodox interpretations. The Revolution is discussed in the chapter "1956: Communism Renewed?" Their basic, opening contention is that "the twin processes of de-Stalinization and Soviet-Yugoslav rapprochement opened up the possibility of renewal for the Communist states of Easter Europe." What they mean by this is that "it was the existence 'outside' of an alternative socialist system, coupled with the genuine desire of Khrushchev to bring

Yugoslavia back into the family of socialist states that made the prospect of renewal genuine." The Swains follow up this claim with a discussion of the new course in Hungary, Khrushchev's attempts to negotiate with Tito, and the effects of the secret speech in February 1956. The lead-up to the subchapter on the Revolution concludes with Tito inviting Khrushchev to Belgrade in September 1956. And the Swains' comment reads, "Together, Khrushchev and Tito seemed to be planning the renewal of communism."

The seven-page subchapter on the Revolution opens with a look at Nagy's writings on Communism in Hungary, the emergence of intellectual opposition to the regime (Petőfi Circle), Rákosi's failed attempt to purge the Party in the summer of 1956, and his subsequent replacement by Gerő. Tito and Khrushchev continued to work together, and Belgrade insisted on the removal of Rákosi and the rehabilitation of Rajk. Following an exposition on the familiar stories of October 22–23, 1956, the Swains present Nagy's dilemma: he was returned to power by the Party, but needed popular support for his vision of Communism to work. And he could not get it exactly because he was associated with the Party. The authors then describe the unfolding crisis (with the third edition carrying extra discussion of Kádár's role) and the establishment of a coalition government with Soviet approval. The Kremlin soon realized that Nagy was not really in control and was forced to make concession after concession.

The Swains then raise the legal justification for stationing Soviet troops in Hungary and claim that the October 30 "Declaration on Friendship and Cooperation between the Soviet Union and other Socialist States" provided Nagy with sufficient grounds to demand troop withdrawal. The Soviet Party leadership gradually drifted towards interpreting the events in Budapest as a "counterrevolution." Nagy sensed this, and declared Hungary neutral in the face of impending Soviet attack. The Soviet invasion is described in the book as a "Soviet-Yugoslav intervention," and the authors claim that Kádár was Tito's choice over Ferenc Münnich for leadership. Moscow went along after the Politburo had met both of them on November 2. In light of the above, it is hardly surprising that the Swains believe that the Hungarians wanted a Yugoslav model revolving around the workers' councils. Their conclusion is in line with their earlier arguments. "Yugoslav-

Soviet cooperation in 'saving socialism' in Hungary fell apart when Khrushchev decided that it was no longer possible to negotiate with the worker's councils" of Budapest after the Revolution had ended.

Ivan Berend's *Central and Eastern Europe* (1996)[32] is a revised version of his earlier book in Hungarian on the same subject. Berend devotes ten pages to the subchapter on "The Hungarian October" and cleverly observes that although the old Stalinists were back in power by 1955, they "could no longer use it as previously." Although Nagy was expelled from the Party, Rákosi "had to face the extremely repugnant and explosive issue of rehabilitating his own victims." Opposition composed of the reform Communists, the Petőfi Circle and the Writers' Union centered around Nagy, and Rákosi's attempt to crack down on them resulted in his own demise. Gerő replaced him, and the victims of the Rajk show trial were reburied on October 6. This five-page introduction is followed by a detailed interpretation of the Revolution itself. Berend states that on October 23 a "spontaneous, elemental, genuine people's uprising erupted," which, as result of the first Soviet attack, developed into "a desperate fight for independence." Nagy was reinstated, and his reform Communist administration was turned into a coalition government, which "was not recognized by the freedom fighters."

Berend calls the developments a "revolution" only after October 28, when Nagy dissolved the secret police, reinstated national symbols, and began negotiations about Soviet withdrawal from Hungary. He reiterates, again and again, that the "power of the government was rather formal and strongly questioned." He arbitrarily conjures up a marked shift to the right, with all forms of socialism rejected. He devotes half a page to what forms of right-wing restoration were rejected by various leaders of the Revolution. He then returns to the narrative at November 1, when Soviet troops made preparations to move back into Hungary, Nagy declared Hungary's neutrality, and asked for United Nations help. The second Soviet intervention reestablished socialist rule and was followed by "brutal repression." Berend's extended discussion of the possible right-wing scenarios is a thinly veiled attempt to introduce the Kádár regime's "counterrevolutionary" propaganda into the discussion of the Revolution in the West. There is a basic contradiction in his otherwise well-written account. By citing extensively the non-Communist leaders of the Revolution (Anna Kéthly, Béla Kovács), and a national communist (József Dudás) who did not want a return of the old, pre-1945 order—without naming the equally prominent right-wing leaders who in his opinion stood for changes—Berend refutes his earlier claim that the Revolution was anti-Socialist by nature. The realistic demands of the Revolution were defined and limited by the presence of Soviet troops. The general consensus, in my opinion, was a third, fundamentally Hungarian way.

The second edition of Piotr Wandycz's *The Price of Freedom* (2001) treats the Hungarian Revolution to four pages in the subchapter on "The Rise and Fall of Revisionism."[33] As one may expect from a prominent historian of Polish background, his focus is on Poland. He begins with the power struggle after Stalin's death and Khrushchev's secret speech, and discusses the Poznan riots and the Polish October first. "The events in Poland," he writes next, "acted as a catalyst on developments in Budapest." He observes a "government-Party dualism" in Hungary, which he deems "fatal for Hungary." His insightful synopsis continues with another clever observation: "Nagy may not have initiated it, but he came to preside over a process that involved a restructuring of administration, raising a new army, permitting a multi-party system, releasing Cardinal Mindszenty, and finally declaring Hungary neutral....and leaving the Warsaw Pact." Wandycz argues that the decision about the second Soviet invasion was taken earlier, and not in response to Nagy's decision on November 1. He draws his additional conclusions and continues his narrative in the Polish-Hungarian comparative framework.

Mark Pittaway's 2004 volume, *Eastern Europe 1939–2000* (2004),[34] is the most recent addition to the field. It has already been adopted in various courses in the United States. Pittaway wrote a typically British social-economic history of the region, and chose a general, topical, rather than country-by-country approach. He discusses de-Stalinization, the Polish October and the Hungarian Revolution in the chapter on "The socialist public sphere and its limits." He claims that by the mid-1950s "the social foundations of socialist rule across the region were virtually non-existent:" people wanted not socialism but better living conditions and more freedom. The gradual loss of legitimacy went hand in hand with the expansion of the state security systems. De-Stalinization raised the possibility of reviewing the earlier show trials, and this again fed into the destabilization of the various East European regimes. "Even small open acts of protest could be met with severe retribution," Pittaway writes. "In Poland, and even more dramatically in Hungary, hatred of the state security agencies played a central role in the upheavals that convulsed both countries during 1956....In Hungary, during October 1956, as the revolution spread from Budapest to provincial towns, the demonstrations that began on their main streets frequently targeted the local headquarters of the AVH." The secret police fired into the crowd in Mosonmagyaróvár and at the radio headquarters in Budapest. And again,

> The most notorious and controversial incident of the revolution was the battle between demonstrators and AVH officers for the control of the Budapest Party Committee building at the end of October, in which the violence of the state security services and the anger of the crowd against them were starkly revealed, both by the violence of the battle and the lynching of the building's defenders by the demonstrators after their defeat.

Another one of Pittaway's brilliant observations is that

> The culture of defeat was bolstered by the widespread belief of many anti-Socialist Hungarians that the West had broken promises, made in radio broadcasts, to intervene to free them from the Soviet yoke. While Kádár's conciliatory policies were built on the culture of defeat created during the period of repression during the late 1950s, they were also underlined by the implicit threat of repression, if certain groups failed to accept the social bargain they were offered. The growing acceptance of socialist rule was based on collective amnesia about the events of 1956, the threat of repression and the development of a broad social contract that differed significantly from the class-war politics of the 1950s.

Pittaway may be sometimes difficult to understand on first reading, but the depth of his argument and the analytical nature of his approach easily qualify his book for graduate seminars, too.

As expected, histories of Eastern Europe in the twentieth century or under Soviet rule represent solid scholarship and an interesting variety of approaches. Held's narrative account differs from Crampton's in so far as the former largely ignores the fraudulent "alternative history" put forward by the Kádár regime, while the latter refutes it. The Swains' fascination with the Yugoslav model, and especially with the workers' councils, reflects one way Western Marxists (cf. Bill Lomax) sought to resolve the apparent contradiction between their idealized version, or even dream, of socialism and the brutal response the Kremlin gave to a level of diversity, represented by Hungary in 1956, which may or may not have negated the whole ideal. Berend was socialized with the propaganda of the Kádár "interpretation of history," which has nothing to do with the actual events, and tries to negotiate a compromise between the official Hungarian version (1956–1989) and the Western interpretations. His work must be treated with the same caution as the Brower textbook in the world histories section. Wandycz uses a Polish-Hungarian comparative framework to present his views of 1956, and while his bias towards Poland is obvious and justifiable, he demonstrates that a short account of the Revolution can be fully reliable and balanced. Pittaway's analytical approach is refreshingly original and insightful, but in undergraduate courses it probably requires some supporting material.

CONCLUSIONS

In Hungary, Kádár developed a network of lies about the "counterrevolution" to justify his regime and Soviet intervention, and the second quote from Pittaway (in the section on East European histories) convincingly explains how it worked. This set of lies was developed into an "alternative history," which claimed that the "counterrevolution" was premeditated and incited by the CIA. Nagy was accused of, and convicted for, conspiracy against the state, i.e. treason, which, of course, he did not commit. And this "alternative history" was exported to the West and was supported with an immense propaganda effort for thirty-three years.

In a recent interview on Hungarian television János M. Rainer, the current director of the 1956 Institute in Budapest, stated that the Revolution is arguably the most thoroughly researched event in twentieth-century Hungarian history. This research has been an ongoing project ever since Hungarians in exile began to discuss the Revolution and Western historians joined in. Since 1989, Hungarian historians in Hungary have also contributed substantially. Besides the 1956 Institute and its American partner, the National Security Archive at George Washington University, independent research groups are also putting in a lot of work, and their findings are regularly published in English also (www.rev.hu). Reliable, sound, historical information is freely available to authors of textbooks that are reprinted every year.

Yet, my preliminary and selective survey of some thirty history textbooks used in American colleges and universities has revealed a wide spectrum of interpretations in terms of depth, quality, and approach. Variety, if based on sound historical foundations, is quite welcome: textbooks with different focuses should address the same issue (in our case the Hungarian Revolution of 1956) in different ways. Wandycz, Thompson, McCormick, and Paxton have demonstrated that short passages can be well-written and accurate. What leaves me with mixed feelings is that I am pleased to see that the 1956 Revolution is always mentioned in connection with Hungary, but I find the overall quality of these accounts surprisingly low. It must be noted, however, that my critical remarks are about the coverage of the Revolution. They are not meant to be value judgments about the overall quality of these history textbooks, nor should they be interpreted as such. I am fully aware of the fact that it is Hungarian historians who must press for the revision of the unreliable passages; nobody else will do it for us. In the past fifteen years or so, textbook publishing has become an industry in the United States, and we must find the appropriate means of feeding into it without engaging in unnecessary confrontations.

NOTES

1. The Kádár regime created its own fraudulent historiography of the events and, together with Moscow and advertised it arrogantly in the West as a "counterrevolution." This surfaces in some of the texts discussed in this fact-finding essay. On the contemporary Hungarian debate see Gyula Hegyi's article in the online edition of the *Guardian.*

2. Thomas F. X. Noble, Barry B. Strauss, Duane J. Osheim, Kristen B. Neuschel, William B. Cohen, and David D. Roberts, *Western Civilization. The Continuing Experiment* (Boston: Houghton Mifflin Company, 1994); the brief edition was published in 1999 by the same company, and the third edition

came out in 2002. The relevant sections in the first edition are in volume C, *Since 1789*, pp. 1173–75.

3. Ibid., vol. 2, *Since 1650*, pp. 700–702. The photo is on p. 701.

4. Ibid., vol. 2, *Since 1650*, pp. 1001–1003.

5. John P. McKay, Bennett D. Hill, and John Buckler, *A History of Western Society* (Boston: Houghton Mifflin Company, 1995). The relevant parts are in volume 2, *From Absolutism to the Present*, pp. 1023–1024.

6. The eighth edition was published by the same company in 2006. The relevant sections are on pp, 1004 and 1006. The page in between is taken up by a profile and photograph of Tito.

7. Donald Kagan, Steven Ozment, and Frank M. Turner, *The Western Heritage. Teaching and Learning Classroom Edition* (Upper Saddle River, NJ: Pearson/Prentice Hall, 2005). The section on the Revolution is in volume 2, *Since 1648*, pp. 697–97.

8. The details are the same as those of the fourth edition. Here the relevant sections are in volume 2, *Since 1648*, pp. 990–92.

9. Jackson J. Spielvogel, *Western Civilization* (Belmont, CA: Thomson/ Wadsworth, 2006), volume 2, *Since 1500*, pp. 830–31.

10. Mortimer Chambers, Barbara Hanawalt, Theodore K. Rabb, Isser Woloch, Raymond Grew, and Lisa Tiersten, *The Western Experience* (Boston: McGraw Hill, 2007), volume 2, *Since the Sixteenth Century*, pp. 936–37.

11. Brian Levack, Edward Muir, Meredith Veldman, and Michael Maas, *The West: Encounters & Transformations* (New York: Pearson/Longman, 2007), volume 2, *Since 1550*, pp. 901, 904, 905–906.

12. William R. Keylor, *The Twentieth-Century World. An International History*, 2nd ed. (New York: Oxford University Press, 1992), pp. 306–308. Suez is discussed on p. 313. Strictly speaking, this is not a college textbook, but I have seen it used in both the UK and in the US. I also use it for reference in many of my own courses in Debrecen.

13. Daniel R. Brower, *The World in the Twentieth Century: The Age of Global War and Revolution*, 3rd ed. (Upper Saddle River, NJ: Prentice Hall, 1996), pp. 326–27; *The World in the Twentieth Century: From Empires to Nations*, 6th ed. (Upper Saddle River, NJ: Pearson/Prentice Hall, 2005), pp. 205–206.

14. William J. Duiker, *Twentieth-Century World History*, 3rd ed. (Belmont, CA: Thomson/Wadsworth, 2005), pp. 148–49 and 163–65.

15. J. Robert Wegs, *Europe Since 1945. A Concise History*, 2nd ed. (New York: St. Martin's Press, 1984), pp. 128–31. This is an old-school textbook from the time when textbook publishing was not an industry.

16. Roland N. Stromberg, *Europe in the Twentieth Century*, 3rd ed.

(Upper Saddle River, NJ: Prentice Hall, 1992), pp. 319–24. The sections on Hungary are on pp. 320– 22, esp. p. 321.

17. Felix Gilbert and David Clay Large, *The End of the European Era, 1890 to the Present*, Norton History of Modern Europe 6, 5th ed. (New York: W. W. Norton & Company, 2002), pp. 404–407 and 438–39.

18. Spencer Di Scala, *Twentieth Century Europe: Politics, Society, Culture* (McGraw Hill, 2004), pp. 573–82. For the discussion of the Revolution, see pp. 580–82. This seems to be a new textbook.

19. Robert O. Paxton, *Europe in the Twentieth Century*, 4th ed. (Belmont, CA: Thomson/Wadsworth, 2005), pp. 526–29.

20. Martin McCauley, *The Soviet Union, 1917–1991*, Longman History of Russia, 2nd ed. (New York: Longman, 1993), pp. 228–38. For the section on Hungary see p. 234.

21. David MacKenzie and Michael W. Curran, *A History of Russia, the Soviet Union, and Beyond*, 4th ed. (Belmont, CA: Wadsworth, 1993), pp. 720– 21. The quote on the domestic impact of the Revolution in the Soviet Union is from p. 715.

22. John M. Thompson, *A Vision Unfulfilled: Russia and the Soviet Union in the Twentieth Century* (Lexington, MA: D. C. Heath and Company, 1996), pp. 387–88.

23. Catherine Evtuhov and Richard Stites, *A History of Russia: Peoples, Legends, Events, Forces Since 1800* (Boston: Houghton Mifflin Company, 2004), pp. 431–32.

24. Thomas A. Bailey, *A Diplomatic History of the American People*, 8th ed. (New York: Appleton-Century-Crofts, 1969), pp. 837–39. The cartoon described is on p. 838.

25. Stephen A. Ambrose, *Rise to Globalism: American Foreign Policy Since 1938*, 7th rev. ed. (New York: Penguin, 1993), pp. 155–56. For his opening remark to the chapter see p. 151, and for his conclusion see p. 157.

26. Walter LaFeber, *America, Russia, and the Cold War, 1945–1990*, 6th ed. (New York: McGraw-Hill, 1991), pp. 187–88. For his conclusion on Khrushchev see pp. 192–93.

27. Thomas J. McCormick, *America's Half-Century: United States Foreign Policy in the Cold War* (Baltimore: Johns Hopkins University Press, 1989), pp. 122–24.

28. Bennett Kovrig, *Of Walls and Bridges: The United States and Eastern Europe* (New York: New York University Press, 1991), 85–89. For the discussion of American policy and options, see pp. 89–102.

29. Joseph Held, ed., *The Columbia History of Eastern Europe in the Twentieth Century* (New York: Columbia University Press, 1992). Held him-

self wrote the chapter on Hungary after 1945. For the Revolution see pp. 221–22.

30. R. J. Crampton, *Eastern Europe in the Twentieth Century* (New York: Routledge, 1994), pp. 288–303. Crampton is an Oxford historian.

31. Geoffrey and Nigel Swain, *Eastern Europe Since 1945* (New York: St. Martin's Press, 1993), pp. 77–101; and Geoffrey and Nigel Swain, *Eastern Europe Since 1945*, 3rd. ed. (New York: Palgrave/MacMillan, 2003), pp. 85–113.

32. Ivan T. Berend, *Central and Eastern Europe, 1944–1993: Detour from the periphery to the periphery* (Cambridge: Cambridge University Press, 1996), pp. 116–26. The references to right-wing elements are on pp. 124–25.

33. Piotr S. Wandycz, *The Price of Freedom: A History of East Central Europe from the Middle Ages to the Present*, 2nd ed. (New York: Routledge, 2001), pp. 250–54.

34. Mark Pittaway, *Eastern Europe 1939–2000* (New York: Oxford University Press, 2004), pp. 121 and 141–43. The two block quotes on the Revolution are from p. 142 and 143 respectively. Pittaway is also British, and he is a faculty member of Open University.

REGISTERS OF REMEM-BRANCE IN ENGLISH PROSE: WHAT THE NORTH AMERICAN READER IS CONFRONTED WITH (*A Brief Overview*)

INTRODUCTION

One of the most exciting aspects of the many memories of the Hungarian Revolution and War of Independence of 1956 is its treatment in English language prose. No attempt has been made since 1956 to survey these works of literature and memory, and the many websites and organizations that deal with the Revolution and its memory in North America have no lists available. Library catalogs and internet databases of second-hand bookstores were used to compile a list of some forty works related to the topic. The most important selection criterion was first publication in English in the United States or Canada between 1957 and 2005. No American or Hungarian political memoirs (not even if translated into English[1]) or histories of the Revolution were included, but eyewitness accounts by American newspapermen (often serving as raw material for novels written afterwards) were. Some of these books have achieved international fame (Michener, Pfeiffer, Fischer, etc.) while others have long been forgotten (Roman, Mingo, Heller, etc.). "Registers" in the title of this essay refers to the various types (and the somewhat mixed quality) of the prose discussed.

The list includes four first-hand Hungarian refugee and six first-hand American journalistic accounts. The seven personal memoirs and family histories (covering a longer period from World War II to 1956) round out the resources for subsequent works of fiction. More than a dozen novels, five mysteries, and four volumes of juvenile fiction make up the other half of the list. In some cases books published outside North America but available in the United States[2] are also discussed, but only when these works offer additional insights. In each case this is explained in detail. Although the Revolution is an integral part of Hungarian history and culture, most of these books are not available in Hungarian.

Hungarian Freedom Fighter Accounts

The intervention of Soviet troops in November 1956 and the treacherous treatment and execution of Imre Nagy and his fellow revolutionaries in June 1958 ensured sustained interest in the Revolution. Accordingly, three of the four first-hand accounts in English were published in 1957 and 1958. László Beke's book was indeed *A Student's Diary*: it was written and illustrated in exile in Canada, and was translated into English by Leon Kossar and Ralph M. Zoltan.[3] Tamás Szabó's *Boy on the Rooftop* was originally written in French, and was translated into English by David Hughes.[4] The dust jacket introduction of the 1958 English edition compares it to *The Diary of Anne Frank*. These two books tell stories of innocence and honesty and provide testimony that can only come from uncorrupted youth and the moral fortitude of the freedom fighters. The tradition of teenage freedom fighters was revived, surprisingly, and with a vengeance, with the publication of Béla Lipták's boyhood *Testament of Revolution* in 2001, for the 45th anniversary.[5] The first two became bestsellers overnight, while Lipták's book received excellent reviews. *Testament* is the only one available in Hungarian.

Andor Heller's *No More Comrades*,[6] however, has long been forgotten. Heller was a star news photographer for MTI, the national news agency in Hungary, and the Nagy government sent him to the West to tell the true story of the Revolution. He was given the first diplomatic passport by the new administration on October 31, and he left Hungary the same day with more than three hundred photographs.[7] His book is a sweeping narrative of the events with dozens of full-page photographs. Heller later testified in the televised open hearings in the

Senate Internal Security Committee, and his book came out in 1957. Unlike the three student freedom fighters, who tell their stories in the simple and straightforward language of Hungarian teenagers, Heller turns his book into an indictment of the Soviet Union and the puppet regime of János Kádár:

> I saw freedom rise form the ashes of Communism in Hungary: a freedom that flickered and then blazed before it was beaten down—but not extinguished—by masses of Russian tanks and troops....I watched a whole nation—old and young, men and women, artists and engineers and doctors, clerks and peasants and factory workers—become heroes overnight as they rose up in history's first successful revolt against Communism. With my own eyes and my camera's eye, I saw Hungary's Freedom Revolution.[8]

Although no translator is named, Heller's book undoubtedly underwent careful linguistic revision. These four books, nonetheless, share a degree of simplicity of language and style.

Hungary has not had such media exposure in the United States since Lajos Kossuth's tour of the New World in 1851–52. While Kossuth's political goals remained unrealized, he helped create the image of freedom-loving and freedom-fighting Hungarians. The three eyewitness accounts from 1957 and 1958, combined with the *Time* magazine cover of the Hungarian Freedom Fighter as Man of the Year for 1956, revived this image and added boyhood innocence to the equation. The fact that even young teenagers fought the Russians, and died in battle or as consequence of trials afterwards, made Communism look even worse. In more general terms, these books provided the basic raw material for future works of fiction, ranging from fight scenes through stories of sexual initiation to accounts of juvenile heroism and escape.

American Journalists in Hungary

Additional raw material for future works of fiction came form the American journalists who covered the Hungarian Revolution on the spot. Although Zsolt Varga wrote an excellent account of the immediate press reactions to the events,[9] it is a little known fact that six American newspapermen later published memoirs in which they recalled their Budapest experiences. Four of these were published between 1957 and 1960, one for the fifteenth anniversary in 1971, and the last one on account of the collapse of the Soviet empire in 1990. While journalistic accounts do not usually qualify as fiction, the best known of the six, James A. Michener's *The Bridge at Andau*, even recently has been cited as a novel.[10] More importantly, foreign correspondents as outsiders carry more credibility than participants, and these reports helped construct the mental picture on which novelists could and would draw quite freely.

The book most Americans associate with the Hungarian Revolution even today is, of course, *The Bridge at Andau*. It became a national bestseller and saw multiple reprints in and since 1957. This 1957 edition appears to have been a work in progress, as Michener sharpened his criticism of the Eisenhower administration for lack of action on behalf of Hungary between the original edition and the first reprint.[11] The book itself is not really a novel, but a reconstruction of the coming of the Revolution, its collapse under Soviet military pressure, and the escape of the refugees to Austria, through refugee interviews and case studies. The bridge itself became the symbol of the passage between the two worlds: tyranny and democracy. As it is pointed out in the essay on Nixon's fact-finding trip to Austria in December 1956, when Ferenc Daday, a Hungarian artist, painted a picture of the scene of the vice president visiting the border, he painted the bridge back into the picture, though he was fully aware of the fact that it had been blown up long before December 21.[12] Thus the bridge, an artifact that does not (and did not) exist anymore, became, and remains, a key icon of the Hungarian Revolution through a work of fiction and a painting.

Michener helped shape the basic Western images and assumptions of the Revolution and launched the first attack on Radio Free Europe. He voices his criticism through a twenty-six-year-old refugee, Ferenc Kobol.

Do you know why Hungarians like me are so bitter against the United States? For six years you fed us this propaganda. For six years the Russians trampled us in the mud. But when we rose in rebellion for the very things you told us to fight for, how many Americans stepped forth to help us? Not one. What tanks did join us in our fight for freedom? Russian tanks. This is a terrible indictment.[13]

This statement is powerful enough by itself, but Kobol felt that the fact that America kept silent about the Revolution in the United Nations was an even bigger blow.[14] The significance of Michener's book lies in the fact that it helped to raise the moral support in favor of the refugees when he openly challenged Vice President Nixon's conclusions about RFE. *Bridge* was a hastily assembled work in progress in 1957: the second printing carries several corrections and additional comments by Michener in the foreword.[15]

Next in line, and showcasing a photo of the ruins of the "Freedom Bridge" over the Einser Canal facing the title page of the book, is Martin Bursten's *Escape from Fear*. It covers not only the Revolution but also the escape and processing of the refugees and the ensuing debate over immigration reform in the United States.[16] Besides being a journalist of some experience, including the coverage of the liberation of concentration camps in Germany in 1945, Bursten was also public relations director of United Hias Service, a major worldwide Jewish relief organization. His book offers the only published account of relief and refugee resettlement work at Camp Kilmer, a military base in New Jersey, now part of the Rutgers University campus. The book carries a wealth of photographs about life in the Joyce Kilmer Reception Center and the organizational chart of the refugee resettlement program.[17] The quality of Bursten's photographic tour de force has been matched only by Robert F. Sisson's photographic essay for *National Geographic* magazine, "Freedom Flight from Hungary."[18]

Barrett McGurn's *Decade in Europe* is a lively record of the reporting experiences of the prominent *New York Times* and *New York Herald Tribune* correspondent from Paris and Rome through Budapest and Moscow back to Rome. Chapter nine, "Revolution: Hungary's Moment of Truth," makes up about one sixth of the book.[19] McGurn's text is perhaps the only impassionate account of the events by an American eyewitness. "[The Soviet evacuation of Budapest] began the Hungarian capital's five hopeful, pitiful days of freedom....All Budapest was jubilantly awake, but all were dreaming."[20] There is a strange air of detachment about the chapter, and "Hungary's moment of truth" is not the Revolution but the Soviet crackdown. McGurn deals with Cardinal Mindszenty extensively, writes freely about the symbols (the torn flag) and myths (no looting of shops) of the Revolution. He also describes life in the American legation between November 4 and his eventual departure from Hungary six days later. The following passage is characteristic of both McGurn's style and message:

> Pitiful calls were coming in. A group at a motion-picture theater was under attack by tanks and could hold out only for another two hours. If the United States were to help it would have to do instantly. Another band, the phone told us, was under assault from tanks, mortars, and medium-sized artillery. They needed "flame throwers and those so-called tank breakers." A youth at the legation door passed a note through the grille. His friends, the message said, were in "death throes" the world could not see. "If you can help us, do so by one o'clock. We will be back for an answer. Otherwise, we are going to die." The young man was told gently that he could spare himself the trouble of a return trip.[21]

After his first, unsuccessful attempt to leave Budapest McGurn explains how Hungarian expectations towards the United States and the United Nations turned into resentment and hope again, when people saw the American flag on their cars when the Western journalists had to return to the legation.[22] He continues by reviewing the refugee issue, and recalls the disenchantment of a British Communist newspaperman, who later was expelled from the Party for reporting the truth about the Hungarian Revolution. The chapter concludes with a late November visit to the Hungarian border and a meeting with a group of disappointed Hungarian guards, who said: "We figure the Russians are sure to go. It's impossible for them to stay against the will of everyone. Of course we could be wrong and if we are we'll leave, too."[23]

Leslie Bain's *The Reluctant Satellites* was the first attempt by an American journalist to offer a comprehensive book-length account and interpretation of the Hungarian revolution of 1956.[24] Bain was born in the States, of Irish and Hungarian parents, but was educated in Hungary between the world wars. He was a magazine writer for *The Reporter* and *Look*, and his book about the Revolution was his third one. Bain added three new dimensions to the discussion of the Revolution: he openly deals with, and refuses to endorse the stories of the participation of "fascist" elements in the Revolution; offers interviews with Czech, Polish and Yugoslav communists; and voices open criticism of the conduct of the United State and Radio Free Europe. In fact, the last but one chapter of his book is a thinly veiled indictment of RFE.[25] In the last pages he touches upon yet another sensitive issue in connection with the events: anti-Semitism.

> That pro-Soviet groups were not loathe to resort to anti-Semitism in Poland was in interesting contrast with Imre Nagy's behavior in Hungary. Both Poland and Hungary have been traditionally anti-Semitic. When, during the revolution in Budapest, signs of anti-Semitism appeared, Nagy and his associates took great care to weed out the Jews from the government and from the high command of the party in order to lessen the effectiveness of the anti-Semitic agitation.[26]

Bain concludes with words of praise for victims of repression: "They have made it possible for men to believe in themselves and to renew their fate in the decency, humanity, and spiritual greatness of their kind."[27]

One of the most interesting books about the Revolution was written by Endre Marton for the fifteenth anniversary.[28] Marton was born and raised in Hungary. He covered the show trials of Cardinal Mindszenty, Interior Minister László Rajk, and American businessman Robert A. Vogeler for the Associated Press during the late forties. He and his wife were sentenced in 1955 to thirteen years in prison, but were released in the summer of 1956. Marton's three hundred-page account covers the story of the Revolution and records Kádár's relative success in consolidating his power by 1971. He offers his own take on the events and raises the question: What could the United States have done? Marton maintains that the Revolution was brought about by the rebirth of nationalism following "liberalization" in the Soviet bloc after Stalin's death.[29] He draws a parallel between 1956 and 1968, postulating that the Soviets simply could not tolerate the defection of their satellites. Contradicting all earlier accounts, Marton claims that help was expected not from the United States but only from the United Nations.[30] He develops the theme of Western betrayal around his claim: the West let East and Central Europe down during and after World War II, and then abandoned Hungary in 1956.[31] *The Forbidden Sky* of the

Hungary that he grew up in became the free sky on his fist flight to the New World, in April 1957. This book was translated into Hungarian in 2000.

Elie Abel covered the end of World War II, the establishment of the two Germanies, the imposition of Communist rule over Poland and the Hungarian revolution of 1956 for the *New York Times*, and the Prague Spring for NBC news. He then taught journalism at Columbia University and at Stanford, but returned to cover the events of the year of miracles, 1989. In the first fifty pages of the book Abel explains the collapse of the Soviet empire and the case of Hungary. A brief and factual summation of the Revolution serves as the introduction to the chapter on Hungary.[32] The real significance of this book lies in the fact that a prominent American journalist revisited the events of the Revolution and established a direct link between 1956 and 1989.

It follows from our discussion above that journalistic memory and treatment of the Revolution faded with time. The fifteen-year gap, between 1960 and 1971, was bridged by Timothy Foote's seven-page article in the *New York Times Magazine* in 1966.[33] The gap between 1971 and 1990 speaks for itself: this is a different generation, and events so far back in time (before the Cuban Missile Crisis, Vietnam, and Watergate) gradually lost their significance for journalists. 1989 revived interest, and the fiftieth anniversary might yield some additional information on the work of American journalists in the field.

PERSONAL NARRATIVES: FAMILY HISTORIES

Seven books, telling stories of Hungarian families, in most cases of Hungarian Jewish families, from World War II to 1956, have been found. These are not just accounts of the Revolution: some of them simply treat it as a point of reference. Two came out in 1958 (Pfeiffer) and 1960 (Kálmán), the other five have been published since 1990. They all share descriptions of family loss and personal tragedy, as well as coming to terms with life in the free world. The publication dates suggest that the authors needed time to digest their own tragedy and waited until after both evils (Nazism and Communism) were gone, and international attention turned toward Hungary again.

The first four books discussed here (Pfeiffer, Petrovics-Ofner, Mandel, and Kenez) are Jewish family histories. What sets them apart from the others (especially Téglás and Porter) is the fact the authors decided to emphasize their Jewishness.

Ede Pfeiffer was a most interesting character: he left Hungary for England in his late teens after the Revolution and wrote *Child of Communism* in Hungarian at the age of nineteen and twenty. It was ably translated into English by Denise Gosztola, and came out in 1958. Later Pfeiffer moved to the United States and became a presidential scholar and World Bank advisor on Hungarian affairs. He died in Pasadena in the spring of 2006. His book became required reading in many schools in Cold War courses. In light of the powerful and eloquent argument put forward on the final page, this is hardly surprising. He invokes the "ghost of Communism" that Marx once wrote about and states that a "new ghost haunts Marx's heirs." He also cites Milovan Djilas, who wrote that "the Communist regimes are a form of constant civil war between the rulers and the people." He compares the Soviet bloc to a gigantic prison. "In one of the cells behind the iron curtain the prisoners broke the lock in the autumn of 1956. The gaoler arrived in time to shut the door, but no locksmith can make the lock quite safe again."[34] The book became an international bestseller and was published in nine languages, but not yet in Hungarian, although translation is under way in 2006.

László Petrovics-Ofner tells an unfortunately familiar story of persecution suffered by a mid-century Jewish family in Hungary. Published in 1990, *Broken Places* is another child's tale of joys and difficulties of Jewish life in Hungary during the war and Communism. Petrovics-Ofner tells his own story through an honest and simple boy, Pisti: his initial admiration for Stalin, his first love, his encounter with a Soviet soldier during the second invasion of Budapest, and his escape from Hungary with his sister, but without the rest of their family. Two visits to Hungary, in 1976 (his first return) and 1989 (after the death of his parents), provide a suitable framework for the book.[35]

Edmund Mandel's *The Right Path* is yet another tragic Jewish family history of labor camps and Communist terror. He dictated what he calls his autobiography to Lynn K. Egerman on a long trip through the Gobi Desert. Mandel fled to Austria and then to the United States, became a successful soccer coach and returned triumphantly to Hungary with an American youth team in 1985. On the basis of the book, he clearly is a man at peace with the world, sober, and free of hate.[36]

Peter Kenez published his personal recollections, *Varieties of Fear*, in 1995. Kenez teaches Soviet and East European history at UC Santa Cruz, California, and has published extensively on both Soviet and Hungarian history during the Cold War. *Varieties of Fear* was successful enough to earn a reprint in 2001. The subtitle of the book, *Growing up Jewish under Nazism and Communism*, gives away both the historian and the refugee in Kenez. He also contributed an oral history interview to an internet database and taught a course on Soviet Cultural Policy at the Central European University in Budapest, in 1999. He is the only historian among the authors listed in this essay.[37]

Lajos Kálmán was a prominent Hungarian lawyer before he fled to the West after the Revolution. He was embraced by the Boston-based Daughters of St. Paul, a Catholic women's organization founded in 1915. Kálmán's memoirs were published in 1960 to reveal "to all classes the diabolical nature and methods of atheistic communism." Richard Cardinal Cushing wrote a foreword to the book, and it became a minor sensation among East Coast lawyers.[38] Kálmán reviewed the systematic deconstruction of the Hungarian legal system and explained how jurisdiction worked in a Communist country. This made the book one of the few first-hand accounts of the show trials (with a separate chapter devoted to the abuses aimed at Americans in Hungary) in English.[39] Kálmán's book defies description: personal information on the author is scarce, while the systematic description of the legal system in Hungary is supplemented with case studies from the author's practice.

Anna Porter recalls long walks along the Danube with her grandfather, Vili Rácz, to tell stories of life before and during World War II and under Communism. Vili, and later Anna Porter, actually escaped to New Zealand. She then moved on to Canada, where she became a successful publisher and author. Her other works include three mysteries. *The Storyteller. Memory, Secrets, Magic and Lies: A Memoir of Hungary* is a stylishly written and well-received book which was originally published in Canada in 2000.[40]

Much like Mandel's autobiography, *Budapest Exit* by Csaba Téglás is a book written by a man at peace with the world. Téglás tells and re-tells the key stories of his life to his two sons in chapters introduced by questions from his siblings. The book is illustrated by Lajos Szalay, another 1956 refugee who became a prominent artist in exile. Téglás's book was first published in the East European Studies series of Texas A&M University Press, the publisher of Lipták's diary mentioned above. *Budapest Exit* was then reprinted in Hungary, but only in English. It has drawn praise from both academics and in the print media for its clarity of style and message.[41]

Personal narratives of family histories covering World War II, Communism, and 1956 border on nonfiction. They place the Revolution and escape from Communist Hungary in the broader context of the suffering the peoples of East and Central Europe experienced in mid-century and tell stories of loss, passage, and rebirth in the free world. Some of the better known fictional accounts drew quite freely on them.

NOVELS

A dozen or so novels of varying quality have drawn upon the raw materials provided in Hungarian and American eyewitness accounts and family histories. Two have been finalists for the Booker Prize, some became bestsellers, and quite a few have long been forgotten. Two bestselling authors have contributed very different books, and the list includes a black sexual comedy with a much-debated movie adaptation. One recurrent theme is initiation by fire and sexual awakening, both byproducts of the teenage freedom fighter trope. Some non-American publications are also included here in order to demonstrate the staying power of the images created by the Hungarian Revolution of 1956.

Three novels by Hungarian authors describe life in Hungary before the Revolution: two from the sixties, and one from the nineties. Two of the three are internationally known, the third is unjustly forgotten. The book we tend not to remember is Békéscsaba-born Eric Roman's *The Best Shall Die*. It is the story of journalist András Orczy and his love, Ilona, a doctor in Sztáliváros in the fifties. Roman tells of András' disappointment with the system, offering a parable for what the Hungarian intelligentsia went through before the Revolution. Roman served in a labor battalion in the world war, was sentenced to death by the Nazis but escaped. He then lived in Budapest before he left Hungary after

November 1956. He wrote the book to earn money to support his doctoral studies.[42] Tamás Aczél's *The Ice Age* is one of the best, and best known, novels of Hungarian life in the fifties. Aczél, a Stalin Prize winner, was a high-ranking Communist who got disenchanted with the regime, fled to the West, and wrote his all-important novel in London between 1959 and 1962.[43] He was coauthor of *The Revolt of the Mind* (1960) with Tibor Méray, another Communist-turned-freedom fighting intellectual. Life in Communist Hungary before the Revolution received a fresh and extremely funny treatment in Tibor Fischer's *Under the Frog* (1992). Fischer is an English-born Hungarian novelist, and the title is a reference to a Hungarian slang expression for something way below par. *Frog* tells of the adventures of two basketball players in Hungary before the Revolution, and was a finalist for the Booker Prize and a *New York Times* Notable Book.[44] Of the three, only Fischer's work is available in Hungarian.

An outstanding American novel that takes place during the Revolution is James Dean Sanderson's *Boy with a Gun* from 1958. It draws freely upon the messages and images of the teenage freedom fighter diaries described above. This is a textbook example of how recollections can be turned into fiction. *Boy* is about Pál, a Hungarian teenager, whose father is an anti-Communist resister. They plan to assassinate M, a high-ranking official, to make a political statement. The Revolution comes by surprise, and Pál's father and brother are both killed. Pál goes on a search-and-destroy mission to kill M.[45] Sanderson, who was film maker, NBC reporter, and chief executive of a public relations firm, capitalized on the popularity of the freedom fighters and linked the story to one of the great villains of the silver screen, Fritz Lang's *M*, the unknown, nameless murderer of Berlin.

Although Vincent Brome's *The Revolution* (1969) was published in England, it is available in the United States and tells of the Budapest events through an American journalist, Gavin Cartwright. Cartwright is a disappointed former American Communist who runs from a failed marriage, finds a new, passionate love in Hungary, and is arrested for murder by the authorities. Unlike in other fictional accounts, there is no catharsis or happy end here; the book ends with Cartwright in Soviet custody in his hotel room, waiting for help that never comes from the American Legation that he cannot even contact.[46]

Another book that deserves mention through it falls outside the scope of the present study is Alan Duff's *Szabad* (2001). Duff, a popular New Zealand writer, tells the story of Attila Szabó, a young freedom fighter torn between ideas and lovers of different ages, on the basis of Hungarian refugee accounts he encountered. In one of the strangest fictional 1956 scenes, he shoots his fatally wounded love while crossing the border. This is clearly a publication with the anniversary in mind, and a successful one: it has everything needed from love, heroism, tragedy, passage, and rebirth.[47] Sanderson and Duff recreate the teenager freedom fighter as an American and a New Zealander would imagine him thirty years apart, in strikingly different narratives, while Brome presents the underlying dilemma of the left (e.g. Albert Camus) in the West after 1956: there was no way to support an ideology that was invoked for the brutal repression of the Hungarian Revolution.

None of these novels are available in Hungarian, but another one, Zsuzsa Bánk's first novel, *The Swimmer* (originally published in German), is. Bánk tells a heart-rendering story about a family that breaks up in the Revolution when the mother leaves for the West without even saying goodbye, and the father goes on an odyssey through Hungary with the his kids. She shows the world through the eyes of the children in a way that earned the unqualified praise of Péter Nádas, one of the most prominent contemporary Hungarian writers: "There is more left unsaid in this heartbreaking novel, and in more subtle ways, than in any other book I know."[48]

A third group of novels places the Revolution in a longer timeline of the lives of its characters. The before-during-after nature of these stories explains why most of these were written during and since the nineties. The one notable exception is a book that has had over one hundred printings and a controversial movie adaptation: *In Praise of Older Women* by Stephen Vizinczey from 1965.[49] *Praise* became quite a hit and started a trend in Toronto called "Cougar" love: older women prowling younger men in bars.[50] The book, a dark sexual comedy, is the story of András Vajda, a boy soldier and "virginal pimp," who fails with one of his peers and goes after older women afterwards. The story was clearly inspired by the sexual initiation theme mentioned above, but András does not get all the women he wants, something that provides the story with a piquant reality check. Another love story before, during and after the Revolution is Julius Ling's *Guiding Stars* (1999). It is based on the author's personal story and experiences. Andrew Dombrady and his love, Kata, flee to Australia after the Revolution, then move on to Canada, and go on long journeys to Europe; it is the story of eternal love born in the flames of revolution in Budapest. Ling actually learned English in Australia, which makes his book written in English a nice achievement. He works and lives in Canada, but the book was published in Florida, which is why it is included here.[51]

Three other novels have characters that have a background in Budapest and the Revolution. Chronologically the first in line is *Anna Teller* (1960) by Jo Sinclair, a well-known Mid-Western writer. Anna's story stretches back in time to rural Hungary in the beginning of the twentieth century, but the actual plot takes place in America years after the Revolution. She comes to America for a family reunion with her son, Emil, and tries to establish matriarchal control over his life, as well as the lives of his family and friends. Using narrative techniques similar to William Faulkner's in *The Sound and the Fury*, Sinclair tries to portray not just a 56-er but an archetype, a Jewish matriarch.[52]

Gabriella Mingo's *Their Fate Was Written* (1974) is the amiable and simple story of five girls from a Budapest university: Klára, Esther, Ágnes, Lidi, and Ilona. They flee Hungary together during the dying days of the Revolution, and illustrate five different lives in exile. The characters and the plot are quite stereotypical (with Klára as the archetypal femme fatale) and flat. The story (especially that of Ilona) is clearly autobiographical,[53] but no further information was found about the author.

The third such character is László Lázár, a gloomy playwright of 1956 background in Andrew Miller's Booker Prize finalist novel, *Oxygen* (2001). *Oxygen* is the title of Lázár's latest play about a mining disaster somewhere in Eastern Europe. He is haunted by an undisclosed story of betrayal, of a friend he probably left to die while escaping, that makes him want to forget everything. Forgetting and absolution come to him through his own death, when, in the very last scene in the novel, he faces a loaded gun to save a friend several years later.[54] Miller, like Sanderson and Sinclair, has no Hungarian affiliation; they all were inspired by the raw material described at the beginning of the present essay.

CRIME FICTION

The Revolution inspired six American mysteries, spy novels, and thrillers. Igor Sentjurc's *Prayer for an Assassin* is a "Day of the Jackal" style story from Budapest, 1956, though it takes place after the Revolution.[55] The book received a very favorable review in the *New York Times*: Sentjurc was compared to Joseph Conrad and Graham Greene for wanting "to write an intrigue thriller that is also a serious novel."[56] The novel has everything a good thriller needs: love, betrayal, suspense, a wily secret policeman, and credible characters that come to life.

In contrast with the little we know about Sentjurc, David Pryce-Jones, the author of *The Stranger's View*, is a well-known English novelist and political commentator. The novel is a mixture of a *Bildungsroman* and a fiction with a search theme: the story of three Englishmen and a Frenchman in search of themselves and love in Hungary and Suez in 1956.[57] Stephen Marlowe's *1956* (1981) is a spy story against the backdrop of Hungary and Suez, a duel between former lovers, an American CIA agent and a young Israeli operative.[58]

David Brierley's *Shooting Star* is a tale of crime, echoes from the past, and love lost in the Revolution and found again in London in the 1980s. Brierley expertly handles the question of together or apart, following an accidental reunion a quarter century after.[59] In 1991 *New York Times* bestselling author Doris Mortman contributed *The Wild Rose*, the story of Gypsy girl Katalin Gáspár, to the ever-growing literature of the Revolution. Exotic, talented, and full of energy, Katalin ("the Princess of the Piano") has two dreams to fulfill: the musical heritage of her late father (a violinist) and the reunion with her love, Steven Kardos, lost in the Revolution.[60] This is one of Mortman's earliest books, and it combines with ease the search theme with lost love, mystery, and tradition.

Eva Byram's *Parallel Roads* from 2005, apparently an internet-based publication, is yet another story of lost love, search, and recovery. Its male protagonist, Robert, ends up in London, makes a mess of his life, and his only chance at salvation, he believes, is finding Julia, his love, who went to New York with her parents after the Revolution.[61] Mysteries using the Revolution as their context all tell familiar stories of lost love and betrayal, and offer some solution: sometimes a happy ending, more often a tragic one. Their common feature is some variation on the search theme that goes back to the hectic days of the Revolution.

JUVENILE LITERATURE

It is only natural that the raw material presented at the beginning of the present essay would produce some juvenile fiction. Children and teenagers fighting for freedom, families escaping sometimes together and sometimes separately (another take on the search theme), and a new, more acceptable life in a more democratic world is cut out for stories for the young. Four such books have been found, and the trend is familiar: an early forerunner was followed by three successors in the nineties. The target is a teenage audience: with simple language and plot, these books tell moving stories and deliver clear messages.

The flag-bearer is Alta Halverston Seymour's *Toward Morning* from 1961, a relatively short family escape story told for children of twelve to fifteen, according to the dust jacket. The book invokes the familiar images of the Szabó and Beke diaries, and of the refugee interviews of Michener, both by its content and by featuring a map of Budapest on the inside cover.[62] Besides Sanderson's novel discussed above, this is the other textbook case of turning memory into fiction.

Helen M. Szablya and Peggy King Anderson's quite successful and popular *The Fall of the Red Star* (1996) tells a similar story for American and Hungarian Scouts. It is one of the few books discussed in this subchapter which is available in Hungarian. Based on Szablya's own family history, this book tells of the flight of the Kőváry family from Hungary. It is illustrated by Anderson, an award-winning children's book illustrator.[63] Judit Makranczy's *We Have to Escape* (1999) is another juvenile family escape story along the same lines.[64]

Eva Wiseman, a Hungarian refugee who ended up in Canada, wrote a heartwarming story about a Jewish girl, Nelly, who stumbles through Nazi occupation, Communist rule, Revolution and a new start in a different world. *A Place Not Home* was published in Canada in 2004, but the original copyright for the text shows 1996.[65] It is a mixture of the family stories and their best novel adaptation, *Anna Teller*.

Juvenile fiction of the revolution tells the same familiar stories of heroism, tragedy, escape, and rebirth, but in a more simple manner than sophisticated novelists would.

CONCLUSION

Together with the Hungarian political memoirs and the various historical interpretations penned by Hungarians in exile,[66] eyewitness accounts described in the first three groups (student diaries, American journalistic accounts, and family histories) have provided the ideas and tropes for the fiction of the Revolution. The general trend seemed to be some early publications (usually on anniversaries) followed by new ones in the nineties, after the collapse of the Soviet empire, when 1956 and 1968 were natural points of reference. Most of the writers are 56-ers themselves, but some English and American authors have also contributed. The fact that the output of fifty years amounts to more than thirty volumes[67] (excluding American journalistic accounts) proves beyond doubt that the memory of the Hungarian Revolution of 1956 is well preserved in North American prose and fiction. It seems fair to say that, as regards East and Central European history, the 1956 Hungarian Revolution and War of Independence is second only to the Holocaust in terms of popularity of topic. Examples cited from New Zealand (Duff), England (Brome), and Germany (Bánk) suggest similar interest outside North America. The most disappointing thing about the various manifestations of remembrance in English prose in North America is that most of it remains unavailable in Hungarian.

NOTES

1. One such example is József Kővágó, *You Are All Alone* (New York: Praeger, 1959). These are legitimate resources for fiction writers, but do not qualify as fiction.

2. Books in this category are available from multiple university libraries in the United States and multiple copies are available from booksellers like www.abebooks.com or www.alibris.com.

3. László Beke, *A Student's Diary: Budapest, October 16–November 1, 1956* (New York: The Viking Press, 1957).

4. Tamás Szabó, *Boy on the Rooftop. An Authentic Account of the Budapest Revolt by a Fifteen-Year-Old Freedom Fighter* (Boston: Little, Brown and Company, 1958).

5. Béla Lipták, *A Testament of Revolution* (College Station, TX: Texas A & M University Press, 2001).

6. Andor Heller, *No More Comrades. A Message form the Freedom Fighters of Hungary* (Chicago: Henry Regnery Company, 1957). The title refers to the famous late evening scene at the Parliament on October 23, when Nagy called the demonstrators Comrades, and they chanted, "We are not Comrades!"

7. Heller, *No More Comrades*, pp. 3–8.

8. Ibid., p. 9.

9. Zsolt József Varga, "Surprised Dailies: Contemporary U.S. Press Coverage of the 1956 Hungarian Revolution" (PhD. diss., Texas Christian University, 2000).

10. Johanna Granville, "Of Spies, Refugees and Hostile Propaganda: How Austria Dealt with the Hungarian Crisis of 1956," *History* 91, no. 301 (January 2006): 70.

11. James A. Michener, *The Bridge at Andau* (New York: Random House, 1957). Note that both the first edition and the second printing came out in 1957. Hereafter, the second printing will be cited.

12. Interview with Ferenc Daday, Yorba Linda, CA, August 6, 2006.

13. Michener, *Bridge*, pp. 249–52. The quote is from p. 249.

14. Ibid., p. 252.

15. Ibid., pp. xi–xiii. For example, reviewers of the first printing had to clarify that Hungarians put the family name first, and the first name last. Originally, Michener stated these were interchangeable. He also inserted comments on Nixon's trip to Austria, on the improved conditions at Camp Kilmer, and on the domestic American debate over immigration reform: pp. xi–xii.

16. Martin A. Bursten, *Escape from Fear* (Syracuse, NY: Syracuse University Press, 1958).

17. Bursten, *Escape*, pp. 155–209. On Kilmer see pp. 155–90; the chart is on p. 171.

18. In the March 1957 issue, pp. 424–36.

19. Barrett McGurn, *Decade in Europe* (New York: E. P. Dutton & Co., Inc., 1959), pp. 213–41.

20. McGurn, *Decade*, p. 218.

21. Ibid., pp. 227–28.

22. Ibid., pp. 216, 234, and 235, respectively.

23. Ibid., pp. 240–41.

24. Leslie B. Bain, *The Reluctant Satellites. An Eyewitness Report on East Europe and the Hungarian Revolution* (New York: Macmillan Company, 1960).

25. Ibid., pp. 186–208: "Aftermath—The Failure of the West."

26. Ibid., p. 232.

27. Ibid., p. 233.

28. Endre Marton, *The Forbidden Sky* (Boston: Little, Brown and Company, 1971).

29. Ibid., pp. 270–71.

30. Ibid., p. 283.

31. Ibid., pp. 286–93.

32. Elie Abel, *The Shattered Bloc: Behind the Upheaval in Eastern Europe* (Boston: Houghton Mifflin Company, 1990), pp. 16–18.

33. Timothy Foote "The Road Back to Budapest," *New York Times Magazine*, November 20, 1966, pp. 16–21. Foote was injured on the hand during the fighting.

34. Ede Pfeiffer, *Child of Communism* (London: Weidenfeld and Nicolson, 1958). The quote is from p. 237. Additional information was provided by Dr. Antal Bejczy in an e-mail dated October 17, 2006.

35. László Petrovics-Ofner, *Broken Places* (New York: Atlantic Monthly Press, 1990).

36. Edmund Mandel, *The Right Path. The Autobiography of a Survivor* (Hoboken, NJ: KTAV Publishing Inc., 1994).

37. Peter Kenez, *Varieties of Fear: Growing up Jewish under Nazism and Communism* (Washington, D.C.: American University Press, 1995; reprint: San Jose: Authors Choice, 2001). The interviews were found and accessed (10/27/2006) at www.memoryarchive.org, under his name.

38. Lajos Kálmán, *The Lawyer in Communism. Memoirs of a Lawyer behind the Iron Curtain* (Boston: The Daughters of St. Paul, 1960).

39. The show trial of American businessman Robert A. Vogeler created a lot of tension between Hungary and the United States. Vogeler was sentenced for, among other things, conspiracy against the state, but his case was retried after 1989 and he was acquitted. After his release from Hungary in the early fifties he wrote a fiery accusation of Hungary and the Soviet Union. See Rober A. Vogeler, *I Was Stalin's Prisoner* (New York: Harcourt, Brace and Company, 1952). Parts of the book were serialized in the *Saturday Evening Post* in 1951.

40. Anna Porter, *The Storyteller. Memory, Secrets, Magic and Lies. A Memoir of Hungary* (Toronto: Doubleday, 2000).

41. Csaba Téglás, *Budapest Exit. A Memoir of Fascism, Communism, and Freedom* (College Station, TX: Texas A & M University, 1998); reprinted Budapest by Mediamix with no publication date indicated.

42. Eric Roman, *The Best Shall Die* (Englewood Cliffs, NJ: Prentice Hall, Inc., 1961).

43. Tamás Aczél, *The Ice Age* (London: Martin Secker & Warburg Ltd, 1965).

44. Tibor Fischer, *Under the Frog. A Black Comedy* (New York: The New Press, 1992).

45. James Dean Sanderson, *Boy with a Gun* (New York: Henry Holt and Company, 1958).

46. Vincent Brome, *The Revolution* (London: Cassell, 1969).

47. Alan Duff, *Szabad* (Glenfield, New Zealand: Vintage, 2001); the shooting scene is on pp. 206–09.

48. Zsuzsa Bánk, *The Swimmer* (New York: Harcourt, Inc., 2004). The German copyright is with S. Fischer Verlag GMBH, 2002. The Nádas quote is from the dust jacket of the American edition.

49. Stephen Vizinczey, *In Praise of Older Women. The Amorous Recollections of András Vajda* (Toronto: Contemporary Canada Press, 1965). The movie version was released in 1978.

50. See: http://www.boingboing.net/2001/12/11/in_praise_of_older_w.html.

51. Julius Ling, *Guiding Stars* (Orlando, FL: Rivercross Publishing Inc., 1999).

52. Jo Sinclair, *Anna Teller* (New York: David McKay Company, Inc., 1960). For the comment in a book review on the matriarch archetype, see Herbert Mitgang, "Big Mama from Hungary," *New York Times*, September 4, 1960. Like Faulkner, Sinclair tells the same story through different characters, and in stream-of-consciousness style.

53. Gabriella Mingo, *Their Fate Was Written* (Philadelphia: Franklin Publishing Company, 1974).

54. Andrew Miller, *Oxygen* (New York: Harcourt, Inc., 2001). The reference to Lázár's shady past is on pp. 110–15, where we are not actually told what happened in 1956.

55. Igor Sentjurc, *Prayer for an Assassin* (Garden City, NY: Doubleday & Company, Inc., 1959).

56. Wirt Williams, "The Assignment Was Murder," review of ibid., *New York Times Book Review*, May 31, 1959, p. 19.

57. David Pryce-Jones, *The Stranger's View* (New York: Holt, Rinehart and Winston, 1967). Pryce-Jones wrote a book about the Revolution as well: *The Hungarian Revolution* (London: Ernest Benn, 1969).

58. Stephen Marlowe, *1956* (New York: Arbor House, 1981).

59. David Brierley, *Shooting Star* (New York: Charles Scribner's Sons, 1983).

60. Doris Mortman, *The Wild Rose* (New York: Bantam Books, 1991).

61. Eva Byram, *Parallel Roads, Opposing Directions* (Frederick, MD: Publish America, 2005).

62. Alta Halverson Seymour, *Toward Morning. A Story of the Hungarian Freedom Fighters* (Chicago: Follett Publishing Company, 1961).

63. Helen M. Szablya and Peggy King Anderson, *The Fall of the Red Star* (Honesdale, PA: Boyds Mills Press, 1996).

64. Judit Makranczy, *We Have to Escape* (Unionville, NY: Royal Fireworks Press, 1999).

65. Eva Wiseman, *A Place Not Home* (Markham, Ontairo: Fitzhenry and Whiteside, 2004; original text copyright 1996).

66. The most important early ones include, besides the Aczél-Méray volume mentioned above, Tamás Aczél, ed., *Ten Years After: The Hungarian Revolution in the Perspective of History* (New York: Henry Holt Company, 1966); and Ferenc A. Váli, *Rift and Revolt in Hungary: Nationalism Versus Communism* (Cambridge: Harvard University Press, 1961).

67. There are about twenty additional books published in England that Americans have had limited access to. These were excluded from the present discussion of North American fiction.

VICE PRESIDENT NIXON'S REFUGEE FACT-FINDING TRIP TO AUSTRIA IN DECEMBER 1956 IN AMERICAN MEMORY

INTRODUCTION

Vice President Richard M. Nixon played but a minor part in White House decision making during and after the Hungarian Revolution of 1956. In December, his primary responsibility was to assess the refugee situation, and the first step in that direction was his brief visit to Austria and Germany between December 18 and 24. He then participated in a widely televised Hungarian Relief Air Show on December 25, and paid a one-day visit to Camp Kilmer, NJ, and New York City on December 27. He submitted his final report to the president on January 1, 1957, and eased out of the project by mid-January, leaving the responsibility to the President's Committee for Hungarian Refugee Relief, headed by veteran relief expert Tracy S. Voorhees. However, Nixon's trip to Austria has largely been forgotten: it is hardly more than a minor episode in both the history of the Hungarian Revolution and in Nixon's long and eventful political career. The only people who seem to remember it are the ones involved personally: refugees he met in Austria and Germany and at Camp Kilmer, and administration officials who participated in the events. Nixon's efforts received extensive press coverage, but soon faded from media memory, too. Strategies of remembering come into the picture with Ferenc Daday, a Hungarian exile and painter, who painted a picture of Nixon at the Hungarian border and donated it to the Richard M. Nixon Presidential Library and Museum in Yorba Linda, CA. The museum staff then decided to put the painting on permanent display in a prominent place, in the open space right near the museum exit—and thus restored these events of late December 1956 to American memory. The present paper first looks at Nixon's involvement in Hungarian refugee relief and then places his contributions to the American memory of 1956 by telling the story of the Daday painting.

THE ANNOUNCEMENT

On December 13, 1956 all major American daily newspapers reported that Vice President Richard M. Nixon would fly to Austria to "to look into what further steps the United States might take to help Hungarian escapees from Russian oppression." The reports were based on an official statement made the day before by White House Press Secretary James C. Hagerty, who also announced the establishment of a presidential committee for refugee relief in the United States to be headed by Tracy S. Voorhees.[1] The statement was issued in Augusta, GA, where Eisenhower was concluding a two-week golf vacation. It had been announced earlier that the US would accept 21,500 refugees,[2] but reports from Vienna made it clear that more was needed: an additional 80,000 refugees were awaiting resettlement in various Austrian and German camps. Nixon did not expect the call to go on the mission, and if he recalls dates correctly in his memoirs, then the president asked him to go on the trip on the very day the news came out, and not before. In fact, Nixon claims that he and his wife were on a Christmas shopping trip to New York City when they were called back to Washington, D. C. by the president.[3] It seems that the idea came on a sudden impulse and that the mission was as much of a public relations trip as a fact-finding mission.

Refugee relief was a moral and political concern, if not obligation, for the Eisenhower administration, especially with the apparent gap between the rhetoric of liberation and the lack of American action on behalf of Hungary and with accusations flying about the dubious role of Radio Free Europe and Voice of America in inciting the Revolution. The president responded promptly by sending Nixon, his vice president and a known anticommunist, to Austria while Soviet troops were at the border, and by doing so over Christmas he added an all-important public relations twist to the mission. He used his own private plane, the *Columbine III*, to fly into the US four Hungarian refugee families on Christmas Day.[4] This was a clear message to the American public, to the Hungarian refugees, to the Austrian and German governments, to doubtful third-world leaders like Jawaharlal Nehru of India, and to the Soviets that the United States meant refugee relief seriously.

As regards the fact-finding trip, it was now up to the State Department and Nixon's staff to decide when exactly to go, who to take on the trip, where to visit, whom to meet, and what to say. The vice president had to be briefed on a number of related issues and background information was needed urgently. Given the short amount of time to prepare for the trip, Horace G. Torbert, Jr. of the State Department and Nixon's staff did an excellent job.

PREPARATIONS

Preparation for the trip began in earnest only on December 13, the very day the press carried the first reports of the vice president's assignment. The initial memorandum on the preparations includes basic information on flight duration, the fueling stops and the aircraft, the weather, official programs suggested by the State Department, and the names of the American ambassador to Vienna and the four Secret Service agents made available in the Austrian capital. It also records the anxiety of Austria to preserve her neutral status as well as Torbert's inexperience in official trip planning. Torbert forwarded Ambassador Llewellyn E. Thompson's invitation for Nixon to stay at his residency, because the Austrians "do not have accommodations for entertain[ing] state visitors overnight." Initial suggestions in this memorandum for the traveling party included Justice Department and USIA representatives as well as Mrs. Pat Nixon, none of whom actually made it to the final list. The report concludes with a summation of a courtesy call from Voorhees, who expressed his delight over the news of the trip and offered his full support in Washington and his staff's help in Austria.[5] From this point on, tasks were properly separated an assigned:

background information was collected for Nixon and assembled into a reading file, the program was worked out, official letters and public statements were drafted. The vice president's briefing for the trip took place on December 17. He was briefed on six major areas ranging from the situation in Eastern Europe and the outlines of the refugee crisis through UN action and American military activities in connection with refugee relief to the work of non-governmental relief agencies and the problems of feeding Hungarians inside Hungary.[6] The list of the traveling party was finalized and made public by the State Department on the day of departure, December 18.[7]

THE TRAVELING PARTY

There was little time for any debate over who should escort the vice president. His traveling party included Deputy Attorney General William P. Rogers, Congressman Robert Wilson of California, International Cooperation Administration Director John B. Hollister, Torbert and Dwight Porter of the State Department, and four Nixon aides: Robert King, Louie Gaunt, John C. Sherwood and Rex Scouten. Two additional members of the party, Dr. Lowell T. Coggeshall of the Department of Health and Medical Affairs and Dr. George Katona, a psychologist from the University of Michigan, traveled separately and joined the vice president in Vienna.[8] The official party was flown to Austria via Lajes, Azores by the president's former aircraft, the *Columbine II*, with a flight crew of eight.[9] Voice of America employee György Otmar served as Nixon's Hungarian interpreter in the refugee camps, while Alfred Puhan of the Vienna embassy provided similar services in German.[10] They left, as planned, on December 18, and returned one day later than planned, on the 24th. This was due to frequent changes in Nixon's program for the trip.

CHANGES IN THE PROGRAM

The proposed program[11] and the final report on the vice president's program on the trip show some two dozen differences.

Major program changes include additional press conferences and informal meetings with the representatives of the American press in Austria, skipping a visit to the State Opera in Vienna and meeting two members of the Budapest legation (December 20), an additional, pre-dawn visit to Andau and a meeting with UN High Commissioner for Refugees August R. Lindt (December 21), leaving for home one day late, inserting an extra stop in Scotland to meet more Hungarian refugees, and turning the proposed fuel stop at Keflavik into a high-level meeting with top Icelandic politicians and a media event by addressing American troops in Europe on the radio. Fog on his arrival in Austria and a snowstorm in Iceland on the way back further complicated Nixon's schedule.[12]

The presence of Soviet troops on the Hungarian side of the border and unconfirmed news reports that the Soviets pursued refugees into neutral Austria represented additional concerns. Austrian authorities tried to persuade Nixon not to go to the border, but he insisted, and went on an additional, 3:30 A.M. visit to Andau on December 21 to observe the arrival of the refugees. This trip, and Nixon's account of it in his memoirs, became an integral part of the mythology of the Hungarian Revolution and inspired the Daday painting mentioned above.[13] It was an act of bravery, an unnecessary risk the vice president did not have to take, but he did. There was a lot more to lose then to gain: if the Russians hit across the border in pursuit of refugees he could get killed by a stray bullet, while an early morning program is not really a photo op, and accounts of it could (and, in fact did) get lost in the press reports of a busy workday.[14] This was Nixon the gambler and the anticommunist: he took a calculated risk to see some real freedom fighters escape from the Soviet Army, and perhaps, to feel the thrill of being so close to enemy troops.

Most of the changes in the program point in the direction of even greater media exposure than planned, while the early morning visit to Andau and the meetings with U.N. High Commissioner August R. Lindt and members of the Budapest Legation expanded the fact-finding nature of the trip. The vice president had an eventful three and a half days between his arrival in Vienna at 5:00 P.M. on December 19 and his departure from his Munich hotel at 7:00 A.M. on December 23. He had four different programs on the 19th, ten on the 20th, thirteen on the 21st, and twelve on the 22nd. This was a professional performance on the part of a politician who had just completed a long election campaign and was called back from a shopping trip to be told to go on this mission.

With limited knowledge of the situation, the vice president needed extensive briefing and background information on various issues ranging from the nature and extent of the US relief effort and the diplomatic background of the matter through the attitude of the refugees towards the United States to the work of the various relief agencies in Austria. He and his staff had so little time that his briefing was concluded on the flight to Austria, and a "reading file" was compiled for him. The selection of information was further complicated by the flood of uninvited contributions from enthusiastic individuals and non-governmental agencies;[15] the question was not what to read but what not to.

AMERICAN REFUGEE RELIEF

The American relief effort before the December 12 announcements by the White House was limited in scope and widely criticized in the press. At the time of Nixon's visit there were still more than 100,000 earlier refugees from Communism (the so-called Displaced Persons) in various European countries waiting for resettlement, and some 160,000 new arrivals from Hungary in Austria alone. Switzerland, Germany, Sweden and Norway received some of them, but in late December an estimated 80,000 still awaited decision. The leftover of the 1956 national and refugee quotas to the United States were filled with 6,500 Hungarians,[16] but most of the remainder in Austria wanted to go to the United States. The arrival of the earliest refugees coincided with Thanksgiving and was covered favorably by the media.[17] Camp Kilmer in New Jersey became a household name in America but it also stood for, as Voorhees later recalled, the inability of the administration to "process" the refugees: "There had been much criticism of the way things were handled at Kilmer, and of the inadequate action of the U.S. in meeting the pitiable emergency needs of the refugees." This "mess at Kilmer" was due to the lack of coordination between the government agencies on the one hand the various voluntary relief agencies on the other. In response to the attacks in the press, the president announced on November 26 that the United States would receive a total of 21,500 refugees from Hungary.[18]

The logical source to turn to for advice was former president Herbert C. Hoover, who had more than fifty years of experience in humanitarian relief and who himself was serving on a voluntary agency, First Aid for Hungary. He had already suggested to the White House to employ Voorhees, who was named Eisenhower's personal representative on Hungarian refugee matters on November 30.[19] Then, after being approached three times in ten days by various representatives of the Eisenhower administration, Hoover drafted a memorandum for the president on December 8. He called for the establishment of two administrative agencies: one made up of the representatives of all the government agencies involved and headed by Voorhees, and another one out of "the eligible voluntary agencies under the chairmanship of the Chairman of the American Red Cross," which should include either Voorhees or a key member of his staff. He had sent a more detailed version of his proposals to Voorhees four days before.[20] Voorhees promptly recruited the available veterans of earlier Hoover relief programs and sent two members of his new team, Hallam Tuck and General Carl Hardigg, to Vienna.[21] On hearing the news of the vice president's trip, Voorhees phoned the White House and offered the services of Tuck and Hardigg to Nixon,[22] while Hoover sent him a copy of his related correspondence and the December 4 and 8 memoranda.[23]

Nixon received two memoranda from the International Rescue Committee (IRC). It was the agency responsible for appropriating the President's Emergency Fund, which was used for Hungarian refugee relief by the administration. One of the reports described the activities of the agency between October 30 and December 12, while other was the record of a fact-finding mission to Austria between November 17 and 27. The former explained the actual work of the IRC, detailing relief activities in Hungary, Austria and the United States, while the latter provided political analysis by discussing the Revolution, the exodus of people from Hungary, and the significance of the events.[24]

This was the state of affairs when Nixon's preparation for the visit to Austria began. He had to come up with suggestions in two areas. Should the US allow more refugees in, and if so, should it be a fixed number or a set percentage of the total number of refugees? And if so, what should be done to the immigration laws of the land?[25]

DIPLOMATIC CONCERNS

The diplomatic situation was no less complex. The Austrian State Treaty was signed the year before. Austria was evacuated and became neutral. Its respect of the terms of neutrality was repeatedly questioned by both Moscow and the new Kádár government in Hungary and there were Soviet troops on the border. On November 23, a Soviet soldier who refused to stop at the border and lay down his arms in Austrian territory was actually shot by the Austrian border guard. The Eisenhower administration had to face the possibility of a Soviet invasion of Austria.[26] Meanwhile, the Austrian government did its best to maintain its neutrality, and resorted to receiving unarmed refugees only. It was announced on November 1 that only the International Red Cross would be allowed to ship supplies into Hungary. Accordingly, a trilateral agreement was signed between the International Red Cross, the Hungarian Red Cross and the Hungarian government on November 17.[27] And the refugees kept coming; according to Gyula Borbándi, their number amounted to 50,000 in December.[28]

Austria's neutrality was a curious mix of what she would have liked to do and what she safely could. Clearly, Austrian sympathies lay with the freedom fighters, but the government wanted to avoid any move that would provoke a Soviet invasion and the restoration of the bad of old days before the State Treaty.[29] All in all, lending full support to Austrian neutrality was a chief consideration for Nixon's staff, but so was securing the cooperation of the Austrian government. Of the 23 items on Nixon's program for December 20–21, nine included discussions with Austrian officials. The vice president was officially informed about the refugee situation, Austria's contributions and future needs. He handled the issue with such tact that the Austrian government expressed its thanks to him via Ambassador Thompson: "[They] are most grateful for the consideration the Vice President had shown of Austrian sensitivity on subject of their neutrality by avoiding actions or remarks that could have been embarrassing to them."[30]

Another, equally perplexing, problem was the state of American-Hungarian relations. Considerations included the accusation that Radio Free Europe and Voice of America incited the "counterrevolution" in Hungary, the fact that Cardinal Mindszenty sought asylum at the American Legation in Budapest, and the status of Edward T. Wailes, the new American minister to Budapest, who refused to present his credentials to the new puppet regime of János Kádár. Wailes advised Nixon of his sensitive situation as early as December 14:

> Were it feasible, I should like nothing better than to drive to Vienna for a day and pay my respects. My position here, however, is somewhat precarious at the moment as I have been in Hungary for six weeks without presenting my credentials due to the Soviet invasion. To leave the country and especially to have it known that I have talked with you would in all probability bring the matter to a head and result in my being requested to present my credentials to the present Soviet stooge regime or leave permanently. This we are trying to avoid in the hope that pressure in the United Nations and from other outside forces might bring forth a more suitable government in the not too far distant future.[31]

Wailes then offered an alternative, which Nixon accepted: "No such problem exists, however, with respect to other officers of the Legation staff and should you wish to have briefing while in Vienna from one or more of them on the current situation in Hungary, it can easily be arranged....Accordingly, Second Secretary Jordan T. Rogers and Military Attache Colonel James C. Todd of the Budapest Legation briefed the vice president late at night on December 21. There is no account of the meeting in Nixon's file, and the official report on his program simply states that "the meeting included a general review of the Hungarian situation and requirements and some speculative discussion as to the probable course of events in Eastern Europe as a whole."[32]

Another memorandum submitted to Nixon on December 17 touches upon American-Hungarian relations with surprising frankness. It first elaborates on the possible ways of taking care of the refugees, then on plans to feed the people inside Hungary, and finally explains the difficulties of dealing with the new Kádár regime. The US, it argues, cannot withdraw her minister from Budapest, because it might lead to the kidnapping of Cardinal Mindszenty, "just as they did

Maléter, Nagy and Rácz." The author urges the vice president to "mention Cardinal Mindszenty with some frequency," and frankly admits that "our legation in Budapest has been alerted to the possibility of an attempt being made to kidnap the Cardinal, even against all diplomatic usage, and that they have been instructed to protect him even with their lives." The conclusion is outspokenly honest: "We could be made to look awful bad if they should take him away from our care."[33] Nixon toed the line carefully and avoided all confrontations with Hungarian authorities. This was achieved in part by carefully drafting various statements for different audiences and by controlling his temper. In his public statements he wisely avoided references to Cardinal Mindszenty.

REFUGEE OPINIONS

Vice President Nixon had to respond to the charges that RFE and VOA had incited the rebellion. To do so, he had to have first-hand information from the refugees themselves. He also had to find out whether they intended to return to Hungary in the foreseeable future or they needed resettlement in and outside of Austria. Public relations and fact-finding again became inseparable. No fewer than ten items on the vice president's program included meeting refugees; from landing in Vienna to the Christmas party in Scotland on the way back, Nixon met Hungarian refugees as well as refugees from before the Hungarian Revolution of 1956.

The background and briefing materials carry targeted questions for the vice president to consider during his trip and in his final report. One briefing memorandum dated December 19 lists eleven groups of questions. Seven of these deal with the refugees and one with the radios: (1) number of refugees to the United States; (2) pre-October 23 refugees; (3) security precautions about the refugees; (4) financial or other aid to Austria to help with the refugees; (5) financial aid for resettlement of refugees outside the US; (9) effectiveness of VOA and RFE broadcasts; (10) recommendations regarding immigration legislation; and (11) refugee students.[34] Additional background materials for Nixon included RFE correspondence rejecting "these baseless charges" against the radio, a USIS report on the public relations side of Operation Safe Haven (the program to fly the 21,500 refugees to the United States), two memoranda on refugee opinions, numerous status reports on refugees in Austria and Germany, and two copies of *The Revolt in Hungary. A Documentary Chronology of Events* compiled and printed in a red-white-green cover by the Free Europe Committee.[35]

In his memoirs Nixon recalls his second, predawn visit to Andau and the conversation he had there with young freedom fighters: "'Do you feel that the Voice of America and Radio Free Europe played a part in encouraging the revolution?' I asked. Looks of surprise came over their faces as my deliberately undiplomatic question was translated. One of them blurted out the answer—'Yes.'"[36] This was a straightforward answer which Nixon nonetheless ignored in his final report. Instead, he and his staff emphasized the positive role of the two stations played in conveying information to people behind the Iron Curtain. This makes the two major reports on refugee opinions and the memorandum Nixon received from former Budapest Mayor József Kővágó at their meeting on December 21 even more interesting.

The first survey was discussed in a USIS-embassy joint message from Vienna dated December 5. It is based upon a public opinion poll conducted among the refugees by Austrian experts between November 22 and 26, and published a week later, on the 29th. The polling took place in two refugee camps at Eisenstadt and Traiskirchen; both were visited by the vice president's party. A total of fifteen questions were asked, and the results were explained in detail in the report. Most of the refugees had arrived within eight days of taking the poll. They expressed their satisfaction with treatment at the camps and identified fear as the main reason for departing. Fifty-three percent said they would return to Hungary if Communism and Soviet occupation were terminated. Forty-four percent said they would not return to Hungary. Forty-three percent of them named the United States as their desired destination, and 27 percent wanted to be relocated to Australia. Twenty-nine percent claimed their personal financial situation was best between 1938 and 1945. Fifteen percent claimed they were best-off before 1938, and 22 percent stated they had never been well-off. Ninty-six percent of the refugees interviewed listened to western radio stations, and some 80 percent identified RFE as their primary source of information. Questions 12 and 13 dealt with the role of the Western democracies: 81 percent would have expected direct military aid in the form of US, NATO or UN troops and/or contraband. The vast majority of the polled thought that the above measures were still not too late to implement. When asked about their "greatest wish at the present time," 47 percent responded by saying emigration as soon as possible, 25 percent wanted a job and continued education, 19 percent placed freedom in Hungary ahead of everything else, 17 percent wanted a peaceful, prosperous life, and 5 percent wished to fight on. Nixon aide Robert King's handwritten comment on the first page of the memorandum says, "This has some good stuff in it."[37]

The second memorandum on refugee opinions came from an unidentified Bela Kornitzer and is dated December 22, Munich, Germany. It is based upon Nixon's visit to a Bavarian refugee camp the same day. It appears that Kornitzer was a member of the visiting party, possibly serving as an interpreter. Refuges told him that "there was a definite hatred and disappointment against the regime" in Hungary, and one coal miner claimed that poverty drove him away from Hungary. The uprising was spontaneous and was triggered by Khrushchev's February 1956 speech on de-Stalinization. The radios (RFE and VOA) played a positive part in the life of the refugees. One of them stated that if he had money he would rather buy a radio than shoes: "You can walk barefoot, but you can hardly live without hope." They all claimed that they never believed any of the Communist propaganda "they were taught in the schools," and that they would return to Hungary if Communism and the Soviets were gone. They had no complaints about the way they were treated in the camp, but they wanted to be out of the camp as soon as possible. Much of the report deals with the refugees' fascination with the vice president. They found Nixon surprisingly young for his office, and they were awed by his willingness to meet them and let them speak their mind. And sincerity did surface in these conversations, too. One refugee claimed that this was just a publicity stunt on Nixon's part, while another one remarked with a grin that his greatest experience as a freedom fighter was to meet the American vice president. They also expressed their conviction that the Western democracies should, and perhaps would, "live up to what they tell the people over the air."[38]

The same subtle criticism is apparent in the memorandum Mayor Kővágó submitted to Nixon during their meeting in Vienna. He was the first real flesh and blood hero from the news the vice president actually met, and it seems an educated guess to believe that Nixon took his comments seriously. In the first half of the seven-page document Kővágó outlines his views of the Hungarian Revolution, its causes, course and effects. His gloomy conclusion is that Hungary is heading for "a horrible national catastrophe." Hungarians want a representative government based on free elections, but what they get instead is "national suicide, chaos, and the dissolution of all legal order." The second half of the *aide memoire* carries thinly veiled criticism of the West. The UN Secretary General should have visited Hungary before the second Soviet attack, and the UN should use the same methods to handle the situation in the Middle East and in Hungary alike. After dealing "a devastating blow to international Communism," the "Hungarians expect an unambiguous answer from the major powers and from all western nations: Do they approve of Hungary's fight for freedom, or do they not? If they do, what exactly are they prepared to do about it?" Hungarian politicians believe that "the major powers and the UN did not go as far in their action as they could have gone without risk of a world war." The United States must take the lead now and find "the ends and means which will lead to securing freedom for Hungary."[39] Having to listen to all this without being able to help must have made this one of the worst moments of Nixon's life thus far.

That notwithstanding, the vice president's meetings with the refugees clarified a number of issues he had to consider. Since the US and the West were not going to fight the Soviets for the independence of Hungary, the vast majority of the refugees had to be resettled outside Hungary. They made it quite clear that their preferences lay with the United States, and this was confirmed by the various news reports on Nixon's trip. This meant that the Austrian government needed additional financial help and that the November 26 quota of 21,500 would have to be expanded. This, in turn, meant immigration law reform. The fact that Nixon insisted on taking Deputy Attorney General Rogers with him and having him on every one of his programs[40] indicates that the vice president actually expected such conclusions to emerge even before his departure from Washington.

Relief Agencies in the Field

Polite and grateful for the helping hand extended to them, the refugees proved reluctant to criticize camp conditions or relocation programs when they met the vice president. The press did, however, and Nixon had secondhand information on wild rumors circulating among the refugees. Perhaps the most striking one comes from Eva Fejer, an interpreter for the refugees working for British authorities: "I was astonished when several of them informed me that they were told by the Americans in Vienna not to go to Britain if possible as they would be put behind barbed wire in concentration camps and even prisons." She also recalls that many of the refugees received empty "holdalls" from some American relief agency.[41] Anglo-American disenchantment over Suez might have contributed to such rumors. If the refugees were unwilling to offer critical remarks and the press carried such exaggerations as the one cited above, he had to talk to American relief experts and the representatives of the various relief agencies working in the area. This was the fourth major issue he was being briefed on before and during the trip, and this was also the cornerstone of Hoover's memoranda, cited earlier.

The Nixon pre-presidential files include a wealth of information on voluntary relief agencies from before, during and after the vice president's trip to Austria. The Voorhees Committee kept the vice president up to date on its work at Camp Kilmer, and in Vienna Hallam Tuck was among the first ones to meet him on December 19. Nixon's files include Red Cross and Catholic Relief Services correspondence as well as individual offers of assistance. The briefings continued during the flight and even in Austria. On December 21 Nixon met with representatives of the International Committee for European Migration, the organization which transported the first refugees to the US before Operation Safe Haven was launched and the American military came to be involved. Later the same day, the vice president received the representatives of the voluntary agencies in Vienna at the US Embassy. Following a frank exchange of ideas, he asked each agency to submit its recommendations in writing.[42] He was later briefed on the Hungarian refugee situation in West Germany, too.[43] There certainly was no shortage of information, and Nixon responded by calling for more aid for the refugees.

The vice president made a public statement before leaving for Salzburg on December 21. He called on "all free nations and the United Nations" to step up their relief efforts in both aiding the Austrian government and accepting refugees. More importantly, he remarked that "the United States must do more than it has already done in order to contribute adequately our share in meeting the problem which has been created for Austria by the bravery and fortitude of those who have fled from oppression by crossing the Austrian border into the free world." Americans, he said, must double their contributions. His staff confirmed unofficially that he was seriously considering the possibility of admitting additional refugees above the 21,500 quota set by the president earlier.[44] From a Displaced Persons camp in Austria he sent a message to Congress to the effect that pre-October 23 refugees must also be taken into consideration. On arrival in Germany he announced that "some of my views concerning the refugees' problems have been changed." On the nature of such changes he said, "I did not realize the many economic problems involved and the highly technical quality of the refugees and the potentiality of their productivity." He promised to "go to bat" for the students once he gets home.[45] Nixon then continued to survey camp conditions in Germany and on the way home in Scotland.

PUBLIC RELATIONS

Nixon's professional handling of the delicate diplomatic situation, the lengthy human interest stories with photographs of his meetings with the refugees in various camps and on departure for the US as well as his carefully worded public statements at various stages of the trip combined for an effective public relations campaign. The Eisenhower administration needed a boost and got it from the vice president.

Voorhees recalls that the administration had such bad press coverage on the refugee situation that one of his first tasks was to do something about it. He had worked on the successful Republican campaign in 1956 and he enlisted the same company again, Communications Counselors Inc., "the highest powered Public Relations organization I could get," to do the job.[46] That this was no empty precaution was made clear by Joseph and Stewart Alsop in their regular "Matter of Fact..." column in the *Washington Post* on the day Nixon arrived in Vienna. They called Nixon's trip to Austria a "most interesting political gesture, but only because of the light it sheds on the domestic political trend." That trend, according to the Alsops, was to present Nixon as young and energetic, perhaps as Eisenhower's choice to succeed him: "An adroit and intelligent man wishing to build himself up to the stature of a future presidential candidate could hardly ask for a better chance than Dick Nixon has now secured for himself."[47] To some degree, the Alsops were right: barring a major diplomatic blunder, a high-level visit to survey the refugee situation in Austria could only be a roaring success in the press. However, discarding Nixon's interest in the problem and his genuine anticommunism to build a case against him even before he had a chance to prove himself was a blow below the belt, especially in light of the risk he would take during his second, predawn trip to the Hungarian border on December 21. Since representatives of the press in the field and traveling with Nixon did a good job, critics had to look elsewhere. Gearing up for the confrontation in Congress over immigration reform, the new accusation was that the Hungarian refugees admitted to the US represented an intelligence threat because many of them were Communist agents. Indicative of this trend is a letter to the editors of the *Washington Post*, printed on January 3, 1957:

> A better alternative would seem to me to be to aid the Hungarians to fight against their oppressors in their own land and save America the fatal mistake of strengthening communism here by the infiltration of an unpredictable number of agents who are sure to be among these people to whom we are now set to give asylum within the confines of the United States.[48]

In such an atmosphere, Nixon had to prove himself a public relations success, and he did. As has been pointed out in the discussion of program changes, he included several additional opportunities to meet the press officially and unofficially, and visited as many refugee camps as he possibly could. This granted him extensive media coverage in the form of sure-to-sell human interest stories with the refugees on the one hand and the opportunity to officially announce and unofficially explain his position on refugee relief and immigration legislation on the other. By allowing his staff to "confirm" a variety of possible figures and percentages that he might suggest to the president, he tried to improve the administration's bargaining position in the impending congressional showdown over immigration restriction.

The *New York Times*, the *Chicago Tribune* and the *Washington Post* combined for more than seventy articles to cover Nixon's seven-day trip to Austria, Germany and Iceland. The image these reports convey is a vice president working around the clock, meeting officials and refugees alike. Seventy-two refugees greeted him on his arrival in Vienna, and he visited at least a dozen major camps in Austria and Germany. On December 22 he saw off a group of refugees at the Munich airport in Germany, and an additional stop and refugee camp visit in Scotland was inserted into his program on the way home. He was shown with refugees peeling potatoes, delivering relief supplies or shaking hands, and accounts were printed of Christmas parties in Austria and Scotland. At the Christmas party at Traiskirchen, Austria, for example, he played the piano and taught Jingle Bells to the kids. He was reported to have "baffled" Austrian authorities on the very first day, when he went to the Hungarian border and freely mixed with Austrians and Hungarians alike. One such report from his program at the Munich airport reads as follows:

> As the Hungarians climbed aboard the United States air force C-118 transport plane, they grasped Nixon's hand, shook it, and said thanks. A girl, 3, wearing a red trimmed bonnet, lifted her hands and Nixon took her in his arms. The child smiled thru happy tears as the Vice President held her while photographers took their pictures.[49]

Building further on this theme, the reports of his arrival in Washington on December 24 carried pictures of Nixon hugging his own daughters.

Preparations for the trip included drafting various basic guidelines for speeches to different audiences for the vice president. Four such drafts have been found in the Nixon papers: a suggested departure statement from Washington, one on "what to say to almost any audience," another one titled "Suggested Statements to an Hungarian Audience," and a list of talking points for a meeting with Austrian union leaders.[50] He made additional public statements on leaving Vienna, Salzburg, Germany and Iceland. One additional element in this public relations campaign to assert the positive role of the United States in refugee matters and condemn Soviet action was the "mortal blow" theme. In the Nixon materials this first surfaced in the second IRC memorandum, then in the meeting with former Budapest Mayor Kővágó, and eventually in the statement he made on his arrival in Washington on December 24: "As a result of [the freedom fighters'] sacrifice, international communism has suffered a mortal blow from which it cannot recover. It has been exposed a gigantic failure."[51] This, of course, became one of the key myths of the Hungarian Revolution of 1956.

The public relations campaign did not end with Nixon's return to the United States. On December 25 he participated in a nationally televised fund raiser for the Hungarian refugees, the next day he briefed President Eisenhower on his ideas, and on December 27 he consulted former president Hoover in New York City and visited Camp Kilmer in New Jersey. He submitted his final report to Eisenhower on January 1, 1957.

Post-Trip Public Appearances

During the press event at Keflavik Nixon announced that he "could not discuss his proposals for increased aid to Hungarian refugees until after he had talked to President Eisenhower."[52] Yet, on Christmas Day, the very day Nixon's return was reported in the press, the public relations campaign moved on. Keeping up the suspense about the contents of the impending report by the vice president to the president and Congress, the *New York Times* announced: "Nixon to Report at Show Tonight. Vice President to Join Stars of Theatre in Benefit for Hungary on TV, Radio."[53] The "show" where the vice president was to "give the nation a report on his trip"[54] was a one-hour, prime-time fundraiser to benefit the refugees. It was only after then, on December 26, that Nixon would meet Eisenhower. This was a most unusual departure from protocol, and the only plausible explanation seems to be that a nationally televised show was too good an opportunity to pass up on.

The show was jointly sponsored by the "American Red Cross, CARE, Church World Service, Catholic Relief services and the United

Jewish Appeal,"[55] and aired from 6:00 to 7:00 P.M. E.T. The vice president opened the show from Washington with a ten-minute address. After thanking all the people who made the program possible, he spoke of the "unforgettable experience" of standing at the border "where thousands of Hungarians had crossed from the slave world into the free world." After recalling some individual cases he praised the Hungarians: "They are fine people, and they are incredibly courageous, and by their actions they have helped the Free World and men who want to be free all over the world, because they have helped to expose communism for the gigantic failure that it is. What they did in Hungary really marks the beginning of the end for international communism." These people need help, and governments can and do help. The US has received 21,500 refugees, but "there are things Governments just can't do, and that is what this program is about." What governments cannot do, voluntary agencies can. But they need money, and "we have done a great deal in our contributions in the United States, but we need to do twice as much as we have already done." By way of conclusion, Nixon recalled that refugees always asked him to thank "the people of America...for what they've done," and wished his audience Merry Christmas in Hungarian.[56] This speech was the summation of the major talking points introduced in the public statements made by Nixon during the trip: it included the emotional appeal for people in need and the praise for the freedom fighters as well as the slogans that American efforts must be doubled and that the Revolution dealt a mortal blow to Communism.

Nixon briefed his boss, President Eisenhower, on December 26. The meeting was attended, among others, by Rogers, Voorhees and Hollister. A subsequent White House statement said that although the 21,500 quota had been filled, the transportation of the refugees to the US would continue until January 10. The president would meet congressional leaders on January 1, and raising the refugee quota would have "top priority" in their discussions. At the same time, Nixon still refused to reveal to the press his actual recommendations.[57] During or after this White House conference Voorhees suggested that Nixon should improve the impact of his forthcoming report by meeting former president and veteran relief administrator Hoover in New York and by visiting Camp Kilmer, preferably in the company of his wife, Pat. The vice president agreed, and the campaign moved on.[58] Another trip had to be arranged in no time.

December 27 turned out to be another busy day for Nixon. He met Hoover in the Waldorf Astoria and they held a press conference together afterwards. Then his party moved on to Camp Kilmer, where he lunched with the refugees in the canteen, addressed them and the press, met with the Voorhees committee behind closed doors, and returned to Washington on the same day.[59]

Whereas the visit to Kilmer added to the positive public relations the refugees and the administration enjoyed, the meeting with Hoover posed some concern for the president and the vice president. The opinions of former presidents are usually sought and respected in times of crisis, and Hoover happened to have experience in humanitarian relief going all the way back to the Boxer Rebellion in China in 1900. Also, many of his former relief assistants were serving on various voluntary and governmental agencies: Fred Dolbeare of First Aid for Hungary, Hollister of the ICA, and Tuck of the Voorhees committee had all served in the American Relief Administration after World War I, Hugh Gibson of ICEM had been a member of Hoover's Council for the Relief of Belgium (1914–17), and Voorhees himself had worked with him on post-World War II relief operations. As has been pointed out, the Eisenhower administration did seek his opinion on three different accounts in late November and early December. This was the right course to take because through the network of his former associates Hoover had a unique overview of the refugee situation. Voorhees even invited him to serve as honorary chairman on the President's Committee for Hungarian Relief, but Hoover refused and chose First Aid for Hungary instead.[60]

This was indicative of two mistakes the administration made. One was disregard for protocol, while the other was not acting on Hoover's proposals promptly. When turning down Voorhees' invitation to serve on the president's own committee Hoover indicated through Tuck that such invitation should come from the president himself—but it never did.[61] Eisenhower never explained why, and we can only guess that he might have been preoccupied with his vision of New Republicanism, and Hoover had no place in it. Seeking Hoover's expert advice and then not going along with it added insult to injury, and turned Voorhees into a mediator between the former president and the administration. Hoover contained his criticism in the joint press conference with Nixon on December 27. He simply offered praise for the Hungarian refugees and called for allowing more of them into the United States. However, he was considerably less reserved in his letter to the president, which Nixon was asked to deliver.

Hoover opens with a bitter remark: "It is not my business to be determining your policies in Hungarian relief matters, but as officials of the Government do me the honor to seek my advice, I will expand a suggestion which I previously made to you, which was in two segments." The first one had been acted upon satisfactorily: an umbrella organization was established to coordinate the work of the voluntary agencies under Voorhees. His second suggestion, however, the establishment of a formal agency to coordinate the work American government agencies (along the lines of the ARA after World War I), had thus far been ignored. He offers a modification this time: this committee should not only be set up as soon as possible, but Nixon should be made its chairman and Voorhees its vice chairman. His two concluding remarks, one at the end of the letter, the other in the postscript, clearly reveal his frustration. Understanding that Nixon might be reluctant to suggest himself as the chairman of the second agency, Hoover writes: "Please pardon my intrusions, but I cannot be advising your subordinates without your being acquainted with this advice—good or bad." The postscript to the letter is equally outspoken: "You might be interested in a statement I made today at a press conference forced by the press on the Vice President and myself."[62]

Hoover's frustration was only in part due to hurt pride for not being asked to head the president's committee. More importantly, he was a relief expert, and saw in the lack of coordination a waste of energy, money and lives. And however frustrated he was over the course of action Eisenhower chose to take, he continued to feed advice to Voorhees. Yet, the president removed him from the equation by delaying his reply until January 8.[63] Meanwhile, Nixon submitted his final report, and Eisenhower met congressional leaders and unveiled his proposed legislative agenda for the new Congress.

NIXON'S FINAL REPORT

Besides the written and oral information collected between December 13 and 27, Nixon and his secretary, Louie Gaunt, had two major sources to work with. One was a collection of five reports by King for Nixon (all dated December 28), the other Hollister's estimate of costs for the refugee program for 1957.[64]

In "Hungarian Refugees—Internal Security" King asserts that all the reasonable precautions are being taken to root out communist infiltrators. He describes the three-step screening process that is started by the Austrians, continued by the INS and completed by the FBI at Camp Kilmer. In "Hungarian Refugee Students" he proclaims that they "as a group offer a special problem and it is one deserving special attention." There are an estimated 5,000 students among the refugees, eighty-five percent have education in the sciences. The problem is that most scholarship offers (a total of 1,000 by December 28) are in the liberal arts. These students will require reeducation not only in the scientific field but also "in our democratic way of life."

In the "Hungarian Situation" King analyzes not the political situation but the possible courses of action the US might take with the refugees. Since most of them would return to Hungary "when and if the Russians were gone" and there exists "the desirability of keeping as many of the refugees as possible in areas close to Hungary so that the eventual return might be facilitated readily," King recommends the use of the Labor Service Organization operated by the US Army and the application of the relevant sections of "the Lodge Bill, otherwise known as 'Alien Enlistment,'" because it would be cheaper in the long run and would help keep available some of the best brains of Hungary so that the Nation is not completely robbed of its future leadership possibilities." In short, only a limited number of them should be relocated to the United States.

In "Radio Free Europe, VOA" King addressed the positive role of the two stations in disseminating news behind the Iron Curtain. As regards the accusations, he claims that,

Apparently there is no indication that any of the broadcasts promised specific aid to the revolutionaries although apparently there was some feeling on the part of many of them that somehow help would be given. There seemed to be no disposition to blame the United States for not coming to the rescue and among the more intelligent there was an appreciation of the difficulties and dangers involved in direct assistance. Apparently almost all of the broadcasts were listened to for their news value and little else [was] being said about the quality of the other parts of the programming activities.

One source, King claims, "stated that many of the Hungarians also remember the 'policy of liberation.'" The fifth report deals with "The Hungarian Revolution" in general. The Revolution, King claims, was "spontaneous—and highly moral." More than half of the refugees were blue-collar workers, the supposed beneficiaries of the system. Thus, the Revolution represented a rejection of not just poverty and the regime but of international Communism itself. The Revolution was "highly moral" and "in several instances the Revolution took on a holiday air." Former AVO chiefs were peacefully expelled from the various towns in the country, with one notable exception, Mosonmagyaróvár, where the secret police fired upon the crowd with machine guns. This brought about "the terrible vengeance which was exacted upon those responsible." The "moral nature of the people's revolt" is also confirmed by the fact that "there was little or no looting of the shops in Budapest."[65] King drew freely upon the records of the Austrian trip, the Austrian poll conducted among the refugees in November 1956, and the Kővágó memorandum submitted to Nixon on December 21.

The Hollister memorandum was equally important and revealing, because the ICA was responsible for federal funding for the refugees. The three considerations Hollister identified were: (1) the total costs in Austria; (2) the costs of moving the 21,500 approved refugees to the United States; and (3) the costs of moving a similar number of people to the US. The Austrians, Hollister writes, "presented a program of $137 million for expenses to date and estimated through calendar year 1957." His estimates were more conservative and applied only to federal funds, not the total costs of the relief operation. Based on a number of considerations he listed, the "total cost can be limited to $40 million if no additional number is taken into this country; and with an additional 20,000 taken, it can be kept below $50 million." $35 million can be used from the 1956 funds, and another $65 million is available in 1957 for various Middle Eastern programs "which will probably not be implemented." Thus, the President's Emergency Fund should support all costs of the Hungarian refugee crisis, and no additional funds will be needed from Congress, "barring some very material new program not at present foreseen."[66]

It is more difficult to trace indirect input, but there is one instance which is obvious. Nixon met Hallam Tuck in Austria and consulted Voorhees in Washington. Their opinions are known from a memorandum Tuck wrote for Voorhees after receiving Hoover's December 4 letter. Besides the technicalities of relief work, Tuck concludes that "the tremendous wave of sympathy for the Hungarian refugees has resulted in an exaggeration of the present size of the problem (certainly not the human suffering)." With somewhat more than 100,000 refugees still awaiting resettlement, this is not a serious challenge: the IRO resettled 650,000 Displaced Persons in two years and the ICEM resettled 10,000 per month. With no sudden increase in the number of Hungarian refugees, "a relatively small central organization would suffice to consolidate and efficiently allocate present efforts in the field, but there should be a central authority."[67] Thus, owing to the efforts of Hollister and Tuck, Hoover's recommendations were finding their way into the decision making process through the back door.

Nixon's final *Report to the President on Hungarian Refugees* totals eleven pages of text and three appendices.[68] In the "Introduction" he praises the Hungarian Revolution, reiterates the "death knell of international Communism" theme and asserts that UN pressure on the Soviet Union to withdraw its troops from Hungary is "the only adequate and permanent solution to that problem." In "Number and Character of Refugees" he echoes his earlier statements with some addition from the King memos. Of the 155,000 refugees, the vast majority are genuine freedom fighters who left the country as a last resort to avoid retaliation. (In fact, the actual number of those who fought with a gun is put at about 15,000, T.G.) Most of them are young and highly skilled, and they intend to return to Hungary if it is safe. They are being screened carefully, and they represent no security threat for the country. If and when relocated, these people will prove to be an asset for the receiving countries. In "Disposition of Refugees to Date" he states that 80,000 of the

155,000 have been relocated, with 15,000 already in the United States. Austria claims that of the remaining 67,000 she can take care of 30,000, leaving a total of 37,000 to deal with. He finds it difficult to offer an "Estimate of Eventual Total Refugee Movement," but he sees one obvious conclusion: "The United States and other free nations must take substantially more refugees than they have agreed to take up to this time."   In a set of "Recommendations as to Future United States Policy on Accepting Additional Refugees" Nixon announces that "it would not be wise for the United States to be tied down either to a fixed percentage or a fixed number" of additional refugees to be admitted. Instead, there should be four major considerations: (1) all free nations, including the United States, should step up their efforts and contributions; (2) the method of paroling refugees into the country above the quota should be continued until Congress acts; (3) Congress must amend the Immigration and Nationality Act to legitimize the refugees paroled into the country and to "provide flexible authority to grant admission to this country of additional...refugees from Communist persecution;" but (4) Congress must also pass legislation so that no "administrative official should have unlimited authority to admit aliens to the United States on a parole basis." Nixon then goes on to present the bill in "Economic Assistance by the United States." US aid to Hungarian refugees has gone through the UN and must continue. Austria must not be expected to foot the bill after years of occupation and in the middle of economic recovery. Aid must also go to the League of Red Cross Societies and even to the voluntary agencies in the field. The president has been able to provide the necessary funds and will be able to continue until the end of the fiscal year, July 1, 1957. Relief efforts have been and will be coordinated by the PCHRR under Voorhees.

The chapter on "General Comments" begins with a disclaimer to the effect that a "more detail report has already been submitted orally to the President." Nixon is convinced that "the American economy can easily and profitably assimilate into our economy the refugees from Hungary who are entering the United States." Next, he offers words of praise for the voluntary agencies and American government officials involved in the relief effort. He then concludes with the familiar image of "the historical significance of this mass migration of people from an area of slavery to an area of freedom." And his final thought:

> The Communist leaders thought they were building a new order in Hungary. Instead they erected a monument which will stand forever in history as proof of the ultimate failure of International Communism. Those people, both inside and outside of Hungary, who had the courage to expose by their actions this evil ideology for what it is deserve all the gratitude and support which we in the Free World are so willingly giving today.

The three appendices present the status of refugees in Austria and at Kilmer, and offer statistics about the parolees admitted before December 28.

Overall, there is little if any information in Nixon's report which he could not have obtained in the United States. It is a very well-written document; not, however, for the president but aimed at the public. Besides reiterating the main themes of the public relations campaign launched with his departure statement on December 18, Nixon offers very little for decision makers. He does not commit to figures either about the number of additional refugees to be admitted or in connection with further aid needed. His program proposal breaks down into two major ideas: (1) we must keep up our joint relief efforts; and (2) recommendations for Congressional action. It follows from the background materials presented in detail above that some of Nixon's conclusions might have been drawn before he had left for Austria and that he, on occasion, disregarded the evidence he himself had collected. Austria did need help, but this the administration knew anyway; something needed to be done about the refugees arriving in the United States, and additional refugees would want to come.

In his report made public Nixon avoided any discussion of the role of the American radio stations in the Revolution. He emphasized the refugees' willingness to return to Hungary, knowing that the conditions for that would not be met for quite some time. When he was assured from different sides that the Hungarian refugee problem was relatively small and could be handled with the financial resources already available, he could safely offer a compromise to Congress: make a gesture towards the refugees and the administration is willing to support legislation to plug a loophole made clear by Eisenhower's decision to create a *fait accompli* by paroling 15,000 refugees into the country while

Congress was in recess. Also, if federal funds were sufficient to take care of the refugees, he did not need to worry about the written recommendations of the voluntary agencies in the field that he had asked for on December 21. And he did not: Ambassador Thompson cabled the materials home from Vienna on January 3, two days after the publication of Nixon's final report.[69]

The vice president's involvement in Hungarian refugee relief proved to be a successful public relations campaign on behalf of an administration that had a credibility problem because of the gap between its rhetoric of liberation and its response to the Soviet attack on Hungary.[70] Nixon's trip to Austria turned out to be more of an unforgettable emotional experience for the vice president than an actual fact finding mission, especially because he freely disregarded some of the important knowledge of the situation that he acquired while in Europe. His final report raised two important questions: How many more refugees would be admitted into the United States? And how would Congress react to the vice president's offer of a legislative compromise?

Disengagement and Fallout

Nixon's disengagement from Hungarian refugee relief actually began with the submission of his final report and was complete by January 9. Eisenhower replied to Hoover's letters of December 8 and 27 only on January 8. He thanked Hoover for his advice and expressed his delight over the fact that the former president was satisfied by the administration's conduct on his first recommendation. As regards the second one, Eisenhower wrote, the work was being done unofficially by Voorhees: he was indeed coordinating the work of the various federal agencies involved in the project. He also made it clear that Nixon wanted no further part in refugee relief:

> After receipt of your second letter, I conferred with the Vice President about your suggestion that he be Chairman of a more formal inter-departmental committee for this purpose. Mr. Nixon feels that it would be difficult for him to do this in addition to the very heavy burden which he is already carrying, and I do not feel that I ought to press him on the matter.

The president assured Hoover that the task of coordinating the work of government agencies was left with Voorhees.[71] So whereas Hoover felt that a better job could have been done on behalf of the refugees, Eisenhower was content with what he already had because all his sources said that the situation was under control anyway, and no additional funds were needed from Congress.

Nixon's desire to get disengaged from refugee relief was made abundantly clear the very next day. A January 9 memo from King to Nixon reported the suggestion from the staff of Senator Walter J. Mahoney that a refugee resettlement agency be set up. Mahoney thought Nixon should be chairman of the agency because he was now being associated by the public with refugee affairs, but the vice president disagreed. His handwritten remark on the King memo reads: "No, I don't want to stay on this. Leave the responsibility to Voorhees."[72]

The situation was indeed under control and the new Congress and the legislative agenda for Eisenhower's second term took priority over refugee matters. Nixon's involvement with Hungarian refugee relief lasted less than one month, from December 12 to January 9. In that short amount of time he put in a professional effort on behalf of both the refugees and the administration, but his refusal to accept long-term commitment goes a long way to demonstrate his reluctance to tie, even in part, his political future and presidential aspirations to this particular issue. And in so doing, he was probably right. The administration did a good job helping the refugees, but its fiery rhetoric of liberation and rollback was discredited by its inaction in October–November and by the limited pressure put on Moscow afterwards. He had firsthand information on the dubious role of Radio Free Europe and Voice of America in the events, and this was likely to come back to haunt the administration once it became clear to the public that these stations were being funded by the CIA.

The United States legally admitted an estimated total of 38,000 Hungarian refugees following the Revolution. Voorhees resigned from his post on February 28, 1957, the Joyce Kilmer Reception Center was closed by May 1, and the refugees arriving after that date were taken to the St. George Hotel in Brooklyn. The President's Committee for Hungarian Refugee Relief submitted its final report and was dissolved by May 15.[73] On April 13 Eisenhower proclaimed that with the lessening of the emergency the number of refugees received would be reduced, and on December 28 he announced the termination of the program. The total costs of the Hungarian refugee relief program amounted to over $71 million. He also noted that during the same period the US admitted 300,000 other immigrants.[74]

The legal status of the Hungarian parolees, the 32,000 on top of the 6,500 for whom there was a quota in 1956, depended on the legislative agenda and willingness of the 85th Congress. The September 1957 amendment to the Immigration and Nationality Act failed to offer a solution to the two major legislative issues highlighted in the Nixon report. An angry president scolded Congress for failing to "provide a method whereby the thousands of brave and worthy Hungarian refugees…might in the future acquire permanent residence looking forward to citizenship," and for not regulating the policy of admitting future refugees into the United States in case of emergency. His suggestion of basing the national quota on the 1950 census instead of the 1920 one was also ignored in the act. The legal status of the parolees was finally settled in July 1958, when passport and visa requirements were waived and legal immigrant status was granted to them.[75]

It follows from the above that Congress was not interested in the legislative compromise offered by the vice president in his January 1 final report. With the three-day miracle of the Revolution gone anti-immigrant sentiments returned with a vengeance. At the same time, the president was not pushing too hard for legislation benefiting the refugees, probably because he expected some solution to emerge following the fait accompli he had created by paroling them into the country. His lackluster effort did not pass unnoticed. On April 29, 1957, Governor W. Averell Harriman of New York "sharply criticized" the president for lack of action at a ceremony honoring the leaders of voluntary agencies on the very day the last ship of Hungarian refugees was to arrive:

While men and women of goodwill have responded magnificently to America's humanitarian responsibilities, our National Government has failed dismally to meet the need for a basic revision of our permanent immigration policy….The President has appealed to Congress for a revised immigration policy, but his leadership is not the kind necessary to obtain action.[76]

Referring to the heated debate in Congress, he pointed to the fact that the good will of the American people had been in part "thwarted by the narrow vision of a few." Arthur A. Markowitz, the author of arguably the best article on American participation in Hungarian refugee relief, offers conclusions that have stood the test of time:

> The United States did, in absolute numbers, admit more Hungarians than any other single nation, yet…in terms of population and natural wealth we ranked pitifully low. Certainly there is no question but that the American economy could have absorbed a great many more refugees than it was called upon to take.…[The anti-immigrant sentiments expressed in Congress] were expectable but nonetheless regrettable. So too was the fact that most of the refugees had to be admitted by executive chicanery and then were denied immigrant status for so long a time. The course which the United States followed was a decently humane one, but there was room for much more generosity.[77]

More attention paid to Hoover's recommendations, more effective mobilization of Republican lawmakers in Congress, and additional support from the president and the vice president for the refugees beyond early January 1957 would have made an otherwise impressive American effort even more convincing. In all this, Nixon played an important role, but also displayed the limits of his willingness to commit himself. He proved himself a reluctant professional in Hungarian refugee relief.

THE MEMORY AND THE PAINTING

The various memoirs of the Eisenhower administration largely ignore Nixon's trip to Austria. In *The White House Years: Waging Peace* Eisenhower devoted a full chapter to the double crisis of Suez and Hungary, mentioned his decision to bring refugees into the States, but completely forgot about Nixon's trip. Robert Murphy in *Diplomat among Warriors* and Sherman Adams in *First-Hand Report* similarly ignored Nixon's contributions and made only passing references to refugee relief.[78] Likewise, Nixon's biographers had little if any to say,[79] and, as has been indicated before, Nixon himself devoted only three pages to this in his own memoirs.

The press also forgot about the trip with one article from Earl Mazo serving as the exception to the rule. Mazo was promoting his biography of Nixon and wrote a short piece for the *Chicago Tribune* on December 13, 1959.[80] In it he recalled Nixon's Christmas party with Hungarian refugee children in Traiskirchen. Of the six American journalists who published memoirs about their tour of duty during the Revolution, only Bursten recalled the Nixon trip.[81]

Another, clearly political, reference was made by Martin Luther King, Jr., during the early stages of the Civil Rights Movement. On January 11, 1957 King invited Nixon to go to the South for a similar fact finding mission. The introduction to the document in the *King Papers* mistakenly claims that the vice president visited Hungary.[82]

It was a huge (six by ten feet, oil on canvas) painting by the Hungarian-born American painter Ferenc Daday that returned Nixon's visit to public memory in the United States. Daday painted the picture in 1971–72, donated it to Nixon, and twenty years later delivered it to the Richard M. Nixon Presidential Library and Museum, where it was put on public display in August 1992.[83] Since then, Daday's painting has been reprinted in *Time* and *American Heritage* as well as in a number of lesser known Hungarian language papers.[84] The Daday painting is the textbook example of how an artifact can return something to memory, a classic case of working against fading memory and of reminding others, yet, incidentally, of a scene the artist never saw.

Daday was born in 1914 as the eighth son of a country teacher in rural Hungary. He enrolled at the School of Industrial Design in Budapest in 1934, and in his sophomore year he walked to Italy to see the most important Renaissance paintings with his own eyes. After college he worked as a set designer in the Hungarian film industry. After the war he joined the staff of the Bureau for Foreign Trade and designed Hungarian exhibits abroad. On one such trip, in Stockholm in 1947, he decided not to return to Hungary, and applied for refugee status in Argentina. He claims he chose Argentine over the United States because it was "more of a virgin land" with less competition, a peaceful and quiet country. He soon got a job painting murals for one of cPeron's projects. Peron had a fund for building children's towns, hospitals and retirement homes for the elderly. Daday worked on fifty such projects. Following the revolution in Argentina now immortalized in films and musicals, he fled to the United States. He and his family landed in Florida. Soon they moved on to Atlanta, where he worked for a small printing firm as art designer. They relocated to California in 1956. Daday first worked for a portrait art studio, where he painted portraits from photos at the price of $5.00 a piece. He soon made enough money to buy a house in Burbank and built a studio there. He still lives in California in 2006, in a gated retirement community south of Los Angeles.[85]

In 1971 the Hungarian community wanted to commemorate the fifteenth anniversary of the Revolution and thank the then president Nixon for his work on behalf of many of them. The initial idea was to have a portrait of his daughters or wife painted, but Daday suggested something else. He heard of Nixon's trip on the evening news on the radio back in December 1956, and he immediately felt this moment had to be preserved by a Hungarian, for Hungarians and others alike. He had the strongest available canvas imported from the Netherlands, made extensive research and preparation, and painted the picture in about a year. He had had the idea all along, but for quite some time he did not have the money or the occasion to do it.

The painting was unveiled on October 6, 1972, at a fundraising dinner during the Nixon reelection campaign in the dance hall of the Ambassador Hotel in Los Angeles. Nixon was represented by Joseph Blatchford,[86] who then was the director of the Peace Corps. The painting was welcomed by the Nixon White House and Daday was invited to the inauguration ceremony in January 1973. During the discussions about the placing of the picture Daday suggested that it should be preserved for the future Nixon Library. This was agreed upon, and he kept the painting in his Burbank studio for some twenty years. When the Nixon Presidential Library was opened in 1990, he moved the painting over. It was first placed in a storage room, then in the conference room in the basement. The library exhibit was finalized in 1992, and the painting was moved to its current, prominent location on August 13. The ceremony, which in fact was the second unveiling, was covered by both the print and electronic media. Daday was later invited by the library to exhibit temporarily the drafts for the painting and some of his other works. The Nixon Library now has about 500,000 visitors from all around the world each year. Daday's dream to return to memory a forgotten event, a major American gesture toward the freedom fighters of the Hungarian Revolution of 1956, has come full circle.[87]

Ferenc Daday's painting, titled *Meeting at Andau* in 1972 and *Nixon at Andau* in 1992, is a curious mix of history, memory and imagination. Daday claims he has depicted "the dramatic moment when a crowd that lost its homeland flows towards a new hope and a better future." On the right we see a village in the distance against a dark background. Storm clouds (with a tinge of red) are swirling over a tree struck by lightning. Three women wave goodbye to the homeland, a man kisses the earth, and another young man carries the Hungarian national flag that has the communist coat of arms cut out. The middle of the picture is dominated by seven refugees and a Hungarian sheepdog (puli). The two figures in the foreground are a woman in a light brown overcoat and an armed freedom fighter pointing backward, towards the flow of refugees. They are met by Nixon and some other refugees who had already made it to safety. Nixon wears his trademark light gray trench coat, and a little girl presents him with a flower. Under Nixon's outstretched left arm we have a peek at the famous bridge at Andau. On the left there are two Red Cross representatives, a father with a kid in his neck waving at the refugees arriving, and three other refugees seated. One is on crutches, another is breastfeeding her baby. The sky above Nixon is white, and in the white sky there are small birds attacked by a black bird from the storm cloud. Daday painted earth and sky as well as fire and water into the picture to highlight the contrast between the two worlds.[88]

The painting was done in part from set pieces, in part form photographs, and in part from imagination. The tree struck by lightning is an actual tree from the San Bernardo Mountains, and Daday still has several sketches of what he calls the "screaming tree." The dominant female figure in the middle was modeled on Éva Szörényi, a prominent Hungarian actress and a key figure of the West Coast Hungarian community during the past fifty years. He also has various sketches of the three figures waving goodbye, while Nixon's face was drawn from photographs acquired from the White House in 1971. The birds in the white sky are skylarks, representing freedom, and they are attacked by an unidentified black bird, like the fiery storm clouds seem to attack the "screaming tree." All the clothes in the picture (except Nixon's) come from his imagination, and he chose this particular sheepdog because it is the oldest known dog associated with the Hungarians.[89]

Daday's truly dramatic painting is a mixture of three different artistic traditions: Soviet and/or German heroic painting from before World War II, the Hungarian rural (both landscape and portrait) tradition, and Biblical representations. The two outstanding heroic elements are the man carrying the flag and the freedom fighter couple in the middle. The rural tradition is represented by the countryside, the refugee family in the middle, and the three figures waving goodbye to Hungary. The left side of the painting is clearly a Biblical image with Nixon positioned as the Savior in divine light with the swirling white sky above. The thick column of refugees walking though the plains is the invocation of the Exodus.

It is not only through mixing of styles that Daday manipulates history and memory: the painting is amazingly inaccurate. Nixon never met actual refugees arriving, and by the time he got to the border the bridge had already been blown up.[90] Hungarian refugees never left in thick columns, they would have been easy target that way. There was no point in carrying a national flag when other things were probably more needed, and armed freedom fighters were not received by the Austrians. One of the more subtle aspects of the manipulative aspect of the painting is that the Soviet threat is represented only by the black bird, the fire in the sky, and the gun of the freedom fighter in the middle, but not by Russian soldiers or military hardware. Consciously or not, Daday tried to create a partly familiar image by painting stereotypical images of the Revolution and the refugees into the picture. The flag, the bridge and the tired refugee faces are all well-known fictional and photographic images of the events. The little girl presenting Nixon with a flower should be familiar from the discussion of the public relations aspect of the vice president's trip above. Interestingly, the image of the teenager freedom fighter (of "the boy with a gun" mould)[91] is completely missing from the painting: the refugees are old people, kids, or people in their prime. The one notable exception is the boy in the refugee family of five in the middle. His arm is in bandage and tied around his neck, but he wears a peasant style shoulder-bag and has a tired and confused look on his face. He looks more like a victim than a hero.

Using various techniques of visual representation Daday chooses to remind and, at the same time, tells his viewers what he wants them to remember. Yet, regardless of the reasons behind the museum's decision to place *Nixon at Andau* in such a prominent place, of Daday's original intentions, or what we see and read into his picture, this painting will serve as a loud reminder of a largely forgotten episode in the history of Hungary's tragic attempt to rid herself of Soviet rule during the Cold War. And it will always stand for unselfish American aid extended to the refugees exhibited at a sacred place for Americans, in a presidential library.

Notes

1. "Nixon Will Fly to Austria Next Week," *Chicago Tribune*, December 13, 1956; "Ike Reveals Trip Aims to Bolster Refugee Aid," *Washington Post*, December 13, 1956.

2. Dwight D. Eisenhower, *The White House Years II: Waging Peace, 1956–1961* (Garden City, NY: Doubleday & Company, 1965), pp. 97–98. Eisenhower claims the announcement was made on December 1, but, it actually happened on November 26.

3. Richard Nixon, *The Memoirs of Richard Nixon* (New York: Grosset & Dunlap, 1978), pp. 141–43. See also Stephen E. Ambrose, *Nixon. The Education of a Politician, 1913–1962* (New York: Simon and Schuster, 1987), pp. 423–26.

4. Clara Koeniger, "The Greatest Gift," *American Heritage* 44, no. 1. (February–March 1993): 33–34.

5. Notes re Austria trip, December 13, 1956, unsigned, 3 pages, Richard M. Nixon Pre-Presidential Papers, Laguna Nigel, CA: Series 354, Box 1: Austrian Trip, 1956 to Munich, Germany: Folder: 12/18/56 and 12/24/56, Austria Trip. The records of Nixon's trip to Austria are held in the Laguna Nigel building of the National Archives and Records Administration: two boxes in Series 354. Hereafter cited as RNPPP, box number, folder title, and document description.

6. Briefing for the Vice President on Austrian Trip, unsigned, undated: RNPPP, Box 1, Folder: 12/18/56: Trip to Austria, RN's Notes. The briefing took place at 3.30 p.m. on December 17.

7. "Nixon Takes Off on Refugee Trip," *New York Times*, December 19, 1956.

8. The Vice President's Trip to Vienna (State Department press release), December 18: RNPPP, Box 1, Folder: 12/18/92, Trip to Austria.

9. Military Air Transport Service memorandum, December 17, 1956: RNPPP, Box 1, Folder: 12/18/92, Trip to Austria.

10. Untitled memorandum from Torbert to Nixon, March 1957: RNPPP, Box 1, Folder: 12/19/56 and 12/20/56, Vienna, Austria.

11. Suggested Schedule for Austrian Visit, Torbert to Nixon, undated, 2 pages: RNPPP, Box 1, Folder: 12/18/92, Austria Trip.

12. Chronological Record of Vice President Nixon's Trip to Austria and Germany (hereafter cited as Chronological Report), unsigned, undated, 4 pages: RNPPP, Box 2: Folder: Trip to Austria—December 1956 Miscellaneous.

13. Chronological Report, p. 2; Nixon, *Memoirs*, 141–43. See also "Nixon Urges More U.S. Aid for Refugees. Pays Secret Visit to Border," *Chicago Tribune*, December 22.

14. The *New York Times*, the *Washington Post*, and the *Chicago Tribune* all covered the trip as the last item in their daily reports.

15. On the briefing on the plane, see Chronological Report, p. 1: the entry on December 19. The reading files are in the second box in RNPPP in two folders. RNPPP, Box 1: Folder: 12/18/56, Trip to Austria. RN's Notes carries several of these uninvited contributions.

16. Arthur A. Markowitz, "Humanitarianism versus Restrictionism: The United States and the Hungarian Refugees," *International Migration Review* 7, no. 1 (Spring 1973): 46–59. The reference is on p. 47.

17. For example on *NBC Today*, the network's premier morning show.

18. Tracy Stebbins Voorhees, "The Freedom Fighters: Hungarian Refugee Relief, 1956–1957" (Prepared in 1961, revised in 1968 and 1971), 30 p., Tracy S. Voorhees Papers, Alexander Library, Rutgers University, NJ: Box K, Mission to Berlin/Defense Advisor/Hoover Commission/Mutual Weapons Development Program/Hungarian Refugee Relief [part], Folder: Hungarian Refugee Relief Essay. The reference is from pp. 1–3. The Voorhees papers will be cited as: TSVP and by box, folder and document information.

19. Voorhees, "Refugee Relief Essay," p. 1. Voorhees' first notes about Hoover's ideas date back to November 24. He cabled the news of his appointment to Hoover on November 30. TSVP, Box K, Folder: Documents, Herbert Hoover.

20. Hoover's letters to Eisenhower and Voorhees were found in the Nixon papers: RNPPP, Box 2, Folder: Austria Trip (1/2) RN's Reading and Other Material. Voorhees was also briefed on Hoover's position on November 4 in a handwritten memorandum from Hallam Tuck: TSVP, Box K, Folder: Documents, Herbert Hoover.

21. Voorhees, "Refugee Relief Essay," pp. 8–9.

22. This information was included in the first briefing memorandum for the vice president. For details see note 5.

23. Hoover's cover letter was dated December 14. For details see note 20 above.

24. "The Sorrow and Triumph of Hungary," Report of the Donovan Commission of the IRC to Study the Hungarian refugee Situation in Hungary, December 10, 1956, 15 p.: NRPPP, Box 1, Folder: 12/18/92; and Special Report to the Board of Directors on IRC Hungarian Refugee Relief, December 12, 1956, 12 p., RNPPP, Box 1, Folder: 12/18/56, Trip to Austria: RN's Notes.

25. Hungarian Refugees, Percival F. Brundage to Nixon, undated, 2p. and attachments: RNPPP, Box 1, Folder: 12/18/56, Trip to Austria: RN's Notes. The same folder contains a set of eleven questions to consider for Nixon, dated December 19, 1956.

26. Johanna Granville, "Of Spies, refugees and Hostile Propaganda: How Austria Dealt with the Hungarian Crisis of 1956," *History* 91, no. 301 (January 2006): 62–90, esp. p. 71. For a somewhat different Austrian interpretation, see Michael Gehler, "From Non-alignment to Neutrality: Austria's Transformation during the First East-West Détente, 1953–1958," *Journal of Cold War Studies* 7, no. 4 (Fall 2005): 104–36.

27. Ellsworth Bunker (American National Red Cross) to Nixon, December 17, 1956; and International Committee of the Red Cross, Geneva Press Release No. 538b, November 17, 1956. Both in, RNPPP, Box 1, Folder: 12/18/56, Trip to Austria: RN's Notes. Granville, "Spies," p. 84; Gehler, "Neutrality," pp. 123–24.

28. Gyula Borbándi, *A magyar emigráció életrajza, 1945–1985* [Profiles of Hungarian Emigration, 1945–1985], 2nd. ed. (Budapest: Európa Kiadó, 1989), vol. 1, pp. 406–07. For the most recent study, see Julianna Puskás, *Ties That Bind, Ties That Divide. One Hundred Years of Hungarian Experience in the United States* (New York: Holmes and Meier, 2000), pp. 270–78.

29. For details, see Granville, "Spies," and Gehler, "Neutrality," pp. 121–26.

30. FYI memorandum from Robert King to Nixon, based on a phone call from the State Department, with information from a cable from Ambassador Thompson, December 28, 1956, 1 p., RNPPP, Box 1, Folder: 12/19/56 and 12/20/56, Vienna, Austria.

31. Wailes to Nixon, December 14, 1 p., RNPPP, Box 1, Folder: 12/18/56, Trip to Austria, RN's Notes.

32. Chronological Report, p. 2.

33. Measures: Some Immediate and Long-Range Considerations,

Memorandum for Nixon, December 17, 2 p., RNPPP, Box 1, Folder: 12/18/92, Trip to Austria.

34. This is the December 19 memorandum quoted in note 25.

35. These documents are in the two reading files in Box 2 of RNPPP.

36. Nixon, *Memoirs*, pp. 141–43.

37. Austrian Opinion Survey of Hungarian Refugees, Jack M. Fleischer, USIS Vienna, to USIA Washington, December 5, 1956, 11 p., RNPPP, Box 2, Folder: Austria Trip (2/2), RN's Reading and Other Material.

38. Notes from Bela Kornitzer, December 22, 3 p., RNPPP, Box 1. Folder: 12/18/56 and 12/24/56, Austria Trip.

39. Aide Memoire, December 22, 7 p., RNPPP, Box 1, Folder: 12/18/56 and 12/24/56, Austria Trip.

40. Notes from RN re: Austria Trip, December 15, 1 p., "Bill Rogers is ranking man on this trip and should be included in all of the events RN takes in." RNPPP, Box 1, Folder: 12/18/56 and 12/24/56, Austria Trip.

41. Eva Fejer's cable to the editor of *Manchester Guardian*, undated, 1 p., RNPPP, Box 1, Folder: 12/18/56, Trip to Austria, RN's Notes.

42. Chronological Report, pp. 1–2.

43. Briefing Notes for Vice President Nixon on Hungarian Refugee Situation in Germany, unsigned, undated, 3 p. and Hungarian Refugees admitted in the Federal Republic, unsigned, undated, 2 p., RNPPP, Box 1, Folder: Austria Trip (2/2), RN's Reading and Other Material.

44. "Finds Need of More Aid for Victims," *Washington Post*, December 22, 1956.

45. "Nixon Changes Refugee Views," *Washington Post*, December 23, 1956. "Nixon Expects Longer Refugee Airlift," *Chicago Tribune*, December 23, 1956.

46. Voorhees, "Refugee Relief Essay," pp. 5–6.

47. Joseph and Stewart Alsop, "Nixon to Austria," *Washington Post*, December 19, 1956.

48. David Talbot, "Communist Agents," *Washington Post*, January 3, 1956.

49. "Nixon Expects Longer Refugee Airlift," *Chicago Tribune*, December 23, 1956.

50. The first three are in Folder 12/18/92, Trip to Austria; the fourth is in Folder: 12/18/56 and 12/24/56, Austria Trip, both in RNPPP, Box 1.

51. "Nixon Returns Singing Praise of Hungarians," *Chicago Tribune*, December 25, 1956.

52. "Nixon Flying Home, Sees Iceland's Chief on Way," *Chicago Tribune*, December 24, 1956.

53. "Nixon to Report at Show Tonight," *New York Times*, December 25, 1956.

54. "Nixon Returns Home Singing Praise of Hungarians," *Chicago Tribune*, December 25, 1956.

55. "Nixon Urges Doubling of Refugee Aid," *Chicago Tribune*, December 26, 1956.

56. The four-page speech is in RNPPP, Box 1, Folder: 12/18/56/ and 12/24/56, Austria Trip.

57. "Act to Let in More Refugees. Ike Orders Processing of Requests," *Chicago Tribune*, December 27, 1956; "Brownell Is Told to Process Papers; President, Nixon Confer for Hour," *Washington Post*, December 27, 1956, Herbert Brownell was Eisenhower's attorney general.

58. Voorhees, "Refugee Relief Essay," pp. 13–15.

59. For details see: RNPPP, Box 2, Folder: 12/24/56, Trip to New York City and Camp Kilmer. For the press coverage, see "Nixon Sees Top Officials On Refugee Resettlement," *Washington Post*, December 28, 1956.

60. Handwritten memorandum, Hallam Tuck to Voorhees, December 4, TSVP, Box K, Folder: Documents, Herbert Hoover; Voorhees, "Refugee Relief Essay," p. 10: "I endeavored to get him to serve as Honorary Chairman of the President's Committee, but he declined because he felt that not enough was being done by the Administration for the Hungarian refugees."

61. This is in the Tuck memorandum cited in note 60.

62. Hoover to Eisenhower, December 27, 1956, TSVP, Box K, Folder: Documents, Herbert Hoover.

63. The Hoover-Voorhees correspondence continued well into 1957. Eisenhower's reply to Hoover is discussed below.

64. As will be discussed later, the written reports from the voluntary agencies that Nixon had asked for on December 21, 1956, did not arrive until January 3, 1957.

65. All five King memoranda are in RNPPP, Box 1, Folder: 12/18/56 and 12/24/56, Austria Trip.

66. Estimate of Probable Costs of FY 1957 for Hungarian Refugee Program by Hollister, December 28, 4 p. The Cover letter is dated December 29, 1956, RNPPP, Box 2, Folder: RN's Material for Austrian Trip Report.

67. This is the same memorandum that was cited in notes 20, 60, and 61.

68. Both the RNPPP and the TSVP have several copies of the report. The full text was printed by the *New York Times* on January 2, 1957.

69. Future of Voluntary Agencies in the Hungarian Refugee Problem, State Department cable from Thompson in Vienna, dated January 3, 1957, 4 p., the stamp on Voorhees' copy shows that he received it only on January 9, 1957, TSVP, Box K, Folder: Documents, Herbert Hoover.

70. Agnes Heller and Ferenc Feher, *From Yalta to Glasnost. The Dis-*

mantling of Stalin's Empire (Cambridge, MA: Blackwell, 1991), esp. chapter one, "Eastern Europe's Long Revolution Against Yalta."

71. Eisenhower to Hoover, draft, January 8, 2 p., TSVP, Box K, Folder: Documents, Herbert Hoover.

72. RNPPP, Box 2, Folder, Austria Trip (2/2), RN's Reading Material.

73. Voorhees, "Refugee Relief Essay," p. 29.

74. Markowitz, "Humanitarianism," p. 57.

75. Ibid., pp. 56–57.

76. "Harriman Scores Immigration Law," *New York Times*, April 30, 1957.

77. Markovitz, "Humanitarianism," p. 58.

78. Eisenhower, *Waging Peace*, pp. 58–99; on the refugees, see pp. 97–99. Robert Murphy, *Diplomat among Warriors. The Unique World of a Foreign Service Expert* (Garden City, NY: Doubleday and Company, 1964), pp. 427–32; and Sherman Adams, *First-Hand Report. The Story of the Eisenhower Administration* (New York: Harper and Brothers, 1961), pp. 254–57, 284–86. The only mention of Voorhees is on p. 258. Adams was governor of New Hampshire and assistant to the president between 1953 and 1958.

79. Fawn M. Brodie, *Richard Nixon. The Shaping of His Character* (New York: W. W. Norton and Company, 1981), p. 378; Stephen Ambrose, *Nixon. The Education of a Politician, 1913–1962* (New York: Simon and Schuster, 1987), pp. 422–26; and Tom Wicker, *One of Us. Richard Nixon and the American Dream* (New York: Random House, 1991), p. 157.

80. Earl Mazo, *Richard Nixon. A Personal and Political Portrait* (New York: Harper and Brothers, 1959).

81. Martin A. Bursten, *Escape from Fear* (Syracuse, NY: Syracuse University Press, 1958), pp. 120–21. This is also the first detailed description of the work at Camp Kilmer.

82. "To Richard Nixon," *The Papers of Martin Luther King, Jr.*, vol. 4, *Symbol of the Movement, January 1957–December 1958* (http://www.stanford.edu/group/King/publications/papers/vol4/570111.037-To Richard Nixon.htm), access date: October 21, 2006.

83. Interview with Ferenc Daday, Yorba Linda, CA, August 6, 2006. Daday was kind enough to meet me in the Nixon Library so that I could I ask my questions about his painting while looking at it. Hereafter: Daday interview.

84. *Time*, August 24, 1992, p. 11; *American Heritage* 44, no. 1 (February–March) 1993: 108–09; *Amerikai Magyar Hírlap*, August 21, 1992; *Új Világ*, August 21, 1992; and *Új Idők*, August 1, 1996.

85. Daday interview.

86. "Az elnöki kampány fogadása," [Reception in the presidential campaign], *Kaliforniai Magyarság*, October 13, 1972.

87. Daday interview.

88. Ibid.

89. Ibid.

90. Daday told me he was aware of the fact that the bridge was no longer there when Nixon visited the border.

91. Tamás Szabó, *Boy on the Rooftop. An Authentic Account of the Budapest Revolt by a Fifteen-Year-Old Freedom Fighter* (Boston: Little, Brown and Company, 1958); and László Beke, *A Student's Diary: Budapest, October 16–November 1, 1956* (New York: The Viking Press, 1957) are the two classic teenage freedom fighter (in Hungarian, *pesti srác*) accounts. The first fictional interpretation was James Dean Sanderson, *Boy with a Gun* (New York: Henry Holt and Company, 1958).

APPENDIX

THE 50TH ANNIVERSARY COMMEMORATIONS

On October 31, 2006, *Washington Post* columnist Anne Applebaum noted in her commentary that, "with a clutch of new books, a multitude of speeches and a score of conferences already underway, no one can claim that the 50th anniversary of the 1956 Hungarian Revolution has gone unmarked." Indeed, the documents in the appendix provide only a small sample of the activities that helped to reinforce old memories about 1956 and contributed to the creation of new ones.

Universities and colleges all over the United States hosted conferences and lectures. The academic participants offered traditional and revisionist interpretations about the various aspects of the 1956 Revolution, including the international milieu. The Hungarian Cultural Center in New York acted as a facilitator by setting up a panel of experts, the "traveling scholars," who visited a number of leading universities and presented their various views on the Revolution. The panel fit readily into the program of broader conferences, such as the one that was held at Harvard University.

The Hungarian Cultural Center, however, aimed to attract more than just the attention of academics and university students. The two giant Broadway billboards, showing images of the Revolution, were made to appeal to the imagination of the average New Yorker and the tourists. The purpose of the "ad campaign" is ably described in a document included in this appendix.

The Hungarian-American communities also partook in the commemoration with enthusiasm and organized various programs of remembrance. To their efforts leaders on various governmental levels, from President George W. Bush to New York Mayor Michael R. Bloomberg, responded with proclamations, letters, and speeches that describe the historic significance of Hungarian Revolution, which had attempted to overthrow totalitarian communism and end Soviet domination.

It is too soon to assess the collective impact of the various anniversary activities on society, yet they all seem to buttress Professor Glant's claim that the 1956 Hungarian Revolution is deeply rooted in American memory.

PETER PASTOR

ACADEMIC ACTIVITIES

COMMEMORATIONS OF THE
1956 HUNGARIAN REVOLUTION

NOVOSTI   Winter/Spring 2007
Newsletter of the Davis Center
for Russian and Eurasian Studies
Harvard University

To commemorate the 50th anniversary of the 1956 Hungarian revolution, the Harvard Project on Cold War Studies sponsored three events at the Davis Center in October 2006. The first event, on October 2, was a two-seminar presentation by László Borhi, a senior fellow of the Institute of History within the Hungarian Academy of Sciences. Borhi spoke initially about "Hungary's Postwar International Position and the Origins of the 1956 Revolution" and then gave a follow-up lecture on "The Fate of the 1956 Revolution and Its Legacy in Hungary Today."

The second commemorative event, a special symposium held on October 10, featured four distinguished scholars speaking about "The 1956 Hungarian Revolution in Retrospect: Failed Illusions?" The symposium was chaired by Mark Kramer, and the main speakers were Charles Gati, a professor of international affairs at Johns Hopkins University's School of Advanced International Studies; Csaba Békés, director of the Cold War History Research Center in Budapest; Attila Szakolczai, a senior research fellow at the Institute for the Study of the 1956 Hungarian Revolution in Budapest; and Federigo Argentieri, a professor of politics at John Cabot University in Rome. They covered both the domestic and the international dimensions of the 1956 revolution. Also attending the conference was the Hungarian ambassador to the United States, András Simonyi. More than 75 people in the audience took part in a lively discussion and question-and-answer period following the main presentations.

The third and largest commemorative event was a day-long international conference held on October 30, "The Hungarian Revolution in Historical Perspective: 50th-Anniversary Reassessments." The conference was divided into four panels: "The Crises in Hungary and Poland," "The 1956 Crises and the Soviet Union," "The Hungarian Revolution, the Soviet Bloc, and the West," and "The Aftermath and Legacy of the Hungarian Revolution." Each panel included four speakers who addressed different aspects of the panel's topic. Most of the speakers were prominent experts on the 1956 events who have done extensive research in former East-bloc archives as well as in Western archives. Three of the participants were connected either directly or indirectly to the 1956 upheavals—Julius Várallyay, a student leader in Budapest during the revolution; Sergei Khrushchev, the son of the Soviet leader Nikita Khrushchev; and Thomas W. Simons, Jr., the former U.S. ambassador to Poland. In addition to the participants from the United States, Hungary, and Russia, other countries represented at the conference included Italy and Germany. Each panel began with presentations by the speakers and then featured considerable time for discussion and debate. More than 120 people attended the conference, including some who had been in Hungary during the revolution. Several of them recounted their own experiences during the rebellion and the Soviet invasion, and they explained whether their opinion of those events had changed at all after the passage of 50 years.

Despite the diversity of views among the speakers at the three commemorative events, a few broad themes emerged. First, the participants generally agreed that the most crucial turning point in the 1956 revolution came on the first day, October 23, when the Soviet Presidium made its fateful decision to send Soviet troops into Budapest to help quell the unrest. This decision was approved on the evening of October 23 by Khrushchev and his colleagues after remarkably little debate. By 2:00 A.M. on October 24, the first Soviet troops were moving in. Far from putting an end to the rebellion, however, the entry of Soviet troops led to more intense fighting and large-scale bloodshed. What had begun as predominantly a revolt against hard-line Stalinist rulers in Hungary was transformed, by the introduction of Soviet forces, into an anti-Soviet uprising and a war of independence. One of Khrushchev's closest aides, Anastas Mikoyan, had warned about this danger when the Soviet Presidium met on the evening of October 23, but the other Presidium members brushed aside his concerns as they strongly endorsed the proposal for military intervention. The Soviet decision on October 23 did not mean that the much larger Soviet invasion on November 4 was inevitable, but it did mean that the odds of averting a full-scale crackdown by Soviet troops were much lower than they otherwise might have been. If the Hungarian authorities had been urged to restore order on their own, it is conceivable that they could have brought the unrest under control without endangering the Communist system in Hungary. But the entry of Soviet soldiers drastically changed the dynamics of the revolution. In that sense, the Soviet Union's initial military intervention in Hungary markedly narrowed the range of options available to Soviet leaders as the revolution unfolded.

A second point that emerged from the three commemorations was the inability of the reformist Hungarian Communist leader, Imre Nagy, to rise to the occasion. Nagy had implemented important reforms in Hungary when he served as prime minister from 1953 to 1955, but he had been removed by the Stalinist faction of the Hungarian Communist Party in the spring of 1955. When the unrest broke out in Budapest on the afternoon and evening of October 23, 1956, one of the main demands put forth by the protesters was for the return of Imre Nagy as prime minister. Had Nagy come to the main site of the unrest, delivered a stirring speech, and urged the protesters not to resort to violence, he very likely could have emerged triumphant as a reformist leader of what still would have been a Communist state. But Nagy failed to meet the protesters' hopes. He instead offered lackluster comments and seemed to fall back on the training he had undergone in the Soviet Union in the 1930s. Nagy's failure to take charge of the revolution during the first several days meant that it quickly slipped beyond his control. Although he did try to emerge as leader of a revolutionary government on October 28, he no longer had the authority he would have commanded on October 23. Nagy did establish a semblance of order by the beginning of November, but by then it was too late. All the structures of Communist rule in Hungary were disintegrating, and Soviet leaders had decided that they would have to resort to a much larger invasion to forestall the complete collapse of Communism in Hungary and to keep Hungary within the Warsaw Pact. Nagy's weaknesses as a leader thus contributed, in some measure, to the failure of the 1956 revolution. Nonetheless, the participants agreed that later on, when Nagy was imprisoned from late 1956 through mid-1958 and then executed, he did finally show immense courage, as he held his ground against the attempts of his Soviet-backed captors to humiliate him.

One final point that emerged was the importance of the Soviet invasion of Hungary in consolidating the Soviet bloc. Newly available documentation makes clear that the revolutionary ferment in Hungary was spreading into neighboring Communist countries, particularly Transylvania (in Romania), southern Slovakia, and western Ukraine. Even in more distant regions of the bloc, such as the Baltic states and Soviet Georgia, the Hungarian revolution sparked mass rallies of support and widespread restiveness. Moreover, the Hungarian revolution began at the same time that a crisis was still under way with Poland, where anti-Soviet unrest had reached an acute point. If Soviet leaders had not prevented the collapse of the Communist system in Hungary or had permitted Hungary to leave the Warsaw Pact, the consequences elsewhere in the bloc would have been enormous. The events of 1989 in Eastern Europe showed that the collapse of Communism in one Soviet-bloc country could rapidly spread to others. By resorting to a large-scale invasion in 1956, Khrushchev preserved the Soviet bloc. Many commentators and world leaders in 2006, when noting the 50th anniversary of the Hungarian revolution, had described the Soviet invasion as the "first nail in the coffin of the Soviet bloc" and the "first step in the collapse of Communism." In reality, as the commemorative events at Harvard showed, the precise opposite is true. The Soviet invasion of Hungary actually preserved the Soviet bloc for many years—a bloc that otherwise might have come unraveled in 1956–57. So long as Soviet leaders were willing to use ruthless force, if necessary, to hold the bloc together, they could preserve Communist rule in Eastern Europe. Not until Mikhail Gorbachev came along some 30 years after the Hungarian revolution did the calculus in Moscow fundamentally change. Thus, despite the significance of the 1956 events and the immense courage of many of the Hungarian fighters, the 1956 revolution in Hungary ultimately was a failure. Truly drastic change did not come until more than three decades later.

MARK KRAMER
Director, Project on Cold War Studies
Harvard University

HUNGARIAN REVOLUTION COMMEMORATED AT INDIANA UNIVERSITY

Bloomington, IN   October 25, 2006

Fifty years ago, protesters convened for a peaceful demonstration in Budapest, Hungary. Suddenly, the police attacked the group; many of the group had to fight with their bare hands against the firearms of the police.

In commemoration of that day, the Indiana University Hungarian Cultural Association and the Department of Central Eurasian Studies sponsored an event Monday to celebrate the country's independence, which was achieved after the attack inspired a nation-wide revolution against the government.

"What we celebrate is how the Hungarians used their bare hands to defeat the (pro-Soviet communists)," said Ágnes Fülemile, Hungarian chair in the Central Eurasian Studies Department.

The event, recalling the day known as the 1956 Hungarian Revolution, was also cosponsored by the IU Inner Asian and Uralic National Resource Center and the IU Russian and East European Institute.

The celebration opened with a speech by Fülemile describing the history and the causes of the revolution.

Fülemile is a native Hungarian, who grew up at a time when speaking of the revolution was forbidden, she said, because "they wanted to black paint the memory."

The commemoration brought Hungarian-born participants from around the state, to engage in a reception.

Among the attendees were older adults invited because of their Hungarian heritage and ties. The formal reception held afterward in the Indiana Memorial Union University Club President's Room hosted a variety of Hungarian dishes.

Fülemile said the revolution proved that a nation could stand up and fight for freedom.

"I hope that among the many historic events, those who attended understand [the] personal and emotional burden [of those] who lived through it," Fülemile said. "And also to discover and reveal what is believed in and how those who went through it, how they might have lived [during the time]."

SHANNON McENERNEY
Indiana Daily Student

TRAVELING SCHOLARS

The Traveling Scholars are three leading Hungarian historians—two from Hungary, one from George Washington University—who will visit the major universities on the East Coast to give lectures on the Revolution. Included will be visual presentations of the Revolution including photographs, video, film, and sound.

FILM PREMIERE EVENT: *A Hot Autumn in the Cold War*
    October 6th, 7:00 P.M.
    Hungarian Cultural Center (New York City)
    Screening of a new documentary *A Hot Autumn in the Cold War* by Judit Kóthy (in Hungarian with English subtitles).
    Q&A with the Traveling Scholars after the screening

ADDITIONAL LECTURES:
   October 2nd, 7–10:00P.M.
   The New School Transregional Center for Democracy (New York City)

   October 3rd, 12–1:20P.M.
   Princeton University (Princeton, New Jersey)

   October 4th, 4–6:00P.M.
   George Washington University (Washington, D.C.)

   October 5th, 5:30–8:00P.M.
   European Union Studies Center (CUNY) (NYC)

   October 9th, 3–5:00P.M.
   New York University (New York City)

   October 10th, 12–3:15P.M.
   Harvard University (Cambridge, Massachusetts)

REVOLUTION, IDEOLOGY AND MEMORY:
   October 24th, 7:30P.M.
   Hungarian Cultural Center
   An evening cosponsored with Radical Society Panelists Agnes Heller, Paul Berman, and Csaba Békés use the occasion of the 50th anniversary of the Hungarian Revolution to examine the relationship between revolution and ideology in today's world.

RESISTANCE AND REBIRTH:
   October 27th–November 16th, 2006
   Walter Reade Theater
   Lincoln Center together with the Hungarian Cultural Center is organizing a three-week long Hungarian Film Festival where 1956-related films will top the agenda.

Please visit www.culturehungary.org for updates.
For more information:

Hungarian Cultural Center
447 Broadway, New York, NY, 10012
212–750–4450 or info@culturehungary.org
Press inquiries: Stefany Anne Golberg, stefanyanne@culturehungary.org

Fifty Years' Perspective
on the Hungarian Revolution of 1956

Office of Interdisciplinary Programs and Centers
College of Arts and Sciences
Case Western Reserve University
Cleveland, OH   September 18–20, 2006

The program included keynote addresses by Professor István Deák (Columbia University), President Gregory Eastwood (Case Western Reserve University), Mrs. Edith Lauer (Hungarian-American Coalition), Professor Csaba Békés (Cold War Research Institute, Budapest), Professor John Grabowski (Case Western Reserve Univerity and the Western Reserve Historical Society), the Honorable George Herbert Walker, III (former U.S. Ambassador to the Republic of Hungary), Professor Kenneth Ledford (Case Western Reserve University), and Mr. Max Teleki (American Hungarian Federation) participated in a three-day conference commemorating the 1956 Hungarian Revolution. The program also included presentations on Hungarian immigration to Cleveland, roundtable discussions with Clevelanders who experienced the Revolution, a presentation on the "Freedom Fighters 56" Oral History Project, films and discussion. The conference was held at Case Western Reserve University in September 2006 and was sponsored by the College of Arts and Sciences, the Baker-Nord Center for the Humanities, the Department of History at Case Western Reserve University, and the Ohio Humanities Council, with the generous support of Mrs. Edith K. Lauer.

THE HUNGARIAN CULTURAL CENTER

*The Hungarian Cultural Center in New York is open-
ing the series of the celebration with a billboard campaign at the gate
of Times Square. Between September and November the 1st two huge
black and white 1956 contemporary photos will deliver a message that
there was a revolution in Hungary which had a global significance and
the country is still proud of this historical occurrence.*

This October 23rd commemorates the 50th Anniversary of the
1956 Hungarian Revolution. The Hungarian Cultural Center in New
York celebrates this event with a billboard campaign in the heart of
Times Square. Displayed from September to November 2006, two
billboards with photographs by professional photographer Erich Lessing and amateur Hungarian photographer Jenő Kiss, display the
phrase "Our Revolution Was Not A Movie." They deliver a message
that the revolution in Hungary had global significance and that the
country is still proud of this historic event. The billboard presents his-
tory-as-advertisement, presenting provocative images in a commercial
format that both tries to sell history as sexy and relevant while cri-
tiquing its own agenda. But perhaps most importantly, these poignant
photos and the message they portray the notions of courage and democratic freedom.

What is the relevancy of revolutionary ideas in 2006? Can mass
movements lead to positive social change anymore? This past June
President Bush traveled to Hungary to speak about '56; his visit
touched on what the role of the West can or should be in popular uprisings in other nations and the different ways the concept of "freedom"
is viewed. Although the '56 Revolution took place in Hungary, the
repercussions transcended time and place. It is often viewed in the context of the Cold War, which in some aspects confines the realities of the
Revolution. However, the intention of the billboard and the surrounding programming is to bring this historical event—its ideas and feelings, and the philosophical investigation of revolution—to the doorstep
of the American public.

We hope that the Times Square billboard campaign promotes dialogue and inquiry around a sometimes forgotten but nonetheless important historic occurrence.

BILLBOARD PHOTO ON BROADWAY. Courtesy of the Hungarian Cultural Center, New York.

BILLBOARD PHOTO ON BROADWAY. Courtesy of the Hungarian Cultural Center, New York.

BILLBOARD PHOTOS ON BROADWAY. Courtesy of the Hungarian Cultural Center, New York.

GOVERNMENTAL PROCLAMATIONS

UNITED STATES CONGRESS RESOLUTION ON THE 1956 HUNGARIAN REVOLUTION

By a unanimous and recorded vote, the House of Representatives passed H. Res. 479 on December 6, 2005. The resolution, which had been introduced by Congressman Tom Lantos (D-CA), recognizes the 50th anniversary of the 1956 Hungarian Revolution and enjoyed the support of the American Hungarian community and its various organizations.

The American Hungarian Federation declared that "With this resolution, the Congress has eloquently recognized the extraordinary sacrifices made by Hungarians 50 years ago, reaffirmed the historic ties and close friendship between the United States and Hungary and acknowledged the tremendous contribution made by Hungarians forced to flee tyranny and start a new life in the United States."

FULL TEXT OF H. RES. 479

WHEREAS on October 23, 1956, university students marching through the streets of Budapest were joined by workers and others until their numbers reached some 100,000 Hungarian citizens protesting against the communist government of Hungary and its domination by the Soviet Union, whereupon the Hungarian Security Police opened fire on the crowd and killed hundreds;

WHEREAS the Hungarian government under Prime Minister Imre Nagy released political prisoners, including major church leaders, took steps to establish a multi-party democracy, called for the withdrawal of all Soviet troops from Hungary, announced Hungary's withdrawal from the Warsaw Pact, and requested United Nations assistance in establishing Hungarian neutrality;

WHEREAS the Soviet Union launched a massive military counteroffensive against the revolt on November 4, 1956, sending tens of thousands of additional troops from the Soviet Union and launched air strikes, artillery bombardments and coordinated tank-infantry actions involving some 6,000 tanks which, remarkably, the outnumbered and under-equipped Hungarian Army and Hungarian workers resisted for several days;

WHEREAS Prime Minister Imre Nagy was seized by Soviet security forces despite assurances of safe passage for him to leave the Yugoslav Embassy in Budapest where he sought asylum, and he was taken to Romania and was subsequently tried and executed; Whereas an estimated one thousand two hundred Hungarians were tried and executed by the post-1956 Hungarian government;

WHEREAS an estimated 200,000 Hungarians fled their country in the aftermath of the Soviet suppression of the Hungarian uprising, and over 47,000 of these people eventually were able to settle in the United States, where they have contributed to the cultural diversity and the economic strength of this country;

WHEREAS the uprising of the Hungarian people in 1956 dramatically confirmed the widespread contempt in which the Hungarians held the Soviet Union and the underlying weakness of the communist system imposed by Soviet authorities in Central and Eastern Europe, as well as the strength of popular support for democratic principles and the right of the Hungarian people to determine their own national destiny;

WHEREAS on October 23, 1989, the Republic of Hungary proclaimed its independence, and in 1990 the Hungarian Parliament officially designated October 23 as a Hungarian national holiday, indicating that the legacy of the 1956 Revolution continues to inspire Hungarians to this day;

WHEREAS the people of Hungary are beginning a year-long celebration to mark the 50th anniversary of the Hungarian Revolution of 1956;

WHEREAS on March 12, 1999, the Government of Hungary, reflecting the will of the Hungarian people, formally acceded to the North Atlantic Treaty and became a member of NATO and on May 1, 2004, Hungary became a full member of the European Union; and

WHEREAS Hungary and the United States continue to expand their friendship and cooperation in all realms: Now, therefore, be it

RESOLVED, THAT THE HOUSE OF REPRESENTATIVES

(1) commends the people of Hungary as they mark the 50th anniversary of the 1956 Hungarian Revolution which set the stage for the ultimate collapse of communism in 1989 throughout Central and Eastern Europe, including Hungary, and two years later in the Soviet Union itself;

(2) expresses condolences to the people of Hungary for those who lost their lives fighting for the cause of Hungarian freedom and independence in 1956, as well as for those individuals executed by the Soviet and Hungarian communist authorities in the five years following the Revolution, including Prime Minister Imre Nagy;

(3) welcomes the changes that have taken place in Hungary since 1989, believing that Hungary's integration into NATO and the European Union, together with similar developments in the neighboring countries, will ensure peace, stability, and understanding among the great peoples of the Carpathian Basin; and

(4) reaffirms the friendship and cooperative relations between the governments of Hungary and the United States and between the Hungarian and American people.

PASSED THE HOUSE OF REPRESENTATIVES
DECEMBER 6, 2005.

WHITE HOUSE ISSUES PROCLAMATION COMMEMORATING THE 50TH ANNIVERSARY OF THE 1956 HUNGARIAN REVOLUTION

THE WHITE HOUSE, Office of the Press Secretary
(Greensboro, North Carolina)

50TH ANNIVERSARY OF THE
HUNGARIAN REVOLUTION BY THE
PRESIDENT OF THE UNITED STATES OF AMERICA

October 18, 2006

A PROCLAMATION

On the 50th anniversary of the Hungarian Revolution, we celebrate the Hungarians who defied an empire to demand their liberty; we recognize the friendship between the United States and Hungary; and we reaffirm our shared desire to spread freedom to people around the world.

The story of Hungarian democracy represents the triumph of liberty over tyranny. In the fall of 1956, the Hungarian people demanded change, and tens of thousands of students, workers, and other citizens bravely marched through the streets to call for freedom. Though Soviet tanks brutally crushed the Hungarian uprising, the thirst for freedom lived on, and in 1989 Hungary became the first communist nation in Europe to make the transition to democracy. The lesson of the Hungarian experience is clear: liberty can be delayed, but it cannot be denied. Today, this beautiful country has held democratic elections, established a free economy, and inspired millions around the world.

The United States is grateful for the warm relationship between our countries and for Hungary's efforts to expand freedom and democracy around the world in places such as the Balkans, Iraq, Afghanistan, and Cuba. By spreading the blessings of liberty, Hungary is helping to lay the foundation of peace for generations to come.

As we celebrate this anniversary, we also recognize the many ways Hungarian Americans have enriched and strengthened our country. Their spirit and hard work have contributed to the vitality, success, and prosperity of our Nation, and we continue to be inspired by their courage and conviction.

NOW, THEREFORE, I, GEORGE W. BUSH, President of the United States of America, by virtue of the authority vested in me by the Constitution and laws of the United States, do hereby proclaim October 23, 2006, as a day of recognition in honor of the 50th Anniversary of the Hungarian Revolution. I encourage all Americans to observe activities.

IN WITNESS WHEREOF, I have hereunto set my hand this eighteenth day of October, in the year of our Lord two thousand six, and of the Independence of the United States of America the two hundred and thirty-first.

GEORGE W. BUSH

THE HONORABLE GEORGE W. BUSH
PRESIDENT OF THE UNITED STATES OF AMERICA
WASHINGTON

October 20, 2006

Dear Mr. President,

It is with great appreciation that we Hungarians have read the proclamation you issued on the occasion of the 50th anniversary of the Hungarian Revolution and Freedom Fight declaring October 23, 2006, a day of recognition of those bloody yet uplifting days half a century ago. I would like you to know that your noble gesture underlining the strong friendship and ever closer ties between our nations and expressing the American people's recognition for our heroic struggle to rid ourselves of tyranny has touched my fellow Hungarians.

The memory of 1956, when a small nation stood up courageously against the mighty forces of a brutal communist dictatorship, will always live on in Hungary. This event of history has also acquired new significance as more and more people across the globe express the desire to live in free societies. Hungary is proud to make common efforts with the United States to help all these forces in their quest for democracy. I look forward to working with you on further enriching bilateral relations, achieving our common goals, and making the world a safer and better place.

Sincerely yours,
LÁSZLÓ SÓLYOM
President of the Republic of Hungary

STATE OF NEW YORK
EXECUTIVE CHAMBER

PROCLAMATION

WHEREAS, the citizens of the Empire State have a longstanding tradition of acknowledging significant milestones and events of great importance in history and, thefore, we are proud to join with the Hungarian community both here in New York State and worldwide to commemorate the 50th anniversary of the 1956 Hungarian Revolution and Freedom Fight; and

WHEREAS, throughout the history of mankind, the cause of freedom has been the single most compelling and important objective of nearly every conflict among nations, religions, and political ideologies, and its fundamental relevance to the success of any country is witnessed in the legacy of Hungary, its people and a wonderful culture spawed by ideas that are the outgrowth of a free and progressive society—the events that unfold 50 years ago in Budapest on the evening of

October 23, 1956 are remembered for their profound influence on the history of this great country as they inspired the national pride of the Hungarian people that burns strongly today; and

WHEREAS, as a group of students gathered to call for a peaceful demonstration against the Communist regime and its repressive policies, they were joined by 200,000 of their fellow citizens in a march for national independence and democracy; tragically, their calls for justice were met by gunfire, and courageous Hungarian battled highly trained Soviet soldiers and their state-of-the-art weaponary, and not until heavy reinforcements arrived from Moscow was the uprising finally suppressed; and

WHEREAS, the global community of humankind has never forgotten the thousands of men, women and children who died fighting in the streets, the thousands who were imprisoned and executed, or the thousands of others who were forced to flee their homeland, many of whom found refuge in the United States of America and in New York State; and

WHEREAS, anyone whohas a love of country and freedom shares a special relationship with the Hungarian Freedom Fighters, whose spirit remains one of the greatest examples of human courage the world has ever seen, as their unrelenting commitment to justice, liberty and human rights—despite overwhelming odds—was a defining moment in the lives of millions around the world and so crucially important that we join to commemorate the anniversary of the 1956 Hungarian Revolution and Freedom Fight and the noble example of the Hungarian people with whom I proudly share my ancestral heritage;

NOW, THEREFORE, I GEORGE E. PATAKI, Governor of the State of New York, hereby proclaim October 23, 2006 as the

50TH ANNIVERSARY OF THE
1956 REVOLUTION AND FREEDOM FIGHT
IN HUNGARY DAY

in the Empire State.

State Seal

> Given under my hand and the Privy Seal
> of the State at the Capitol in the City of
> Albany this twelfth day of
> October in the year two thousand six.

Signed
JOHN C. CAHILL
Secretary to the Governor

Signed
GEORGE E. PATAKI
Governor

OFFICE OF THE MAYOR
CITY OF NEW YORK

PROCLAMATION

WHEREAS: Fifty years ago, a courageous group of Hungarians asserted their right to self-rule, fighting for freedom against communist oppressors. The Soviet Union brutally thwarted the Hungarin Revolution of 1956—but the bravery of those freedom fighters inspired men and women in Hungary and throughout the world to dream of a brighter future. Today, the Republic of Hungary is a free, multi-party democracy.

WHEREAS: The Hungarian Cultural Center in New York is commemorating this important anniversary with two billboards in Times Square with inspiring photographs from 1956, celebrating the incredible daring and resolve of real heroes who stood up against oppression. In addition, the the Hungarian [Cultural] Center will be launching reimaginefreedom.org a Web site with essays, photographs, time lines, a discussion forum, and more—a detailed tribute to the 1956 revolution that will allow Hungarians, New Yorkers, and people around the globe to better understand this historic event.

WHEREAS: Thucydides, the ancient Greek historian, wrote that "the secret of happiness is freedom, and the secret of freedom, courage." For centuries, New York has stood as a beacon of freedom and opportunity, countless immigrants, many of them Hungarian, have come to our shores to pursue their dreams. Today, we honor the legacy of the Hungarian patriots who fought in the name of the burning desire for liberty that we all share.

NOW THEREFORE, I, MICHAEL R. BLOOMBERG, Mayor of the City of New York, in recognition of this important anniversary, do hereby proclaim Monday, October 23rd, 2006, in the City of New York as

HUNGARIAN REVOLUTION OF 1956 DAY

City Seal

IN WITNESS WHEREOF I have hereunto set my hand and caused the seal of the City of New York to be affixed.

Signed
MICHAEL R. BLOOMBERG
Mayor

ACTIVITIES BY THE HUNGARIAN-AMERICAN COMMUNITIES

WEST COAST:

LOS ANGELES: 1956-RELATED ACTIVITIES AND EVENTS

The "Remember Hungary 1956" Coordinating Committee chaired by Éva Szörényi (Kossuth Prize-winning actress of the Hungarian National Theater), organized and sponsored a series of events and activities to commemorate the fiftieth anniversary of the Hungarian Revolution and War of Liberation.

EXHIBITS: The photographs of the 1956 October events in Hungary, taken by the Austrian Erich Lessing, were shown at the Doheny Memorial Library of the University of Southern California in Los Angeles, from September 17 to December 17, 2006. A similar photo exhibit was also on view at Stanford University in Palo Alto, from September 19 to December 19, 2006.

INTERNATIONAL COMPETITION: A call for a suitable music composition honoring the 1956 Revolution and Freedom Fight attracted a number of submissions. On October 14 the prizewinner, composer and organ virtuoso András Gábor Virágh from Budapest, performed his *Elegia-1956*, a composition for voice and organ, at the American-Hungarian Baptist Church of Alhambra,. The vocal part was sung by operatic soprano, Ms. Ella Lee.

COMMEMORATIVE ASSEMBLY: On October 22, 2006, about eight hundred people attended the nearly two-hour long ceremony at the Memorial Statue of the 1956 Hungarian Revolution on Cardinal József Mindszenty Square in McArthur Park. Wreaths and countless bouquets of flowers were placed at the foot of the monument by some thirty organizations and many individuals. The artistic part of the program included music, and choral songs. Patriotic poems appropriate for the occasion were also recited. The keynote address was presented in English and in Hungarian by the former Los Angeles Consul General of the Hungarian Republic Szabolcs Kerek-Barczy, while a letter of greetings from the President of the Republic of Hungary László Sólyom was read by Consul General Ferenc Bösenbacher. Several 1956-related proclamations from federal, state, and local office holders were also read to the delight of the cheering crowd. Among these were the Proclamation of the President of the United States George W. Bush, the Proclamation of the Governor of New York State George Pataki, and a letter from the Governor of California Arnold Schwarzenegger. Letters from the mayors of Los Angeles County, and the City of Los Angeles were also read to the assembled. The festivity at the Memorial Statue was followed by an evening memorial program at the Magyar Ház [Hungarian House] in downtown Los Angeles. During this last event Consul General Bösenbacher presented the commemorative medal, the "Hero of Liberty," accompanied by a certificate signed by President Sólyom, Prime Minister Ferenc Gyurcsány, and by the doyen of Hungarian historians, Domokos Kossáry, the president of the Hungarian '56 Memorial Committee that issued the decoration. Over fifty locals received the medal.

PROMOTION OF THE HUNGARIAN FESTIVAL CONCERT: The Pacific Symphony Orchestra of Orange County, and the "Carpathian Folk Quartet" visiting from Hungary performed at the Orange County Performing Art Center on October 23, 26, and 29, 2006. They played works of Béla Bartók, Johannes Brahms, and Zoltán Kodály. The introductory narrative was by Carl St. Clair, the music director of the orchestra.

RELIGIOUS COMMEMORATION: A high mass was celebrated by Cardinal Roger Mahoney in memory of the 1956 Hungarian Revolution in the new Cathedral of Our Lady of the Angeles on November

5, 2006. The mass included the *Missa Brevis* of Zoltán Kodály, performed by the Saint Charles Choir under the direction of Paul Salamunovich.

COINING OF A MEDAL: A commemorative medal was designed under the supervision of the Coordinating Committee and minted in limited numbers by the Mint of Hungary, Inc., in Budapest. The medals are in silver, and bronze, and were already available for sale in late 2005. The net income was used to support ongoing activities and events for the commemoration of the fiftieth anniversary.

AUDIO-VISUAL MATERIAL: At the request of the Coordinating Committee, a thirty-minute documentary film on the 1956 Hungarian Revolution was produced pro bono by DUNA TV in Budapest. DVD copies have been made available at no charge to any responsible party for public presentations.

THE HISTORY OF THE REVOLUTION IN PRINT: One thousand copies of an eight-page illustrated pamphlet commemorating the 1956 Hungarian Revolution was purchased from its publisher, the Hungarian Cultural Society of Connecticut, and distributed at no charge to interested guests attending '56-related activities. The pamphlet was written by Csaba Téglás, and was first printed by Texas A&M University Press in 1998.

BOOK PROJECT: The publication of *Remeber Hungary: 1956. Essays on the Hungarian Revolution and War of Independence* by Professor Tibor Glant of the University of Debrecen, Hungary, was fully sponsored by the "Remember Hungary 1956" Los Angeles Coordinating Committee. The author also received from the committee a six-month stipend, spent at Montclair State University, NJ, for the research and preparation of the manuscript for publication. The book is published by the Center for Hungarian Studies and Publications, Inc., which prints the works of Hungarian historians in English. These are distributed by Columbia University Press.

Reported by
ANTAL BEJCZY

MEMORIAL STATUE WITH THE MYTHICAL TURUL BIRD
József Mindszenty Square, McArthur Park, Los Angeles, CA

MEMORIAL STATUE OF THE 1956 HUNGARIAN REVOLUTION
József Mindszenty Square, McArthur Park, Los Angeles, CA

CEREMONY AT THE MEMORIAL STATUE ON OCTOBER 22, 2006
József Mindszenty Square, McArthur Park, Los Angeles, CA

GOVERNOR ARNOLD SCHWARZENEGGER

Ms. Eva Szorenyi   October 6, 2006
President
Remember Hungary 1956 Committee
4537 Craft Avenue
Studio City, California 91602

Dear Ms. Szorenyi,

Thank you for inviting me to speak at your event to commemorate the 50th anniversary of the 1956 Hungarian Uprising. I am honored by your invitation and continue to be impressed by your efforts to memorialize this extraordinary event in world history.

Although I unfortunately cannot attend your event, I want to pass along my tremendous respect and admiration for those who took part in Hungary's historic fight for freedom. As a teenager, I remember the faces of the Hungarian refugees flooding over the Austrian border, and as someone who went on to move around the world to pursue the dream of freedom and opportunity, I continue to be greatful for the heroic sacrifies made by the Hungarian freedom fighters.

It is an honor for me to help you commemorate the remarkable sacrifices these freedom fighters made in the name of economic, political and spiritual freedom. I cannot overstate my appreciation for all this movement did to promote our unique way of life, and I am so proud that thousands of Hungarian freedom fighters and refugees found their way to our Golden State to pusue this same dream of freedom, tolerance and opportunity.

I join you in honoring the Hungarian fighters who gave so much so that all of us could pursue lives free of tyranny and oppresiion. We will always remember that they made the ultimate sacrifice so taht this promise of freedom could be extended to new generations.

With warm regards and best wishes for a succesful event,

ARNOLD SCHWARZENEGGER

THE WHITE HOUSE
WASHINGTON

Hungarian Freedom Fighters Federation   November 22, 2006
Studio City, California

Dear Friends:

Thank you for the Hungarian Freedom Fighters' 50th Anniversary gold medal. I was honored to accept this important award.

Thank you for your efforts to commemorate the great history of your people. The lesson of the Hungarian Revolution is clear: Liberty can be delayed, but it cannot be denied. As people across the world step forward to claim their own freedom, they can draw inspiration from your example and hope from your success.

May God bless you, and may God continue to bless the people of our two nations.

Sincerely,
GEORGE W. BUSH

LOS ANGELES COUNTY PAYS TRIBUTE TO THE 50TH ANNIVERSARY OF THE 1956 HUNGARIAN REVOLUTION

AMERICAN HUNGARIAN   October 20, 2006
JOURNAL

On October 10, 2006, the Los Angeles County Board of Supervisors paid a special tribute in honor of the 50th Anniversary of the 1956 Hungarian Revolution. During its regular meeting, the Board, presided over by County Mayor Michael Antonovich, issued a resolution which proclaimed that the County proudly joined the

Hungarian people in this commemoration which honors the courage of Hungarian Freedom Fighters who fought so valiantly for freedom and democracy. Attending this memorable presentation was a distinguished delegation of diplomats and Hungarian community leaders consisting of 1956 freedom fighters and former 1956 refugees, religious, academic and organization representatives, Hungarian scout leaders, and the Karpatok folk dance members.

With the delegation standing on stage behind the Board of Supervisors and Scouts holding the Hungarian colors, Mayor Antonovich, a great friend of the Hungarian community, presented the resolution to Ms. Éva Szörényi, delegation chair, in the company of Dr. George Osopay, cochair, Ilona Reksz, coordinator, and County Commissioner Dr. Frank de Balogh. Miss Szörényi accepted the beautiful resolution and with heartfelt words expressed her thanks on behalf of the Hungarian community. Consul General Ferenc Bösenbacher conveyed the thanks of the Hungarian Government and read the official U.S. Congressional resolution marking the 50th Anniversary of the Revolution. He was followed by Polish Consul General Krystyna Tokarska-Biernacik, who described the solidarity and friendship of Poland and Hungary during the crucial events of 1956.

The Hungarian delegation then expressed its appreciation to the Board by making a special presentation to each County supervisor for his past support of Hungary. Mayor Antonovich asked County Commissioner de Balogh to coordinate this presentation. The Commissioner began by noting that the Board had been very supportive of Hungarian community causes, commemorations, and cultural events for more than two decades. An important example of that was in 1999 when the Board passed a resolution sponsored by Supervisor Mike Antonovich endorsing the admission of Hungary into NATO. This endorsement by the nation's largest county of 10 million persons was very helpful in obtaining subsequent endorsements from the California State Legislature and from California Governor Gray Davis. Those contributed to winning the support of the Congress and the White House for Hungary's NATO membership.

HIGHLIGHTS OF FORMER CONGRESSMAN ERNIE KONNYU'S SPEECH COMMEMORATING 1956

FIRST UNITED METHODIST CHURCH   October 21, 2006
Palo Alto, California

U.S. Senator John F. Kennedy, said in his October 23, 1957, speech on the first anniversary of the Hungarian Revolution:

> October 23, 1956, is a day that will live forever in the annals of free men and nations. It was a day of courage, conscience and triumph. No other day since history began has shown more clearly the eternal unquenchability of man's desire to be free, whatever the odds against success, whatever the sacrifice required.

Here I stand in a church today, a Hungarian born former U.S. Congressman, quoting a great political leader, John Kennedy. Indeed I am expressing our political thoughts about the 1956 Hungarian revolution. Yet in the Hungary...yes! the Soviet Union dominated communist Hungary...of the 1950s such expression could have gotten us, commemorators, a jail sentence or worse. For our anti-state activities we could have been hung by the neck and left twisting in the wind. And all that for political expression that did not adhere to the Stalinist line demanded by the ruling party Chief, Mátyás Rákosi, led Communist Party of 1950's Hungary....

The horrible treatment of the people was expressed this way by the noted Hungarian poet, Gyula Illyés, in a portion of his poem titled, "One Sentence On Tyranny":

> Where there is tyranny there is tyranny;
> Not only in the gunbarrel, not only in the prison cell.
> Not only in the torture rooms, not only in the nights,
> In the voice of the shouting guard; there is tyranny.
> Not only in the speech of the prosecutor pouring like dark smoke,
> In the confessions, in the wall tapping of prisoners. There is tyranny....

As we watch history roll by us we can see how Hungarians learned to hate communism. Ronald Reagan in his 1987 speech in Arlington defined the hate developed for communism this way, "How do you tell a communist? Well! It's someone who reads Marx and Lenin. And how do you tell an anti-communist? It is someone who understands Marx and Lenin." The protesting Hungarian students and the proletariat workers were forced to read Marx and Lenin by the government. As a result they understood. So they marched in protest, called out for economic change and for removal of the occupying Soviet troops from Hungary. They knew the danger they were creating for themselves but desperate people do desperate things.

So what could the repressed citizens in a failed economy of 1956 Hungary do but revolt! On October 23, 1956, the people were led by students who sensed no political freedom after graduation. They were led by factory workers who saw no economic hope. Their wages were so low and their freedoms were so limited that leaving their jobs to face Soviet tanks seemed like a wise choice. Charging with rifles and Molotov cocktails, first hundreds, than thousands than tens of thousands of brave Hungarians exploded in harms way.

It was magnificent! That charge caused the dictatorship to fall, for even the rulers sensed that the people were with the freedom fighters! The Hungarian Army joined the side of the Revolution with its leader, General Pál Maléter. The general announced that he will accept the orders of the provisional government now headed by the popular former prime minister, Imre Nagy. The commanding Soviet general listened to the revolutionary leader's demands for Soviet troops to leave Hungary and they abandoned the streets of Budapest to the freedom fighters.

By October 30 the revolution appeared totally victorious! Prime minister Imre Nagy declared Hungary a democratic republic and the country announced it's military neutrality by abandoning the Soviet-run Warsaw Pact. That stroke seemingly destroyed for the first time in the Soviet block of countries one key national column propping up the Soviet hegemony in central Europe....

To the sorrow of the Revolution, victory was short lived. The Soviet Red Army attacked Hungary in force on November 4, 1956, and crushed the newly born legitimate government. Thousands of Hungarians were killed during the fighting or afterward in judicial murders carried out by the new Soviet created puppet government of Communist Party Chief János Kádár....

For more than thirty years Hungary's Kádár regime tried to break the backbone of the nation, ruled by repression, created the so-called "goulash communism" but generally mismanaged the economy. Facing total political bankruptcy, in the summer of 1989 the Communist government surrendered and agreed to start roundtable negotiation with the opposition parties. At the end of September an agreement was signed. The peaceful transformation of the system to democracy was achieved.

Seventeen years ago, on October 23, 1989, a democratic republic was proclaimed from the balcony of the Hungarian Parliament, where thirty-three years earlier a revolutionary crowd demanded independence and the withdrawal of Soviet troops from Hungary....With the free elections held five months later the process was completed, Hungary became a republic and a western-type parliamentary democracy....

We American-Hungarians have every reason to be proud of the historic role Hungarians played in undermining the Soviet empire in 1956....Indeed, the blood of the 1956 Revolution was a key development in redeeming the West from the Evil Empire! We must not allow this historic event to be forgotten or overshadowed....

Finally, I raise my right arm to the 1956 freedom fighters in this church today. Let me as a retired major in the United States Air Force Reserve, and as a former United States Congressman salute you for the freedom you gave the Western world. Thank you freedom fighters. Thank you for all of us!

ERNIE KONNYU

Ernie Konnyu is a Hungarian-born American residing
in Saratoga, California, and is a former member of both
the United States Congress and the California Legislature.
While he was a State Assemblyman, Konnyu secured
funding and location for the statue "Gloria Victis" erected
in memory of the 1956 Hungarian Revolution
in the courtyard of the San Francisco State Office Building.

GLORIA VICTIS STATUE
by Olga Rozsa
Dedicated on October 23, 1986,
in the Courtyard of the California State Building
San Francisco, CA

SAN FRANCISCO AND SEATTLE: 1956-RELATED ACTIVITIES AND EVENTS

SAN FRANCISCO: The commemoration of the fiftieth anniversary of the 1956 Hungarian Revolution was held on the evening of October 23, 2006. The Renaissance School Children Choir opened the ceremonies with the national anthems of Hungary and the United

States, followed by prayers for peace by leaders of several religious denominations. Following the welcoming remarks of Honorary Consul General of the Republic of Hungary Eva E. Voisin, the U.S. Congressional Resolution was read by Representative Tom Lantos. The message of California Governor Arnold Schwarzenegger was then presented, followed by Senator Jackie Speier's reading of the Resolution of the California Legislature. The Proclamation of the City and County San Francisco, declaring October 23, 2006, as "Hungarian Freedom Fighters Day in San Francisco," was read by Gavin Newsom, mayor of the city and county of San Francisco. Following the ceremony a reception was held.

SEATTLE, WA: The commemoration events started at the Congregational Church on Mercer Island on the evening of October 20, 2006. The movie presentations *Cry Hungary* (1986), and *Freedom's Fury* (2006) were followed by a panel discussion. The panelists were eyewitnesses to the Revolution of 1956. This event was geared especially toward those who were too young at the time to remember the actual details of the Revolution.

RELIGIOUS COMMEMORATION: On October 21 an Archdiocesan Mass was held at the St. James Cathedral. The mass was celebrated by Bishop Joseph Tyson and the Opus 7 Choir sang the *Missa Brevis* by Zoltán Kodály. After the communion the Protestant Pastor, Rev. Sándor Szabó, also gave a sermon. The mass was followed by a reception attended by dignitaries, including the lieutenant governor, and the attorney general of Washington State.

MEMORIAL CONCERT: On October 22, 2006, the award-winning international pianist Endre Hegedűs, professor of the Liszt Ferenc Academy of Music in Budapest, gave a concert at Benaroya's Nordstrom Auditorium.

UNIVERSITY LECTURE: On October 23 an in-depth discussion was held in the Walker Ames Room of Kane Hall, on the University of Washington campus. The topic was Hungary, its past, including the 1848 and 1956 Revolutions, and its future in the European Union. Dr. Péter Dobay, professor at the University of Pécs (Seattle's sister city in Hungary), made the presentation and moderated the discussion. The guests included David Hughes, president of the Hungarian-American Chamber of Commerce of the Pacific NW, former

US commercial attaché to Hungary, founder of the American Chamber of Commerce in Budapest, and eyewitness to the political transformation of Hungary in 1989.

Reported by
ANTAL BEJCZY

EAST COAST

FAILED ILLUSIONS — PRESENTATION OF PROFESSOR CHARLES GATI'S NEW BOOK ON THE 1956 REVOLUTION

EMBASSY OF HUNGARY   September 20, 2006
Washington

On September 20, the Embassy of Hungary hosted the presentation of the recently published book *Failed Illusions—Moscow, Washington and the 1956 Hungarian Revolution* by Charles Gati, Senior Adjunct Professor at Johns Hopkins University School of Advanced International Studies.

Professor Gati, who is considered among the top U.S. scholars on the politics of Central and Eastern Europe, left Hungary in 1956 after having participated in the revolution. Gati deals with the topic from unorthodox perspectives while his book reveals surprising new findings about the revolution and its international political context.

Ambassador Simonyi opened the event and introduced the author as a friend and an exemplary Hungarian and American patriot. He underlined the spirit of freedom that the revolution in 1956 symbolized. Professor Gati presented his book and his main theses. He addressed the question of the unfortunate timing of the revolution in terms of the international political environment; the controversial role, and often indecisive behavior, of the martyr Prime Minister Imre Nagy; the hesitation on the part of the Soviet leadership on military intervention and the crackdown after the lynching on Republic Square. He elaborated on his hypotheses, according to which the revolution could have succeeded given some of the mistakes had not been made in 1956.

Approximately 250 guests attended the lecture and reception at the Hungarian Embassy. Among the guests of honor were Secretary of Commerce Carlos Gutierrez; Hungary's Minister for Foreign Affairs Kinga Göncz; Director of the CIA General Michael Hayden; former National Security Advisor Zbigniew Brzezinski; Former US Ambassador to Hungary Philip Kaiser; Pál Maléter, Jr., son of the late Pál Maléter, Defense Minister of the Imre Nagy government and martyr of the revolution; Jackson Diehl, editor of the Washington Post; New York Times reporter Neil Lewis; Professor Mark Kramer.

During the Q&A session, Secretary Gutierrez, Minister Göncz and Brzezinski emphasized the significance of the revolution for the eventual democratization of Central and Eastern Europe as well as for the future of those nations still suffering under oppression.

Representatives of the U.S. and Hungarian media, many former 1956 revolutionaries, and the leaders of Hungarian American organizations also took part in the event, which was recorded by C-SPAN television.

ANDREW VAJNA'S *CHILDREN OF GLORY* [SZABADSÁG, SZERELEM] PREMIERS IN THE U.S.

AMERICAN HUNGARIAN   November 10, 2006
JOURNAL

Producer Andy Vajna and movie director Krisztina Goda enjoyed a special honor on Sunday, October 29th: their jointly helmed film was the first Hungarian movie shown privately to a U.S. President and his guests. The event was a tribute by the White House and the President's guests to Hungary and the 50th anniversary of the revolution.

The screening is of distinctive importance given that movies are rarely shown at the White House. It is also an extraordinary gesture from George W. Bush that despite his numerous duties he devoted nearly five hours to *Children of Glory*.

Apart from Vajna and Goda the White House also hosted at the exclusive screening of the movie Nancy Goodman Brinker and April H. Foley, the former and the current U.S. Ambassador to Hungary. George Pataki, Governor of New York State, András Simonyi, Hungarian Ambassador to the United States and György Oláh, Nobel Prize Laureate in Chemistry also attended. In representation of the movie industry, Tony Curtis was also present and Hungarian tycoon Sándor Demján, executive producer of the film, and his wife attended, as well. Kossuth Prize Laureate Actress Éva Szörényi presented a Certificate of Appreciation to the President from the "Remember Hungary 1956" Committee.

The end credits were ensued by sustained applause and the First Lady and the President both expressed their heartfelt congratulations to Vajna.

Children of Glory remains a huge attraction in Hungary. Over 128,000 people have already watched it in cinemas nationwide. Meanwhile, the international career of the movie continues. *Children of Glory* was screened at a special gala on November 2 in Los Angeles.

GUEST LIST FOR THE *CHILDREN OF GLORY* SCREENING AND DINNER AT THE WHITE HOUSE

AMERICAN HUNGARIAN   November 10, 2006
JOURNAL

THE PRESIDENT and *MRS. BUSH*
    The Honorable Judy Ansley, Special Assistant to the President and Senior Director for European Affairs, National Security Council

MR. STEPHEN ANSLEY, Spouse of the Special Assistant to the President and Senior Director for European Affairs

The Honorable *JOSHUA BOLTEN*, Assistant to the President and Chief of Staff, *MRS. STACY BOLTEN* (Mother)

MR. TONY CURTIS, Actor, *MRS. JILL ANN CURTIS*

MR. SANDOR DEMJAN, Chairman, TriGranit Development Corporation, *MRS. LIDIA DEMJAN*

MR. GEORGE DOZSA, President, Hungarian American Coalition, *MRS. MATILDA B. DOZSA*

The Honorable *APRIL FOLEY*, United States Ambassador to Hungary

DR. KATALIN ILONA FULOP, Director of Communication, Intercom Rt.

MS. KRISZTINA GODA, Director, Flashback Kft.

MRS. ANN HADLEY (Wife of The Honorable *STEPHEN J. HADLEY*), Assistant U.S. Attorney, U.S. Department of Justice

MR. LASZLO HAMOS, President, Hungarian Human Rights Foundation, *MRS. ZSUZSA ERDELYI HAMOS*

MR. STEPHEN HARMATH, Regional Vice President, USA, Free Hungarian Journalist Association, *MRS. ILONA HARMATH*

MR. JOHN S. KOROSSY, JR., President, United Hungarian Society of Cleveland/ World Federation of Hungarian Veterans

MRS. ILDIKO KOROSSY, President, Magyar Club of Cleveland

The Honorable *STEVE C. LATOURETTE*, United States Representative, *MRS. JENNIFER LATOURETTE*

MS. ANDREA LAUER-RICE, Founder and CEO; Member of The Hungarian American Coalitions Board of Directors, Lauer Learning, *MR. CHARLES BARTON RICE, JR.*

MRS. AGNES LENDVAI-LINTNER (Spouse of *MR. EMERY LENDVAI-LINTNER*)

MR. PÁL MALÉTER, son of former Hungarian Defense Minister Maléter, *MRS. ANDREA MALÉTER*

MR. LESLIE L. MEGYERI, Chief Financial Officer, American Hungarian Reformed Federation, *MRS. KATHRYN MEGYERI*

DR. GEORGE OLAH, Nobel Laureate, *MRS. JUDITH OLAH*

DONALD P. AND KATHERINE B. LOKER, Distinguished Professor of Organic Chemistry, Univesity of Southern California

MR. LASZLO PASZTOR, National President Emeritus and Member of the Presidium of the National Federation of the American Hungarians, Inc., Honorary President; Hungarian Freedom Fighters Federation, *MR. LASZLO PASZTOR, JR.* (Son)

The Honorable *GEORGE E. PATAKI*, Governor of New York, *MRS. ELIZABETH ROWLAND PATAKI*, First Lady of New York

MS. MONICA SELES, Tennis Pro, *MRS. ESTER SELES* (Mother)

His Excellency *ANDRÁS SIMONYI*, Ambassador of the Republic of Hungary, *MRS. NADA P. SIMONYI*

MS. ÉVA SZÖRÉNYI, President, Remember Hungary 1956, *MR. STEVEN ORMENYI* (Son)

MR. MAXIMILIAN N. TELEKI, President, Hungarian American Coalition, *MRS. WENDY TELEKI*

MR. ANDREW G. VAJNA, Producer, *Children of Glory*

The Honorable *GEORGE H. 'BERT' WALKER III*, Former American Ambassador to Hungary

MR. DAMON WILSON, Director for Central and Eastern Europe, National Security Council

New York's Coordinating Committee for the Commemoration of the 1956 Hungarian Revolution

ISAAC STERN AUDITORIUM,   October 15, 2006
Carnegie Hall

New York City's Carnegie Hall hosted a Gala Memorial Concert commemorating the 50th Anniversary of the 1956 Hungarian Revolution organized by the Coordinating Committee for the Commemoration of the 1956 Hungarian Revolution. Dr. Paul Szilagyi, Chairman on the American Hungarian Federation's 1956 Committee, initiated the effort working with Geroge Lovas of the Hungarian Freedom Fighters Federation who would work to establish the Coordinating Committee for the Commemoration of the 1956 Hungarian Revolution. Numerous AHF members, local organizations and individuals joined the effort leading to this tremendous success. AHF seeded the fundraising effort with it's first $5,000.00 and later provided accounting and good offices, enabling contributions of almost $250,000.00! The long-term plan is to finance, through donations, a permanent Memorial to the 1956 Hungarian Revolution to be located in New York City. Support this worthy cause. AHF would like to extend special thanks to it's members who played a key role on the committee, providing both financial and logistical and strategic help: Sandor Murray, AHF and NY 1956 Committee Treasurer; Stephen Varga, AHF President ex-Officio and Chairman of the William Penn Association; Arpad Drotos of the Hungarian Reformed Church of New York; Csaba Teglas; and George Lovas.

The Governor of New York George Pataki opened the Gala. Ambassador of Hungary András Simonyi read the greetings of His Excellency László Sólyom, President of Hungary. Hungarian Members of Parliament, Zsolt Németh, the president, and Vilmos Szabó, the vice president of the Parliamentary Committee on Foreign Relations, were present.

The performing artists included the Takács Quartet (strings), Péter Frankl (piano), Viktória Vizin, (mezzosoprano), András Molnár (tenor) and the Yale Philharmonic Orchestra with conductor Shinik Hahm. The orchestra played and the singers sang compositions by Bartók, Liszt, Kodály, Berlioz, and Erkel.

The program also included a world premiere: "Path of the Extraordinary," a symphonic poem by young Hungarian composer Ádám Balázs, which was commissioned for the occasion. Read more about the performers and program on the official Coordinating Committee Web page www.hungary1956nyc.org or on the New York Hungarian Culture Center Web page, www.culturehungary.org.

The concert was preceded by a Memorial Mass at 12:00 noon at St. Patrick's Cathedral.

For pictures, and article on the event in Hungarian by AHF's László Papp, and additional information, see www.gimagine.com.

FERENC DADAY, *VICE PRESIDENT NIXON VISITS ANDAU*, The Richard Nixon Library, Yorba Linda, CA

THE *CHILDREN OF GLORY* SCREENING AT THE WHITE HOUSE, October 29, 2006

ACTRESS ÉVA SZÖRÉNYI, PRESIDENT GEORGE W. BUSH, LAURA BUSH, AND ISTVÁN ÖRMÉNYI, White House

NAME INDEX

Abel, Elie, 56, 132, 143
Aczél, Tamás, 54–55, 136,
    144–145
Adams, Val, 64, 176, 186
Alsop, Joseph, 162, 184
Alsop, Stewart, 162, 184
Ambrose, Stephen, 109–112,
    123, 181, 186
Anderson, Peggy King, 140,
    145
Anderson, Raymond H., 58
Andropov, Yuri, 106, 115
Ansley, Judy, 229
Ansley, Stephen, 230
Antonovich, Michael, 220–221
Apple, R. W., 22, 55
Applebaum, Anne, 189
Archer, Thomas, 62
Ardry, Robert, 45–46
Argentieri, Federigo, 191

Bailey, Thomas, A., 107–110,
    112, 123
Bain, Leslie B., 44, 130–131,
    143
Baker, James, 79, 82
Balassa, Béla A., 40
Balázs, Ádám, 232

Balogh, Frank de, 221
Balogh, Joseph, 40
Bánk, Zsuzsa, 137, 141, 144
Bartók, Béla, 214, 232
Bartók, László, 37, 60
Bede, István, 10
Beebe, Les, 39
Bejczy, Antal, 143, 215, 227
Beke, László, 63, 126, 140, 142,
    187
Békés, Csaba, 191, 197–198
Berecz, General Béla, 13
Berecz, János, 15, 51, 53
Berend, Iván T., 117, 120, 124
Bergold, Harry E., 78–79
Berle, Adolf J., 57
Berlioz, Hector, 232
Berman, Paul, 197
Bethlen, István, xxii
Binder, David, 9, 13, 19, 26–27,
    30, 37, 41, 52, 54–55, 57–
    58, 61, 63, 69
Blatchford, Joseph, 178
Bloomberg, Michael R., 190, 211
Bohlen, Celestine, 53, 63
Bolten, Joshua, 230
Bolten, Stacy, 230
Borbándi, Gyula, 154, 183

ABOUT THE AUTHORS

TIBOR GLANT is associate professor and chair of the North American Department at the University of Debrecen, Hungary. He majored in history and English at Debrecen (1986–91), and holds an MA (1992) and a Ph.D. (1996) in American history from the University of Warwick, UK. His main focus of research is American history and culture, and American-Hungarian relations in the twentieth century. His books include *Through the Prism of the Habsburg Monarchy: Hungary in American Diplomacy and Public Opinion during World War I* (1998), and *A Szent Korona amerikai kalandja, 1945–1997* [The American Adventure of the Holy Crown, 1945–1978] (1997).

ISTVÁN DEÁK, Seth Low Professor Emeritus, specializes in central and east central European history. He received his Ph.D. from Columbia in 1964. His publications include *Weimar Germany's Left-Wing Intellectuals: A Political History of the "Weltbühne" and Its Circle* (1968); *The Lawful Revolution: Louis Kossuth and the Hungarians, 1848–1849* (1979); *Beyond Nationalism: A Social and Political History of the Habsburg Officer Corps, 1848–1918* (1990); and *Essays on Hitler's Europe* (2001). Coeditor: *Eastern Europe in the 1970s* (1972); *Everyman in Europe: Essays in Social History* (1974), and *The Politics of Retribution in Europe: World War II and Its Aftermath* (2000). He is working on a book entitled *Europe on Trial: Collaboration, Resistance, and Retribution in Europe during and after World War II*. He is a frequent contributor to the *New York Review of Books* and the *New Republic*.

BOOKS PUBLISHED BY THE CENTER FOR HUNGARIAN STUDIES AND PUBLICATIONS

CHSP Hungarian Authors Series:

No. 1.   *False Tsars.* Gyula Szvák. 2000.

No. 2.   *Book of the Sun.* Marcell Jankovics. 2001.

No. 3.   *The Dismantling of Historic Hungary: The Peace Treaty of Trianon, 1920.* Ignác Romsics. 2002.

No. 4.   *The Soviet and Hungarian Holocausts: A Comparative Essay.* Tamás Krausz. 2006.

CHSP Hungarian Studies Series:

No. 1.   *Emperor Francis Joseph, King of the Hungarians.* András Gerő. 2001.

No. 2.   *Global Monetary Regime and National Central Banking. The Case of Hungary, 1921–1929.* György Péteri. 2002.

No. 3.   *Hungarian-Italian Relations in the Shadow of Hitler's Germany, 1933–1940.* György Réti. 2003.

No. 4.   *The War Crimes Trial of Hungarian Prime Minister László Bárdossy.* Pál Pritz. 2004.

No.   5. *Identity and the Urban Experience: Fin-de-Siècle Budapest.*
Gábor Gyáni. 2004.

No.   6. *Picturing Austria-Hungary. The British Perception of the
Habsburg Monarchy, 1865–1870.* Tibor Frank. 2005.

No.   7. *Anarchism in Hungary: Theory, History, Legacies.* András
Bozóki and Miklós Sükösd. 2006.

No.   8. *Myth and Remembrance. The Dissolution of the Habsburg
Empire in the Memoir Literature of the Austro-Hungarian
Political Elite.* Gergely Romsics. 2006.

No.   9. *Imagined History. Chapters from Nineteenth and Twentieth Century Hungarian Symbolic Politics.* András Gerő.
2006.

No. 10. *Pál Teleki (1879–1941). A Biography.* Balázs Ablonczy.
2006.

No. 11. *The Hungarian Revolution of 1956. Myths and Realities.*
László Eörsi. 2006.

No. 12. *The Jewish Criterion in Hungary.* András Gerő. 2007.

No. 13. *Remember Hungary 1956. Essays on the Hungarian Revolution and War of Independence in American Memory.* Tibor
Glant. 2007.

No. 14. *Reflections on Twentieth Century Hungary: A Hungarian
Magnate's View.* Baron Móric Kornfeld. 2007.